AN
ANTHROPOLOGY
OF
WANDERING

AN ANTHROPOLOGY

OF

WANDERING

HOW ADVENTURE CAN ALLEVIATE A FEARFUL CULTURE

JUSTIN S. BAILEY

THOSE WHO WANDER PRESS
BLOOMINGTON, 2026

Copyright © 2025 by Justin S. Bailey

All rights reserved. This book or any portion thereof may not be reproduced or used in any manner whatsoever without the express written permission of the publisher except for the use of brief quotations in a book review.

Those Who Wander Press

First paperback edition February 2026

For information about special discounts for bulk purchases, please visit jsbailey.org

Paperback ISBN: 979-8-9935991-0-6
Ebook ISBN: 979-8-9935991-1-3

Book cover and layout design by Alan Hebel
Cover illustration composition by Alan Hebel using Shutterstock

*To my father, Mark S. Bailey,
for all the lessons in the outdoors and
for teaching me how to overcome my fears.*

CONTENTS

Prologue: To Wander, or Not to Wander?............ 1

Chapter 1: Those Who Do Not Wander: Arriving Without Traveling............................ 15

Chapter 2: Those Who Wander: The Restless Few ... 49

Chapter 3: Perspectives Through Adventure: Grappling With Change and Continuity.......... 85

Chapter 4: A Nation Suffering From OSD (Obsessive Safety Disorder): Context For Our Brave New World............................ 123

Chapter 5: Our Ancient Brains Meet the Brave New World: Evolutionary Baggage and Cognitive Bias 161

Chapter 6: Media and the Modern Paradox: Paranoia and Confusion in the Age of Information....... 195

Chapter 7: Agents of Fear: Responsibility, Trust,
    and the Choices We Make................... 227

Chapter 8: The Trade-Offs of Adventure,
    Part I: The Benefits of Wandering................... 255

Chapter 9: The Trade-Offs of Adventure,
    Part II: The Challenges of Wandering 279

Epilogue: To Wander 307

Acknowledgements 327

Notes 329

Selected Bibliography.......................... 349

Index 353

PROLOGUE
To Wander, or Not to Wander?

"I went to the woods because I wished to live deliberately, to front only the essential facts of life, and see if I could not learn what it had to teach, and not, when I came to die, discover that I had not lived. I did not wish to live what was not life, living is so dear; nor did I wish to practise resignation, unless it was quite necessary. I wanted to live deep and suck out all the marrow of life, to live to sturdily and Spartan-like as to put to rout all that was not life, to cut a broad swath and shave close, to drive life into a corner, and reduce it to its lowest terms, and, if it proved to be mean, why then to get the whole and genuine meanness of it, and publish its meanness to the world; or if it were sublime, to know it by experience, and be able to give a true account of it in my next excursion."
—Henry David Thoreau, *Walden; or, Life in the Woods*

Entering the summer of 2014, I had just graduated from Indiana University with a degree in anthropology and history. My partner, Hilary, had also just graduated with degrees in anthropology and Spanish. Hilary had spent a healthy portion of her young adult life tramping around Spain and South American countries, immersed in the cultures of Peru, Argentina, and Chile. We met two years before at an archaeological field school in the mountains of western Wyoming, where I was on my second expedition of archaeological training. Upon reaching the end of an undergraduate career, unemployed and with that nagging feeling of insurmountable debt corroding the brain, the first thing any sensible person ought to be doing is seeking employment and paying off loans. Not me. Being a responsible adult was going to have to wait because I had an irresistible itch to do something memorable, adventurous, even reckless if necessary. I had to try to get something out of my system.

Were we going to start looking for jobs immediately or take the opportunity to do what we both deeply loved: travel? And not the lethargic slow-roast-your-ass-on-a-beach type of vacation travel, but the feel-it-in-your-bones roughing it kind of travel. The Appalachian Trail was always something deeply compelling to me, and it didn't take much to encourage Hilary to join me, as she was curious to explore more of her home country after being steeped in culture abroad for the last few years. We also didn't have much money, so sipping Chianti at an Italian villa would have to wait.

We began our research and training many months before graduation. While sharing our plans and reading about others' experiences in books and blogs, I noticed an interesting trend in the way we all talked about adventure in our culture. As with all things unknown, and especially at an early age, we initially view such experiences as daunting, incomprehensible, and something to be appropriately apprehensive about. We found ourselves swarmed by many unsettling questions and concerns about the dangers and privations of what we were about to undertake; "Where will you sleep; how are you going to eat; how will you stay clean; aren't you worried about wild animals; what about the bears, snakes, ticks, mosquitoes, and flies; what about diseases like giardia and Lyme disease; what if you get lost; what if you get hurt or sick; what about the "weirdoes;" haven't you heard people have been murdered on the AT; are you going to carry a gun; what about money; aren't you worried about your career; are you crazy; why would you want to do something like this?" My eyes widened, and my mind strained; this barrage of questions and trepidations left me momentarily stunned and self-conscious. I would later have the insight that this was probably the momentum of fear and anxiety that breaks or arrests the development of many aspiring adventurers when they initially look for and begin to plan their adventures.

Now, I certainly don't fault people for being worried about someone's safety and future well-being. These were all legitimate concerns that we too felt obligated to ask and answer ourselves. However, it did feel as though the tone from some of these questions hinted at a lack of confidence in our capabilities or perhaps some passive-aggressive way of letting us know how foolish they thought we were, instead of having a genuine interest in what we were doing and why we were drawn to an adventure like this. All meant well, but this subsequently had a substantial psychological effect on me, initially resulting in troubling feelings of self-doubt and guilt in my naivety. Restless nights abounded. I began to second-guess this decision. "Should we be doing this? Is this just a ridiculous waste of time? What if something bad *does* happen to us? How will I live with that, if I live at all?"

Only in hindsight would we realize how ill-conceived or just plain silly many of these initial apprehensions turned out to be and how right we were in not conceding to our and others' fears. These topics of fear and insecurity in society related to adventurous undertakings and their origins have had me thinking and researching ever since.

AN ANTHROPOLOGY OF WANDERING

My working hypothesis is that all of us are far more capable and resilient than we realize, yet are easily persuaded into passivity or taking the more cautious paths through life. Is there a link between the fears in our society and a lack of adventure in our lives? Could learning habits, values, and goals that structure adventure into our lives more frequently help ease a lot of our anxieties and fears and guide us toward developing a more mindful, fulfilling, and enriched life and society?

○

We were now convinced that doing a thru-hike of the Appalachian Trail would be a fairly benign and uplifting experience, so long as some pragmatism and common sense were applied. Yet, how some people questioned our sanity for wanting to embark on this adventure, one would think we were planning to tour Mars. All these anxious and foreboding questions speak volumes to our modern lifestyle and insecurities. They indicate that many of us living comfortably in "modern" society are pretty far removed from our relationship with adventure, and more specifically (as the aforementioned list of interrogating questions suggests) nature. As any serious college student knows, research is hammered into your head incessantly, and we had done a considerable amount of it preparing for our excursion. Importantly, this helped justify and validate our confidence. We suspected that most of these concerns were likely founded in myth, hysteria, and plain inexperience, along with a few highly publicized, but rare cases of things going horribly wrong on the AT.[1] But regardless of how low an instance of violence is likely to befall us, our brains—wired for survival—involuntarily assault us with *what if, what if, what if…*and that can make all the difference in whether we decide to prioritize and structure adventure into our lives or not.

I tried to reassure myself with the fact that we were both in good shape and had extensive outdoor experience. Despite all the rationalizing, a great deal of anxiety continued to overwhelm and creep into my consciousness. For some reason, I had built this idea of backpacking the AT up in my mind as a monumental endeavor, something only a few superhumans were able to endure and accomplish. Irrationalities still got the best of me. Thoughts and ill-fated scenarios involving bears, guns, snakes, and "crazies" lumbered and crawled and slithered through my head in the nights leading up to our departure for the trail. So much was uncertain. So much could go wrong, right? How to anticipate all of this? Numerous people had gotten lost for good on the AT. That could be us! We might even have to eat each other!

We found it difficult to anticipate the changes we would undergo in the following months as we adapted to a radically different daily life of backpacking on the Appalachian Trail. We asked ourselves endless questions of introspection that were tinged with recurring apprehension. "What is this lifestyle like? Will we enjoy it? Will we hate it? What will we learn? What kind of people will we meet? What stories might they have to share? How much will we change? How often will we fight with one another? Will we face conflicts with others? Will we even finish? If we don't, does that mean we've failed at something? Is this even worth doing? Should we be more concerned about finding jobs? Is this something we will regret? What are we going to gain from this, if anything? What am I forgetting? What do I not need? Is this dangerous? What if we get lost, injured, or sick? *What if, what if, what if...?"*

Only after we started to experience the reality of *being present* on the trail and realizing we weren't the only "fools" out there did we realize just how trivial and nonsensical many of our apprehensions were. And the further we hiked, the more at ease and less anxious we felt with the landscape and the people around us. Even concerns about the world at large seemed to dissipate and take on a different perspective. What was happening here? Later on, I had another insight that there was quite a noticeable contrast taking place between preconceptions and reality; our *perceived fears* often turn out to be very different from our *actual risks* when we have the opportunity to see them play out in the real world. This awareness paradoxically only arrives long after we've made the plunge into the depths of a voyage. That said, we would soon come face to face with some of those prior apprehensions and would have to deal with several unexpected and troubling events in time...but we did live to tell this tale, and we are much better off because of it.

○

There is no way to measure the loss of a grand experience not ventured. Individual lives cannot be science experiments. We cannot test out different life choices, then hit rewind and choose the best life course. Because of this, we often understandably choose the path of least resistance—"better safe than sorry," we too frequently say. What about the counterpart to this—"nothing ventured, nothing gained?" How often have we all given in to a fear of some unknown adventure, only to be plagued later by a tiny disquieting feeling in our head telling us that perhaps we should have gone through with it? We all possess an adventure left untaken, unexplored, unlived. What exactly is stopping us from taking part in one of the most ancient and instrumental behaviors of our species—an intoxicating mix of serendipitous wondering and wandering?

The British travel writer Bruce Chatwin once sought to answer the question 'Why do men wander rather than sit still?'[2] Why humans wander is also the central motif of this book, yet in our modern times, we are often restricted from pursuing our innate wanderlust. To my mind, we must first address the question of what holds us back from manifesting all those adventures we dream about. Ask yourself, is your life as adventurous as you'd like it to be? Chances are that the answer is a sheepish "no." As untroubled children first eagerly learning to explore our environment, many of us dream of "seeing the world" when we get older, yet how many of us can confidently say, right now, that we've stayed true to this youthful yearning for adventure? Why did we have those dreams to trot the globe, to begin with? Was this simply a childish impulse or something deeper that we've learned in time to suppress?

As we age into adulthood, many things inevitably create impediments to our inherent wanderlust that make it challenging to sustain. Living in the fast-paced, status-seeking society that we do, we live under enormous social, cultural, and economic pressures to earn our keep, outcompete one another, and "maximize efficiency" from the cradle to the grave. We get caught up in the grind of our careers. We build families, communities, and businesses. We become tied to seemingly endless debts and responsibilities. If we are lucky and not tied too much to our work, we might have time to take our annual one-week vacation each passing year to destress and "recharge" as if we've become human batteries in the *Matrix*. However, we are certainly not immersing ourselves in the kind of travel and exploration many of us, I imagine, still desire to do "at some point down the road." "Someday," we say, but not now, not today. Is all this simply because this is just what growing up is—forfeiting things we want to do for things we have to do? Or is there something else happening to rationalize the abandonment of our adventures and creative outlets? What else might be going on to encourage our increasing passivity and sedentism?

The obstacle at the center of what prevents many of us from structuring adventure into our lives, one that we may not recognize or want to acknowledge, is *fear*. Fear manifests itself in various forms. We live evermore in a culture of fear and misinformation that subtly disorients us, heightens our anxieties, and prevents many of us from leading a more fulfilled and adventurous life. What if the source of alleviating many of our apprehensions about the world is paradoxically something we are afraid to do in the first place? Could adventure be an antidote to our modern unrest? And how do we begin to renew and restructure adventure back into our hectic modern lives?

I suspect there are many lessons that we can discover from those who wander, i.e., travelers and adventurers, that may enable us to overcome some of our major modern societal ailments—our fears, cynicism, anxiety, and disillusionment with humanity. I believe we *must* understand the origin of these deeply unsettling problems and what we can do to alleviate them, both at an individual and societal level. I believe getting more of us to travel, experience, and appreciate adventure more qualitatively has a large role to play here. As another British author, Alain de Botton, wrote in *The Art of Travel*,

If our lives are dominated by a search for happiness, then perhaps few activities reveal as much about the dynamics of this quest—in all its ardour and paradoxes—than our travels. They express, however inarticulately, an understanding of what life might be about, outside of the constraints of work and the struggle for survival. Yet rarely are they considered to present philosophical problems—that is, issues requiring thought beyond the practical. We are inundated with advice on *where* to travel to, but we hear little of *why* and *how* we should go, even though the art of travel seems naturally to sustain a number of questions neither so simple nor so trivial, and whose study might in modest ways contribute to an understanding of what the Greek philosophers beautifully termed *eudaimonia*, or 'human flourishing'.[3]

Before we can learn *why* and *how* to wander and take our plunge into a renewed life of travel and adventure, it is important that we first understand the forces preventing us from doing so, and that will be the task of most of this book because, it turns out, it is as complex as it is fascinating.

First, our shared outlook on the world is perplexing, to say the least. When we reflect on our contemporary society and gauge "the state of the world", it's not hard to sense the overwhelming weight of confusion, fear, alienation, and insecurity that persists within culture and society. But why is that? Are we living at a uniquely terrifying time relative to all other periods of human history? If we consult some of the general data and the researchers mapping out the trends of human development over the last few centuries, several of them seem to have nothing but *good* news to share, which completely contradicts the horrendous narratives we endlessly hear on television or gawk at on the internet. The few researchers who compile and interpret this uplifting data inform us that we live in an astounding "age of information" with gadgets of unprecedented supercomputing power. We are incredibly privileged by the standards of human history. How do we explain this paradox, and what does adventure have to do with alleviating a culture of fear?

The anthropologist in me has a strong sense that a wandering ethos—an inner urge or calling to explore—to venture far and wide is a deeply embedded feature of our humanity and one that has played a vital role in our evolution and survival as a species. From my study of hunter-gather societies, I believe, as Bruce Chatwin did, that "evolution intended us to be travellers" and that "we are travellers from birth."[4] Much travel literature often describes adventurers' reflections on their soon-to-be travels in similar poetic musings. The 14th-century traveler Ibn Battuta, upon departing for his initial 3,000-mile *hajj* or pilgrimage from his hometown of Tangier to Mecca, described his original yearning for the adventure to come as being "swayed by an overmastering impulse within me and a desire long-cherished in my bosom to visit these illustrious sanctuaries."[5] What exactly is it that captures and has captured the minds of so many wayward travelers, nomads, pilgrims, and explorers throughout history? Is this a shared human universal or present in only a select few restless risk-takers?

As a social and cultural phenomenon, we're incredibly fascinated by mythical tales and stories of adventure and the wanderers of each passing generation—from Odysseus to Robinson Crusoe, from Ibn Battuta and Marco Polo to Lewis and Clark, from Amelia Earhart to

Yuri Gagarin. We've likely been entranced by these legendary figures since time immemorial—predominantly living as hunter-gatherers, nomadic herders, and agriculturalists. Although a vast number of our species now live in a sedentary industrial society, some of us still manage to pursue this wandering ethos in diverse and creative ways. Regrettably, this human behavioral trait and cultural expression of wandering is rarely a subject of modern anthropological discussion (even though it is the basis for why so many anthropologists get involved in the study of anthropology in the first place). Indeed, the motto of anthropology could very well be that we desire to see the world through another's eyes. This anthropological longing for perspective is the same for the world traveler and seeker of adventure. I have therefore summoned this phrase of the "anthropology of wandering" to pursue the questions related to human wandering across time and space.

Many anthropological questions align with adventure and are left open for us to contemplate. For instance, at what point in time did the spark to venture out beyond the horizon arise in human consciousness? Did *Homo ergaster* or *Homo erectus*—archaic forms of humans known as hominins living in the middle Pleistocene, some 1.5 to 2 million years ago—possess the mental capacity to share the same restive urge for adventure as us? Were they also compelled to see how far the land goes that wasn't just inspired by a mere craving for food? What exactly is this "wandering ethos" or sense of adventure that compels us to move and explore our environments? Don't *you* ever get restless and bored staying in one place for very long?

We often itch to go and do something different. Where does that feeling come from, and why aren't we all content to just sit on the couch all day? Is a desire to wander not another plausible hypothesis to entertain and explain why our human presence is now global? Nearly all species of the earth with the ability to locomote will explore their environments for a variety of reasons. But at what point in our human lineage did we gain the capacity *to wonder about wandering* to foreign and distant places? Were certain individuals in our nomadic hunter-gatherer days selected to search for new source materials for their tools or find other groups to trade with, all based on their eagerness for adventure? What role might this have played in our evolution? These questions are almost certainly beyond proper scientific hypothesis testing, yet they are still philosophically worth pondering, are they not?

It isn't hard to imagine our earliest hunter-gatherer ancestors reminiscing around a blazing fire deep into the night about their celebrated explorers who led their great-great-grandparents to greener pastures teeming with game and abundant resources. Perhaps they immortalized them in some form on indecipherable cave paintings or etched them into sandstone walls as petroglyphs on one of the tens of thousands of archaeological sites spread across the globe. We find the occasional commentary on the subject of adventure from classic ethnographies from such notable anthropologists as Bronislaw Malinowski, A.R. Radcliffe Brown, Margaret Mead, Ruth Benedict, or Claude Lévi-Strauss.

Thus, our urge to wonder and wander runs very deep in who we are as a species. Modern life has a wonderful array of benefits, but some things are out of line with how we've evolved. There still is a lot to understand, but cognitively, at some point, we evolved a unique capacity to not just remain in a single habitat like most species but to move to and explore all areas of the globe. This deep, restless yearning to toss ourselves into the wild unknown certainly must have found cultural expression long before such adventurous tales as the *Epic of Gilgamesh*,

PROLOGUE

the *Iliad,* and the *Odyssey* were written down. The way some of the earliest poems were written and echoed by bards draped in himations (Romans invented the true toga) hints at a much longer tradition of remembering and transmitting stories orally. We're naturally intrigued and perplexed by those who seem to willingly place themselves at risk for the mere sake of it. Why leave the comfortable abode of our homes? What could possibly be gained from throwing ourselves so aimlessly into bizarre, uncomfortable, and unknown situations?

O

My time on the Appalachian Trail was when I felt the most empowered and the least bit jaded about life, and I've been trying to get back to that state of mind and being ever since we ended our journey on the Appalachian Trail in the fall of 2014. The experiences of backpacking the Appalachian Trail profoundly reoriented my thinking about my life as well as society at large. I've wanted to uncover what it was that made this time so philosophical, adventurous, and life-altering and I want to share this experience and my thoughts on the meaning of adventure with you because I believe it holds significant value to many of us—to learn something imperative about who we've been, how resilient we are as humans, and how important travel and adventure still is for us living in the "modern" world of the 21st century.

I wrote this book, in part, because I often find myself mired in cynicism and disenchanted with our modern world, unable to be as adventurous as I would like, and mystified by why this is the case. I suspect you feel similarly. From time to time, I am certain we all pose this question in one form or another to ourselves, "Is this all there is to life; working an uninspiring job around the clock as a caffeine fiend with a desperate hope that one day forty years from now, I'll finally begin to have that grand adventure in retirement so long as my mind, body, and finances remain somewhat intact?" For me, the predominant life philosophy and work ethic of our culture that tells us to grind ourselves down physically, emotionally, and mentally until we retire is a remarkable gamble that so many of us unquestionably, or perhaps powerlessly, accept. Given we have a single life to live on this planet, I can't help but think that this is a genuinely depressing, dehumanizing, and unwise mode of living our lives. I wonder if there is perhaps a better alternative route we can take through life. Surely there is a healthier, more inspiring, more balanced, and more adventurous way to restructure our lives. But where to begin?

CHAPTER 1
Those Who Do Not Wander:
Arriving Without Traveling

*"The world is a book, and those who
do not travel read only one page."*
—Saint Augustine

Many of us have heard about the Appalachian Trail by now, probably in large part from Bill Bryson's popular book *A Walk in the Woods* or through its film adaptation. We know it's a long trail; it spanned 2,185 miles in the summer of 2014 during our journey, though it too morphs in time. The southern terminus begins in Georgia at Mt. Springer, the northern in Maine at Mt. Katahdin, a colossal mound of rock flanked on all sides by succulent coniferous forests. Most aspiring thru-hikers traditionally begin their trek from Mt. Springer and head north. We couldn't start until after graduation in May, so starting in Georgia wasn't an option if we wanted to do an unbroken stretch, as snow would be setting in by the time we made it that far north, and Baxter State Park, where Mt. Katahdin resides, doesn't allow people in after the snow flies. Plus, we wanted to be unconventional nonconformists, so we started at Katahdin to head south...

○

When I awoke at 5:30 a.m. on Thursday, June 26th, 2014, in room 118 of the Baxter Inn in Millinocket, Maine, I was in a slight haze of confusion. The previous day's twenty-hour drive from Indiana was largely absent from my mind. The window curtains were closed and the room was dark, though not entirely obscured. Enough light seeped into the room to silhouette this dull, unfamiliar place. It took a moment to find my bearings. Groggy, I forced myself up. Once I flipped on the light in the bathroom, a little more became clear. The night before, I'd prepared the complimentary coffee (if these motes of dark dust can be labeled as such) and toggled the cheap plastic switch on.

I looked myself over in the mirror, noted my puffy, eager eyes, and then stepped back out into the main complex of the dim room. Being the first one up, I moved stealthily so as not to disturb Hilary and her father, Steve, who had graciously offered to drive us here to Maine and climb Mt. Katahdin before bidding us farewell on our journey. I moved slowly toward the unexposed window, anticipating a rising sun to mark the beginning of our trek. Romantically, I imagined some kind of soundtrack music like that from a Spielberg film would suddenly begin and follow us on our voyage. I drew back the curtain and cocked my head to peer out into what I fantasized would be a pure bliss of sunshine. In dismay, my heart sank; darkened gray clouds and drizzling rain amidst a poor scene of a dilapidated building and rusting cars were all that confronted me. And no music, just the off-beat pattering of rain on asphalt and tin roofing muffled by a pane of foggy glass. Hilary, more the realist, has always taken great pleasure in scolding me for being overly idealistic. My pride was fortunately spared this time as she still lay snoozing. Before we had even begun, I had already made my first mistake: never expect that things will go the way you anticipate. This would prove to be a relentless lesson over the next eleven days as we trekked from Mt. Katahdin through the Hundred-Mile Wilderness into the small, charming town of Monson.

While we checked in with the ranger in preparation for our 10.4 round-trip mile ascent and descent of Katahdin, he forewarned us that this was the most difficult and strenuous section of all the 2,185 miles making up the current length of the Appalachian Trail. He estimated it would take us around ten hours to finish this section, seeing as how we weren't accustomed to the trail yet. I scoffed condescendingly to myself at this and thought, "No way will this take *that* long. I just hiked 10 miles in four hours in Indiana wearing my fucking sandals!" Damn, was I ever wrong, and was he ever right. It took almost exactly that amount. It was unbelievably taxing, and I was confronted bluntly with a second hard lesson: bury your ego at the base of the mountain, because nature's indifference will quickly take advantage of it if you don't. It might just mean a harsh blow to your pride, or it could turn out to be something far more serious and devastating. Remain vigilant and humble in the woods.

The first mile was fairly easy, though muggy and wet. A faint sticky mist wafted through the forest of pungent conifers in the late June air; their mixing aromas somehow stimulated nostalgia for ancient times. Sweat soon beaded through the pores of our bodies. Bone and blood, tendons and joints, muscle and skin, chemicals and nerves, all fueled and conspired together in an intricate display of unfathomable symbiosis; the biological apparatus of the human body is such a striking, durable machine, uncannily crafted for movement and wandering.

AN ANTHROPOLOGY OF WANDERING

Gnarled and brazen roots bulged through Earth's surface, defining and ever-so-slowly redefining the landscape and the path before us. Moss and lichen coated much of the forest floor and all the debris that lay embedded upon it, like the shaggy puke green 1970s carpet left moldering in your grandparent's basement. The second mile still didn't give much of a challenge, and we were making excellent time. At this point, I confidently maintained my skepticism of the ranger's purported ten-hour day.

The rain began to fade, and the mist dissipated soon after we crossed a wooden bridge that effortlessly carried us across the crashing Katahdin Stream Falls. London, a beginning southbound hiker like ourselves, passed us shortly after. We would only encounter two others that day and come to find later that a majority of the other beginning southbounders had delayed due to the forecast rain; perhaps they, too, shared a similar romance of sun-filled inauguration and Spielberg symphonies. I suspected they might have experienced the same heart-sinking feeling I also felt earlier that morning, but opted for snoozing the day away.

Once we reached the top of a rustic stone staircase, the sun was emerging, and the clouds were clearing up a bit. Droplets of water clung and fell from the dominating conifers. Occasionally, one of us would nudge a tree, shake the water off the succulent needles, and shower us in the process. Around the three-mile mark, the stones lining the trail began to morph and take on a much grander shape, increasing rapidly from that point on with the rising gradient. Water trickled, then streamed down the same path.

Pebbles and cobbles had now become boulders. Panting and perspiring, my skepticism began to erode. We eventually made it above the tree line, where we met the force-ridden wind and the great spine of Katahdin that resembled the grandiose plated back of an eon-extinct reptile. The wind came in powerful gusts that would make the most stable feet budge and second-guess their assurance.

Our pace was slow going now, and the pleasant walking jaunt we began with had now shifted into an intense bouldering exercise as we climbed over and upward on barren rock. Had the white blazes not been painted to indicate the trail's route, one would surely think they'd gone astray from the path. The moment was daunting, yet simultaneously thrilling. As I turned around to look below, an immense white cloud confronted us. Thick and opaque, it blotted out a large portion of the view. Though the scene was ominous, awe and raw beauty were retained in the visible remaining dark greenery, rock, and sky.

We'd made it up the spine and within a mile and a half of the peak. We were walking a fine line between a divided field of boulders, small shrubs and grasses, rare and endangered plant and animal species, a unique butterfly species, islanded by climate, found nowhere else, but on this very site. The chilled temperature amidst the wind and pattering rain summoned goosebumps and uncontrolled shivers. There remained our final incline, though we did not yet know it. London emerged from the mist that was ebbing and flowing, obstructing visibility. He informed us we had less than half an hour until the peak. We exchanged a few words, and within a minute of separation, he'd faded and returned to the mist.

The fog lifted for some time, and there it was at last, the weather-scarred sign of Katahdin not 30 feet away. My eyes widened, and my heart pulsed an even greater throb of excitement. I'd already glanced over dozens of photographs and the blogging words of many others who'd captured their victorious moments here, but I'd never felt the pulsing thrill or been able to fully empathize with those in the blog posts and images in the abyss of Google's search engine. But now, this was my moment. This was our moment. And there it was, as real as ever an experience could be.

A hand-stacked stone cairn five or six feet high stood twenty feet from the sign; a collective monument that would perhaps stand far longer than this weathered wooden sign, yet remain a relic, mysteriously indecipherable and curious of its signifying meaning to those of the long-distant future should the threads of our history be severed.

Even the metal plaque's text that lay close by may very well corrode and diminish its text before the cairn. It declares this piece of land, gifted by Percival Proctor Baxter in the early 1930s, "Shall *forever* be used for public park and recreational purposes, shall *forever* be left in the natural wild state, shall *forever* be kept as a sanctuary for wild beasts and birds, that no road or ways for motor vehicles shall hereafter ever be constructed therein or thereon."[6] Forever is quite a long time. I thought to myself how overly optimistic that statement sounded and asked, "For how long do the mere hopeful words of the past dictate the actions, perceptions, and values of the ever-changing people of the future?" A continuity of values must persist in society for past hopes to be realized.

I found myself back in the drizzling present. For the many northbound hikers, this site signaled a well-accomplished end, for others calling themselves "flip-floppers" the start of the last half of the trek, for still others a successful day hike or check off the bucket list, but for us "southbounders", the thinned out loners of the AT herd, it signified the very beginning. Another salient lesson dawned on me: whatever goal, dream, or adventure one imagines pursuing, make it a reality because pure imagination alone can never fathom the truth and beauty of something left undone.

○

Let's begin with a hard truth about ourselves. Most modern Americans are pampered and predictable travelers, in the traditional sense of the term. Although we may fancy ourselves as travelers when boarding a plane for vacation or taking a road trip across the country, transportation technology has given rise to something unique in our time: the ability for us to *arrive without traveling.* With planes, trains, and automobiles, we have the extraordinary capacity to obliterate space and skip everything between points A and B. Have you ever wondered what you may be missing in that space in between your start and end points? In other words, we may say our modern perspective on travel is "it's all about the destination, not the journey." For generations, we have been spoonfed every line in the book about American exceptionalism—that our history, political system, values, and culture somehow stand out as distinct and destined for eternal greatness. However, when it comes to immersive travel and experiencing the rest of the world firsthand, Americans are rather unexceptional when we consider the places we go and don't go. If we are such a wealthy nation and our standards of living have increased so much, why do so few of us invest in seeing the world more intimately and broadly than we do? Are we as brave as we like to imagine ourselves? How much of a role does fear influence our travel patterns?

Despite the unprecedented influence America appears to have in the world, we no longer seem to be the great, fearless travelers we once thought of ourselves as in our most idolized American myths: think of Lewis and Clark, Daniel Boone, and sailing across the plains on a prairie schooner. When maps still labeled parts of the land as *terra incognita* and the oceans, *mare incognitum,* or when the American West was still envisioned as the "last frontier," many Americans found every reason to dream and move. But now the world appears claustrophobic, filled, discovered, and unenchanting to a great deal of us. We've lost our energy to venture and explore. Because of this, we are suffering from a paralysis of spirit, a disconnect from the still vibrant natural and cultural world. I'd like to encourage many of us to travel more, and I think that's a pretty easy message to share. But what's more difficult to figure out are the *problems* and explanations as to why we don't already.

I want to make the case that traveling and connecting with other cultures and people isn't just a selfish indulgence or simply about having a good time, though it can certainly be that. And it's not something exclusively for the rich, nor is travel necessarily detrimental to the planet. On the contrary, I think not traveling and having adventures is far more consequential to human resiliency and societal well-being than many of us may realize. Innumerable negative consequences likely result from our lack of connection with the rest of the world, both individually and collectively. These things might start small but end up disastrous in the long run: a milieu of poor assumptions and skewed value judgments about people and places we've never seen and known directly creep up within our culture and foment nasty bouts of unrest, violence, and revolution. Ugly shades of prejudice and ignorant ideas of extreme nationalism and xenophobia spawn from this lack of interaction. Cutting ourselves off from one another and severing communication is a recipe for disaster from my anthropological viewpoint. Travel tends to temper such nonsensical ideas and humble us. As Mark Twain once famously observed, "Travel is fatal to prejudice, bigotry, and narrow-mindedness, and many of our people need it sorely on these accounts. Broad, wholesome, charitable views of men and things cannot be acquired by vegetating in one little corner of the earth all one's lifetime." What trade-offs have we unwittingly made for the sake of modern convenience travel—the Caribbean Cruise, the pampering resorts, the frequent flyer miles, and the interstate highways?

○

Whether you're a carpenter, economist, or physicist, at the end of the day, we're all trying to measure something. We're trying to measure something, not for its own sake but to predict something of value, to craft a narrative, and to derive from that narrative a set of morals or ways in which we ought to conduct ourselves. Measuring how we travel and adventure is no different. But how should we go about it? Given the impacts of the coronavirus on travel, let's first consider travel before the pandemic for a more accurate picture of "normal" times. If we merely look at the *quantity* of American travel miles, either from vehicle travel on the road (~3.2 trillion in 2022)[7] or those traveling by plane (U.S. enplaned revenue passengers exceeded 880 million in 2023, the highest ever recorded)[8], the notion that we're failing to travel is outrageously absurd on the surface. We could take nearly 400 round-trip voyages to Pluto with these numbers! From a bird's-eye view, it looks like all we do is move and travel. How can we get away with saying that we're failing to travel?

Think of it this way: if we were granted unlimited funds and a solar-powered commercial plane that would allow ceaseless flight until we ran out of food or filled up the waste tank, one could circumnavigate the globe endlessly and rack up record-breaking numbers for most miles traveled. We'd make it in the Guinness Book, hooray! However, by the second or third trip around, we would come to see just how uneventful and meaningless an experience like this would be. But *why* exactly is that the case? The answer is that this type of travel puts a person in what we may call "spatial limbo", excluded from the more meaningful elements of an actual trip, namely *distance*, *time*, and *place*. These are the crucial ingredients that make the *quality* of an adventure important and that are unfortunately absent in most of our modern travels. When we dissect the statistics and zoom in a little closer to examine our current travel patterns, we will find the picture isn't all that impressive. This pattern reveals an obvious lack of diversity in the places we wander (if we travel at all), despite a good percentage of us having the means to do so.

Perhaps we might feel content with contemporary travel and even counter that we *have* seen and do know the world via the Internet and other media outlets in the forms of high-quality images, breathtaking documentaries, and enticing personal stories we read. For a lot of us, this is enough to fulfill our curiosity and wanderlust. But is this only an illusion? Can we truly gain an accurate sense of the world vicariously through these mediums alone? Perhaps the answer lends itself to nuance—to some extent, yes, but mostly no, I would say. Does watching several documentaries on the Appalachian Trail, reading a few books and blogs on it, and viewing pictures of the trail give you the same sense of accomplishment and reality as someone who lived it day in and day out for four to six months? What does it feel like to be isolated for ten days in the most remote section of the trail, the 100 Mile Wilderness in the dead of the Maine forests? Who do you have to meet and swap stories with during the quiet evenings as your muscles rejoice for relaxation under a waning sun? Do you feel the sweat pouring out of your skin, muscles expanding and contracting with each lumbering step up and over Mount Moosilauke? Though exhausted and despite the fifty-pound pack breaking your back, you still find the emergent explosion of energy to sprint down one side of the mountain in a sporadic moment of elation. How about the grinning smile on your face that emerges when you know that you just successfully exited the southern terminus of the White Mountains and you are about to begin the next leg of your journey? Adventure films, photos, books, and blogs can be great, but they can't give you the most important of experiences.

There is no doubt that it is important to travel in your mind when reading and viewing these accounts of adventure, but our empathetic powers of seeing things from another's perspective this way only get us so far. Pure imagination and vicariousness aren't enough, which is the false promise of a lot of modern technology. If we're not traveling with our bodies and the senses that inevitably enhance an experience, we are only receiving small pieces of a much grander puzzle of life's possibilities and memorable experiences. It is the culmination of *memories* that instill our lives with purpose. Nothing truly compares or impresses the mind with such vividness as an actual encounter with natural and cultural landscapes. There is simply far too much nuance in the world left uncaptured by the pictures, film, audio, and words that we edit, curate, and consume, and too often these days, out of context. What's more, is that it becomes far more challenging to hold the level of ugly contempt so many seem to have of others when they've physically had to rely on strangers in a foreign environment, whether that be in the United States or abroad. Our telecommunications indeed give us these vivid vicarious feelings as though we're connected, but this is partly illusory or, at the very least, unfulfilling when we reflect on it more.

The fact is, collectively, we're currently a stagnant, complacent, fearful culture with an alarming number of citizens enraged about people they've never interacted with, both domestically and abroad. One survey estimates that 53% of Americans fear traveling abroad, and 70% believe Americans are targeted by terrorists if they do travel abroad.[9] In the nearly fifteen years after 9/11, the number amounted to 369 American citizens killed by a terrorist act while abroad.[10] During the same period, a little over 3,000 were killed *within* the U.S. by terrorist acts.[11] Less than 10% of Americans traveled overseas in 2015 despite the 9% increase to international destinations, yet 10% of those trips were strictly for business.[12] Many statistics and books confirm how fearful Americans are of travel, and I believe a steep price is being paid for that fear.

We are failing to witness much of our world firsthand. What might the consequences of this be? The same tremendous technology that gives us a powerful ability to become instantly aware of our world also scares the hell out of us and causes us to stay put (more on this later). We are led to form quick assumptions and ideas about people and places as fast as sound bites and light waves can travel to our screens and speakers. All of this makes for a potentially dangerous mix of overconfidence and condescension in things not truly experienced. With greater encouragement to simply slow down, reflect, and learn to witness the beauty and intricacy of our lives, we may perhaps discover a new pace worth wandering.

○

Let's back up for a moment. The history and context of human movement are important to consider. We have been wandering for a very long time. The *only* method by which our species could travel and experience the world for hundreds of thousands of years (millions when we include our ancient hominin cousins) was via our own two legs. Small boats emerged on the scene perhaps some 50,000 years ago. Then arrived the domestication of the horse, camel, cattle, oxen, and other "beasts of burden" throughout millennia to carry our loads and help us move. Carriages eventually became drawn by horses, and larger vessels began to drift on the seas. Steel tracks soon bore the brunt of railcars and steamships plunged into the artery-like interior riverways of the continents. Automobiles and aircraft coincided and emerged on the scene a little over a century ago, and now high prospects of automated vehicles, magnetic levitating trains in tubes, and ever-enhancing technology seem expected to increase their presence in the coming years. Only a mere *century and a half* has passed since we have been able to experience the world at such enormously high speeds. At some point during this continuum of movement, this speed at which we could be carried abolished the intermission of wandering and gave us the claustrophobic sense that the world was shrinking. This is an illusion, but the psychological consequences are substantial.

Traditionally, getting from A to B virtually anywhere on the globe required an extraordinary amount of planning, imagination, foresight, traversing, and *wonder*, but now this time frame is little more than an irksome layover in one or more airports or a long, tedious drive; a purgatory in which we're anxiously waiting to arrive at our destinations. Don't get me wrong, I love catching up on my podcasts and take pride in my punctuality, but sometimes while driving, I glance out to see a railroad track and wonder if I might just pull over, abandon my car, and start walking just to see where it goes. This abolishment of that intermission in traveling and the high speeds at which we can travel helps explain why we perceive the world as getting smaller and filled up. Today, it has become harder to fathom that Earth is quite a sprawling place and still rich in natural and cultural landscapes. In a world ever more demanding of our time, attention, and energy, it makes sense why efficiency is the pulsing heart of technology and business practice, but we should still bear in mind, as Einstein reflected, that "Logic will get you from A to B. Imagination will take you everywhere." To modern-day adventurers who encourage their fellow travelers to fixate on their travels and not so much on an endpoint, this time frame is most celebrated and captured by the phrase, "It's all about the journey, not the destination," a reversal of our modern perspective on travel we saw earlier.

The world many of us are conscious of today, due to our technological and scientific advancements, is remarkably different from the world in which the majority of our distant ancestors were conscious in the remote past. We evolved as wanderers, and yet rarely do we take a glimpse back at the progress we have made and question how it all came to be and whether we're headed in the right direction. We suffer from an inability to imagine the world without many of our modern technologies and conveniences. As a result, we suffer from "present-centeredness" in that we often unconsciously assume that many of the things we do today are inherently better or wiser than the way people did things in the past. This isn't always the case. Our modern creed is the belief that making things faster and more efficient is inherently noble and without repercussions. It has become the core principle of modern capitalism and entrepreneurship. Seldom do we ask whether efficiency is an intrinsic good. What might we be trading off for its sake? Is technology truly liberating us, or are there unforeseen restraints being placed on us?

In her enchanting book, *Wanderlust: A History of Walking*, author Rebecca Solnit puts forth a compelling argument. By increasing our technologies for the sake of efficiency, we abolish free time by "making it possible to maximize the time and place for production and minimize the unstructured travel time in between. New time-saving technologies make most workers more productive, not more free, in a world that seems to be accelerating around them." For instance, if a car manufacturer finds a clever way to double the output of its cars and thus meets last week's quota by Wednesday instead of Friday, it would be economically unwise to allow everyone to simply take the extra two days off and enjoy the free time in celebration of their hard work. To remain competitive, they're incentivized to take advantage of those two days and continue to crank out more vehicles, and that decision is almost always in the hands of a few with shareholder interests in mind rather than the beleaguered workers.

Anthropologists have likewise noted the dramatic impacts technology has had on society in modern history for some time now. Famed cultural anthropologist Sidney Mintz lends us similar observations as Solnit on the constraints many of us feel toward these time-saving technologies and the remarkable effects they have had on our behavior and society in his seminal work, *Sweetness and Power: The Place of Sugar in Modern History*.

The experience of time in modern society is often one of an insoluble shortage, and this perception may be essential to the smooth functioning of an economic system based on the principle of ever-expanded consumption. Anthropologists and economists have struggled with the paradox implicit in modern society—that its vastly more productive technologies result in individuals having (or feeling they have) less time, rather than more. Because of time pressure, people try to condense their consumption pleasure by consuming different things (such as movies and popcorn) simultaneously. This simultaneous (but often peculiarly unsatisfying) experience seems to individuals to be a "natural" one...*Maximum enjoyment in minimum time* has come to mean both divided (simultaneous) consumption—one eats while walking or working, drinks while driving or watching entertainment—and higher frequency of occasions for consumption. Watching the Cowboys play the Steelers while eating Fritos and drinking Coca-Cola, while smoking a joint, while one's girl sits on one's lap, can be packing a great deal of experience into a short time and thereby maximizing enjoyment. Or it can be experienced quite differently, depending upon the values one holds. Most important, however, people who experience pleasures simultaneously in these ways are taught to think about the consumption itself—not about the circumstances that led them to consume in that fashion, other than to sense that there was "not enough time" to do otherwise.[13]

We are often unaware of just how complex and peculiar our society is structured, and yet it has enormous consequences on virtually all aspects of our behavior and cognition, even down to how we move, think, and feel in the world.

The argument for efficiency, Solnit further notes, "suggests that what cannot be quantified cannot be valued—that that vast array of pleasures which fall into the category of doing nothing in particular, of woolgathering, cloud-gazing, wandering, window-shopping, are nothing but voids to be filled by something more definite, more productive, or faster-paced." Have you tried lately to simply stare at and study the pattern of a leaf *without* being high on some psychoactive ingredient? Try this as a five-minute meditation exercise and notice what emotions may arise. Does anxiety soon creep in after a minute goes by, and you have the sense that you are "wasting time?" The signs of people anxious to get to their destinations as quickly as possible are all around. The advertising and marketing industries are compelled to find endless ways to fill those voids to capture our attention. Perhaps this explains why so many of us are glued to our phones while walking down a street, unaware of our immediate opportunities for direct experience. Even amid the wilderness, such as state and national parks where people visit with the direct intention to remove themselves from the demanding speed of everyday life, one can see traces of people cutting through the brush, anxious to get back to the rhythm of a restless, racing society. Solnit reflects on this observation:

> Even on this headland route going nowhere useful, this route that could only be walked for pleasure, people had trodden shortcuts between the switchbacks as though efficiency was a habit they couldn't shake. The indeterminacy of a ramble, on which much may be discovered, is being replaced by the deter-

minant shortest distance to be traversed with all possible speed, as well as by the electronic transmissions that make real travel less necessary. As a member of the self-employed whose time saved by technology can be lavished on day-dreams and meanders, I know these things have their uses, and use them—a truck, a computer, a modem—myself, but I fear their false urgency, their call to speed, their insistence *that travel is less important than arrival.*[14]

These anxious habits permeate our existence. Once, while on vacation in Hawaii with our three-year-old son, I kept trying to hurry him along to get to wherever we were going when Hilary stopped me and asked what I was hurrying for. We were on vacation, explicitly *to slow down* and take our time, and it dawned on me how hard it is to shake this incessant habit of needing to always get somewhere efficiently to the point where we spoil our experiences, mired in such mania.

This shouldn't be interpreted as some technophobic Luddite rally call to smash our appliances and gadgets all to hell and get back to basics in remote cabins Unabomber style. This is merely meant to show us that trade-offs are taking place right before us at a rapid speed, and it might be wise to understand in what ways these current transitions in technology and culture might be impacting us at a behavioral, cognitive, and societal level. How might the restlessness we all feel be related to our society's efficiency addiction? One of the main concerns as an anthropologist is wondering how all the subtle unconscious changes in our technology and society might impact us for the worse. It's nearly impossible to divorce ourselves completely from the current conditions of life, and most of us are hesitant, if not outright reluctant, to do so when given the occasional opportunity. Once we're cushioned by the convenience of all our gadgets and entertainment, it becomes very difficult to slowly trim it back. However, some salient lessons and values can still be gained and applied to solve some of the personal and collective problems we are facing in the world today. These trade-offs will be discussed in the final chapters of the book, but first, let's examine our typical travel patterns in a little more detail to discover where we go *when we do go*.

○

According to some of the most recent data from the U.S. State Department, 151,814,305 valid passports were in circulation in 2022[15] , which equates to around 46% of the population, and the highest it has been, and also up 20% since 1989 when the U.S. population was 247 million. However, the significant statistical leap isn't due to increased travel but is in large part due to the January 2007 Western Hemisphere Travel Initiative (WHTI) requiring passports for Mexico and Canada.[16] Nevertheless, this shows that roughly 40% of us have taken some action to indicate we are interested in leaving the country at some point. By far, Mexico and Canada are the most consistent places Americans travel to: 41.2 million Americans of the 74 million Americans who traveled to international destinations in 2015 went exclusively to these two countries. This makes sense, though, since they are typically cheaper, closer to get to, less logistically challenging to navigate, have little to no language barriers, and have no radical time zone changes to adjust to. Nonetheless, the fact that 60% of Americans do not possess an active passport is intriguing for a nation of supposed immense wealth, opportunity, and influence. What is also significant to point out is that even if 40% have a valid passport, that still does not mean they have used it or have used it all that much. As mentioned, less than 10% traveled overseas in 2015[17], and the numbers are bound to be lower if we also take into consideration those who travel strictly for business (10%) or military reasons.

This prompts an interesting question for debate. Should travel within these occupations of business and military qualify as adventurous? What about pilots and flight attendants? The question remains open. On the one hand, these vocations seem separate from the same category of vacation time, recreation, or traveling for the sake of travel alone because they are restricted by job duties and strict time schedules that prevent someone from having free rein over their wanderings. Often, things that become routine lose their luster and no longer seem all that exciting. Adventure is largely about indulging in the liberty of *distance*, *time*, and *place*, something often inherently contrary to these professions. On the other hand, one can argue that the experiences drawn from traveling abroad on business or while on a military tour can be widely diverse. They have the potential for someone to acquire intimate relations with locals, experience other cultures, and learn languages and customs, even when their time is constrained. Some anthropologists studying adventure have argued that even military expeditions in the form of peacekeeping missions can qualify as an adventure.[18] Nevertheless, it remains difficult today to sincerely argue for the romance of modern warfare, as was done in previous centuries. As distinguished anthropologist Lawrence Keeley has observed, the 19th century's stories and poems of war are widely celebrated in hindsight as adventurous and heroic, albeit since then, "the Western appreciation of war has changed in literature from an uplifting melodrama to an elegiac tragedy, to a surrealist black comedy."[19]

According to the National Travel and Tourism Office data, within the decade from the years 2003 to 2012, an average of 61.6 million U.S. residents traveled abroad each year.[20] So here we see the discrepancy between those with a valid passport (around 130 million) and those who actively use their passport (61.6 million) in a given year. This figure ends up being a little more than half when using the 2012 data for valid passports in circulation, which were at 113,431,943 at that time.[21] Of that 61.6 million, nearly three-quarters (around 45 million people) traveled exclusively to Mexico, Canada, and the U.K.[22] Geographically and culturally speaking, then, this is not all that diverse, nor is it traveling all that far from home. And even *within those countries*, the vast majority of coveted hot spot destinations can be singled down to those aboard a cruise and luxury resort towns that are often already heavily Americanized, like Cancún and Puerto Vallarta in Mexico, or very specific locales like London in Britain.[23] When Leonardo DiCaprio's character, Richard, arrives in Bangkok in the film *The Beach* and observes the absurdity of American traveling, he laments, "The only downer is everyone's got the same idea. We all travel thousands of miles just to watch TV and check in somewhere with all the comforts of home. And you gotta ask yourself…what is the point of that?" It's hard not to feel some pang of agreement with that sentiment. What much of this data reveals is that, as Americans, we are quite predictable and unimaginative when (and if) we travel abroad.

However, there is something legitimate to be said about traveling within the United States, which has been and still is a rich culture in and of itself and is admittedly quite expansive and diverse in geography. Each state or region can arguably be equal in cultural and natural status to that of another country. As the late British-American journalist and social critic Christopher Hitchens remarks in his memoir *Hitch-22* about his first extended tour of the States, he commented, "...a crucial part of seeing America was also seeing how many Americas there were." To its credit, the United States is an expansive country and does possess many unique and remarkable ecological and cultural faces, an arena of adventure unto its own.

Many Americans have indulged themselves in adventure over several generations now by taking advantage of their public lands. According to the current National Park Service (NPS) statistics, 330,971,689 people visited the national parks in 2016, which ends up appearing as quite a healthy measure of interest in our national parks.[24] However, to be prudent, these figures are likely not absolute and are lower because this figure does not parse out individuals, but represents *visits by an individual*. For example, one person visiting five parks will equal a tally of five persons visiting our national parks, according to the data. Thus, those who visit a national park are more likely to visit multiple parks, therefore skewing the numbers. But that's still a large enough percentage that could help explain the low percentage of foreign travel. Also, we must bear in mind that many foreigners travel to and within the United States, and many of those foreigners also visit the national parks, which will likely bring the figure even lower for the specific tally of U.S. citizens visiting the parks. For instance, during the period from 2003 to 2012, when we had 61.6 million Americans traveling abroad, we had an average influx of 54.6 million international visitors.[25] So, if we wanted to know specifically how many Americans visit our national parks, we would need to take these factors into account to calibrate our figures.

To highlight this point a little more, if we look at the statistics on state park admittance, which is over 720 million per year, this clearly shows a figure more than double the U.S. population.[26] One might also add that there is an endless supply of outfitters and guides for the outdoor adventure tourism industry to equip visitors for boundless outdoor activities such as kayaking, climbing, hunting, fishing, scuba diving, backpacking, bicycling, etc. Thus, the market for commercial adventure opportunities for the modern thrill-seeker abounds, making the incentive to stay in the homeland much more enticing, which, again, might help explain the low numbers of Americans abroad.

How we travel demands some scrutiny as well. Recreational vehicles, which are an ever-booming industry and a classic American tradition, appear to be the number one choice for how many citizens experience travel in America. This makes plenty of sense. They are convenient and comfortable. They carry everything one could ever want and need. They allow us free rein by giving us the power to choose where and for how long we wish to spend our time in a given area. And they empower older generations and those enfeebled by injury or other ailments to take adventures that they may otherwise have been deterred from. These are all great things, and I'm not trying to pick a fight with Grannie and her RV. However, they can also be unsuspectingly constraining. Vehicles are also baggage, especially large ones. They can own us as much as we own them and limit us in innumerable ways, obstructing us from having experiences many Americans desperately need. Edward Abbey, a sharp critic of the American style of traveling, what he termed "industrial tourism," bemoaned over half a century ago in *Desert Solitaire* over the fate of many of the beloved national parks and the nature of American travel:

> They work hard, these people. They roll up incredible mileages on their odometers, rack up state after state in two-week transcontinental motor marathons, knock off one national park after another, take millions of square yards of photographs, and endure patiently the most prolonged discomforts... Industrial Tourism is a threat to national parks. But the chief victims of the system are the motorized tourists. They are being robbed and robbing themselves. So long as they are unwilling to crawl out of their cars they will not discover the treasures of the national parks and will never escape the stress and turmoil of the urban-suburban complexes which they had hoped, presumably, to leave behind for awhile.[27]

Though overtly cynical, Abbey's abrasive words could just as well have been written yesterday to accurately describe the encumbered way in which many of us still attempt to wander. Even after half a century, we're still managing to stifle ourselves as much as we are the national parks. Even the backcountry areas of some national parks are competitively fierce to gain access to. Try getting a backpacking permit in a number of the more sought-after national parks during peak season (sometimes even during the offseason now), and you'll understand the absurd irony of trying to seek solitude in a place originally designed and reserved to be mostly devoid of people. Lottery systems have been employed for outdoor excursions such as white water rafting and kayaking to alleviate crowds in the wilderness, yet create an unfortunate scenario where only a select few get to experience the great outdoors.[28] Crowded destinations signal that we ought to consider venturing to other areas of the country and world to allow some of these places to breathe. We have it within us to dare a bit more to spread out both within and beyond our borders and be creative with where an adventure can take us.

What things like planes, trains, automobiles, resorts, cruises, and RVs all have in common is that they, like our homes, are insulators. They belie the inconvenient truth that we are a cautious and sheltered people. What's more, they demonstrate how dependent—overly dependent perhaps—we are on technology. Humans have always been dependent on technology. There's no shame in that, but in today's age, we outsource nearly all of our adventure experience to corporations and technologies with the hope that they will keep us safe and take us to destinations as quickly and comfortably as possible. What trade-offs do we make when we attempt to make things easier, more efficient, and safer? If we paved the whole stretch of the Application Trail and notched out pull-off areas for our viewing pleasure, stocked every mile with cafes and soda machines, it would surely make things easier and safer for us. But would we appreciate it as much? Could we draw any inspiring hard-won lessons from such a blasé experience? And by the way, I am not exempting myself from these criticisms. I've added myself to the amassing crowds and bumper-to-bumper traffic in our national parks many times. I've consumed more than my fair share of gasoline and maimed and destroyed vehicles zipping back and forth across the country. These criticisms shouldn't be taken to make us feel ashamed and guilty. Rather, they are meant to challenge us and for us to reflect on how we can better preserve and protect these areas without destroying the essence of what these places represent to all of us. The question then is, can we design a system of adventure in our society that is less invasive, yet more fulfilling?

To be frank, wandering should be a distinct chance to live through more raw and challenging experiences in a less encumbered way. Challenges stimulate us to think, plan, and work harder. They make us value things more because of all the time and effort put into reaching the top of the mountain or crossing a surging river. Will we hold the same level of value for those mountains when roads and cars can effortlessly corkscrew us to the top, or bridges ceaselessly carry us across all those canyons, valleys, and rivers? Should machines replace *all* labor? The more efficient and easier things become, the less we are likely to value those things because we'll never be able to relate to all that thinking, planning, and hard work that goes into them.

Thus, there are obvious incentives for staying in the United States when thinking about traveling and adventure: perhaps a stern patriotic belief in putting money into the U.S. economy; cheaper travel; shorter distances to traverse; conveniences; no language barrier; and as my grandfather always commented, "America is so large and so abundant in geography and culture that there's already so much here to see and do." Then again, my grandfather was also terrified of flying. The data bear all of this out and more. As one report explained, "Tourism experts and avid travelers attribute Americans' lack of interest in international travel to a few key factors, including the United States' own rich cultural and geographic diversity; an American skepticism and/or ignorance about international destinations; a work culture that prevents Americans from taking long vacations abroad; and the prohibitive cost and logistics of going overseas."[29] The language barrier is also a very intimidating obstacle that likely explains why the countries (or destinations within those countries) Americans seek are predominantly English-speaking. When we consider all these factors, it is little surprise then that many Americans are deterred from traveling abroad. We don't have the luxury of proximity to many different countries as those in Europe, and there's simply a lot to see and do here that does not require passports, currency exchange rates, and the nightmare of making it through Customs and groping by the valiant and laudable TSA & Friends if we so choose to hit the open road instead.

○

There are legitimate reasons why someone cannot afford to travel much. Costs can be expensive. Go figure! For instance, it has been noted for some time that there is a positive correlation between income and the number of passport holders.[30] In 2011, repeat traveler households reported $129,000 annual income, and the average cost of international airfare per person per trip was $1,237, with an additional average of $1,487 for expenditures. Thus, the obvious point is that the richer you are, the more likely it is that you have a passport and have the means to travel regularly. This is also true for education and several other political, economic, and cultural factors.[31] What is surprising, now in 2025, is that average airfare has remained constant at $1,237[32], and the average daily cost of a vacation is around $324, with lower budgets averaging around $121 per day and luxury budgets around $923 per day.[33]

However, these are just a few statistics, and anyone who's looked at enough statistics by now knows they can vary widely. I personally don't put much stock into them and only treat them as a rough estimate anyway. Besides, we should not read all this as a determination of our circumstances, nor let it deter those of us with less education or less money, because it could very well be our *high standards* that are driving up these prices and expectations. Plus, there are websites, such as Pomelo and Going, that offer low airfare alerts and only require some diligence and quick action to snag up some incredibly low deals. Also, the cost of air travel has dropped significantly since the 1970s, and overall costs in other forms of transportation, like trains, buses, and vehicles, have become more affordable. As far as expenses go, that is up to our standards. Most hostels, the world over, are reasonably cheap, and the ability to prepackage dry foods for meals is just the few options that can radically reduce expenses while abroad. There is an overwhelming number of creative ways to be cost-effective in our adventures if we so choose to learn and adopt them.

Friends and colleagues with similar salary and student debt levels as me have been overheard time and again saying they wish *they* could go to Italy, or whichever country is brought up in discussion. So why don't we? I will be blunt here. Failure of imagination. Failure to be bold. Failure to prioritize. Failure to be savvy with our time and money. Failure to want to wander. Failure to actively overcome fear. We prefer all the luxuries of home (televisions, game consoles, cars, bigger houses, land, boats, guns, lots and lots of toys, and all the bills and insurance policies that we know will inevitably fasten themselves to those toys) while neglecting to put money away for adventures. The fact that we choose to overburden ourselves with all these material things versus experiences like travel and adventure indicates that many of us, in fact, do possess the means to wander; we just don't value travel and adventure as much. But if we want to scrounge up money, look no further than the food in our trash can. The average American family throws away about $1500 of food annually.[34] That's a round-trip flight to just about anywhere in the world nowadays. Frugality can be your friend if you let it.

For many of us, it's not that we can't financially afford to go places; it is that we don't prioritize or *value* it like we do our material items, and we're not diligent enough with how we save and budget. As author and an expert on the overworking and overspending American, Juliet B. Schor, elaborates, many of us are locked in a vicious cycle of work and spending where we "see, want, borrow, buy" and repeat.[35] Largely in the pursuit of status and obsessed with our self-image, we chase after luxury goods and fall into overwhelming debt, emulating lifestyles of those in our society that far exceed our bank accounts. Schor's research has shown that "the more TV a person watches, the more he or she spends…what we see on TV inflates our sense of what's normal."[36] All in all, we don't seem willing to break out of this cycle and sacrifice some material possessions for something we perceive as a mere intangible experience, such as an adventure, despite how many of us still dream of "seeing the world." Cognitive dissonance be damned.

There also tends to be a stigma that travel is only for rich elitists. As Sarah Palin once reportedly claimed, "I'm not one of those who maybe come from a background of, you know, kids who perhaps graduate college and their parents get 'em a passport and give 'em a backpack and say go off and travel the world. Noooo. I worked all my life…I was not, uh, a part of, I guess, that culture."[37] One might be surprised to find that backpacks and passports aren't all that expensive, and most world travelers you meet aren't garnished with Louis

Vuitton boots and bags. Backpackers are some of the most financially conservative travelers you are going to find. And for the record, I've been working since I was fifteen, all through high school and college. I provided myself with my passport, plane tickets, and backpack, and I am still years away from paying off student debt. Working as a contract archaeologist in the United States gets you not much more than $50,000 a year, and that's factoring in your per diem. I'm here to call bullshit on the idea that one needs to be spoiled rich to travel and isn't exclusively for the haves.

Many of us do not realize that many opportunities for adventure are incredibly inexpensive. In fact, in the four months on the Appalachian Trail, the two of us *combined* only spent around $2,500. While costs for a thru-hike can vary considerably, many have claimed to do it for under $1,000 for the entire length of six months by being incredibly thrifty. This is where savviness, frugality, and imagination come into play. It merely takes some ingenuity and willingness to prioritize finances and time if one desires to go somewhere and explore. If we can get ourselves out of the mindset of wanting to live like kings and queens every place we go and consider these points, then we can do away with the myths of travel being expensive and only for the well-off.

○

Contemporary Americans are a restless bunch, wound up like a spring. But are we still "leading lives of quiet desperation" in the words of Henry David Thoreau? It's apparent our lives, in many ways, have improved significantly since Thoreau's time in the mid-19th century, and few of us would admit to leading a meager, desperate existence. This is rather harsh and myopic. However, in everyday conversation, when we speak of our greatest dreams and desires, many of us often chime in that we still wish to "see the world", yet the cold, hard truth is many of us never do in any physical sense. We treat our adventures as fleeting "what if" experiments, never allowing them to materialize. It is telling that one of the wealthiest, most influential countries on the planet and in history fails to experience other areas of the world, other geographies, and alternative ways of doing and thinking about things. It is commonly known among social psychologists that contact with others causes us to indulge in perspective-taking and, as a result, we gain a greater affinity for one another. There is much that many of us are missing out on. Failing to wander is failing to take part in one of humanity's longest-cherished activities.

We can begin to see that many things operate to keep us in place: mortgages, finances, family, friends, community, career responsibilities, and the overall comfort and security of a place. There's nothing wrong with us not wanting to travel the world because we cannot afford it, or we love being with our friends, family, or community, or simply enjoying where we are and what we're doing in life. I adore playing the role of homebody nowadays nearly as much as I love being a restless wanderer. Plus, travel is not for everyone, and that is fine. However, from what we've reviewed so far, we still must face some inconvenient truths about ourselves: The fact is, Americans are fearful and worried about many things these days, despite the colossal amounts we spend on our safety. The fact is, Americans don't invest much in adventure and a diversity of natural and cultural experiences. When we do travel, we don't travel very far from home or for very long. Trust is significantly down, and we are continuously fighting among ourselves about nearly every issue under the sun. We spend an inordinate amount of time consuming large amounts of insipid information on television and the Internet. We are divided and skeptical about almost everything, and we seem entirely consumed by an obsessive work culture that fuels an even grander obsession with material assets. And despite being such a wealthy nation with many of us having the means and opportunities to travel quite extensively, we don't. Altogether, it becomes apparent that fear and unrest probably have something to do with our failure to wander. How we spend our money, time, and attention strongly indicates what we value. To date, wholesome adventure is not one of those things for most of us.

We are all searching for meaning. We all want something out of life. More than anything, we want purpose. What gives our lives meaning? Where do we derive happiness from? We might believe that we obtain happiness and meaning from the tangible objects of our desire, but if this were true, by now, surely the abundance of our materialist culture that we've been accumulating for more than half a century would have satiated this urge and made most of us content by now. That doesn't seem to be the case, and I'm confident that's a dead-wrong life philosophy to have. Life satisfaction has much more to do with the psychology of our minds, the sensations we discover in new experiences, and the memories we construct with one another. When we learn something new, it generates certain feelings within us. Coming to know how the world truly operates is what grips us the most, and there's no better way to achieve this than through serendipitous feelings of wondering and wandering. By shedding fears and indulging in an adventure, we become reacquainted with the qualities of *distance, time,* and *place,* which serve as catalysts, enabling us to capture what we're all ultimately seeking: community, identity, structure, and purpose. In the end, the Appalachian Trail fulfilled this model for humanity like an elegant mathematical equation and inspired me to begin a quest to better understand those who wander.

CHAPTER 2
Those Who Wander:
The Restless Few

"For all its material advantages, the sedentary life has left us edgy, unfulfilled. Even after 400 generations in villages and cities, we haven't forgotten. The open road still softly calls, like a nearly forgotten song of childhood. We invest far-off places with a certain romance. This appeal, I suspect, has been meticulously crafted by natural selection as an essential element in our survival. Long summers, mild winters, rich harvests, plentiful game—none of them lasts forever. It is beyond our powers to predict the future. Catastrophic events have a way of sneaking up on us, of catching us unaware. Your own life, or your band's, or even your species' might be owed to a restless few—drawn, by a craving they can hardly articulate or understand, to undiscovered lands and new worlds."
—Carl Sagan, *Pale Blue Dot*

Katahdin was now at our backs, shrinking in the picturesque, humid scene of the lush Maine summer. And again, another mistake was made, though it wouldn't be known to us for another four days. We'd made a miscalculation from the comforts of my room amid planning last winter that it would take us eight to ten days to make it from Katahdin to the small town of Monson on the other end of the Hundred-Mile Wilderness. Little did we know, it takes a good day and a half just to enter the Wilderness from Katahdin, especially strenuous for those who have yet to acquire their "trail legs." The Hundred-Mile Wilderness is considered the most secluded and rugged section of the Appalachian Trail. A wooden sign at the trailhead cautions, "It is 100 miles south to the nearest town at Monson. Do not attempt this section unless you have a *minimum* of 10 days of supplies and are fully equipped. This is the longest wilderness section of the entire AT, and its difficulty should not be underestimated. Good hiking! Maine Appalachian Trail Club (MATC)."

We were certainly "fully equipped", overly equipped in fact, my pack idiotically bulging at nearly 60 pounds. This is a frequent mistake among novice backpackers rooted in admirable fear—the fear of starving. And yet, despite so much excess weight, we had packed enough food for only ten days for the entire time, starting from Katahdin to Monson. In hindsight, we should have allotted our rookie selves a generous twelve days and packed lighter, more nutrient-dense foods. And here we thought we'd prepared so well. Weariness and hunger seemed to be in our future, but luckily, we came upon our first instance of "trail magic" very early on: lavish, ready-to-make chili dangling in our destined first shelter of the Wilderness. Hats off to the kindness of strangers, known on the trail as "trail angels" who leave random assortments of food, supplies, and the occasional joint hanging from trees to aid the wearied, ill-planned, or discouraged thru-hiker.

Our second day had revealed itself to be clear and cool with a comfortable aura of the sun radiating through the trees. The scene was one of those occasional early mornings where everything strikes you as fresh and stimulating. The air was clean and crisp, hardly in motion, much unlike our vigorous selves, soundly tramping toward the trailhead with huge grins of contentment spread across our faces. I can't quite recall now if I had tears in my eyes then or not, but I recall my excitement was potent and the moment felt ethereal. It is not easy to convey how meaningful this beginning moment of setting out on a journey was for me. I'd dreamed in sleep, dreamed in the day, and lived vicariously through various novels and personal accounts about wayward lifestyles, and here the reality was unfolding before me. The road beneath my rhythming feet and the weighted pack of obsessively calculated necessities upon my back gave me the greatest reassurance of a well-made decision.

As if my fortune couldn't be any better, I had someone to share all this experience with; something else I'd never anticipated in all my previous youthful dreaming of such life adventures. Hilary, petite but tenacious, hobbled along in front, her feet already quickening with pain from her plantar fasciitis. With a problem like that, no sane person would dare attempt such a challenge as backpacking the entire Appalachian Trail. Her brown mop-top curly hair, freshly cut short, was not visible from my perspective as the top of her pack eclipsed her head. She was merely a pack with legs, as I loved to tease her, who would occasionally give out a deep guttural sound to express the abnormal amount of phlegm collecting in her throat. In my best David Attenborough impersonation, I would make social commentary on "this elusive creature with a habit of generating what is known in the American vernacular as a 'loogie.'" We all become a little feral as a consequence of living ruggedly. Though I'd deemed her "trail name" to be Cactus because of her prickly but under-the-surface calming personality, it became apparent only later that a more fitting name might have been "Problems." And damn would she soon have some problems.

Questions haphazardly arose from time to time as we strolled along. "Why were we doing this?" This particular question morphs for virtually every hiker at some point from the tone of a pondering philosopher to a crazed, desperate person at the end of their wits, sped up to become "why the fuck are we doing this!?" and often followed by many other expletives. Meditative questions came buzzing into our brains as we walked, "What was so alluring about walking for months in the woods for people? Did it have something to do with the precariousness of it all? Were we trying to escape from something or in search of something? Why did other people do this? Maybe they have some of the answers. We should ask them...."

We hiked an additional two miles from Abol Campground to the trailhead that we momentarily missed in a laugh of embarrassment. Through that mistake, we were, fortunately, able to chat with the park ranger who had checked us in the morning before. I mentioned I'd scoffed when he told us it would take us ten hours to climb and descend Katahdin. He returned only with a humble smile. He told us a bit more about himself, how he too had hiked the AT, the perils, and rewards of being a park ranger, and gave us some worthy advice to simply go the trail at a steady and patient, yet persistent pace. We bid him farewell as he rumbled slowly down the dirt road, the truck rocking as its tires dipped into the water-filled divots. He was off to take care of one of those perils, outhouse maintenance.

Immediately upon entering what seemed a quaint and harmless

forest, my jovial, carefree expression turned into a wry, sour grimace as a swarm of mosquitoes lunged for our exposed skin. It was an absurd milieu for the first few miles as we angrily thumped along aimlessly, swatting the air and smacking ourselves foolishly, burning soon-to-be much-needed calories. By the time we reached our first memorable vista of Daicey Pond, the buzzing bastards seemed to have had their fill and subsided somewhat. We stopped momentarily for a Clif Bar and soon after, plunged ourselves in the wrong direction for about twenty minutes. I had mistaken a white mold or lichen-marked tree for what I assumed was a faded and distorted white blaze, the rectangular signature of the AT stamped 165,000 times roughly every 70 feet along the 2,200-mile route.[38] After a while of encountering only blue blazes that signified another trail, I scolded myself with multiple insults, and we turned around and found our way again. The trail provided many of these minor challenges and irksome lessons for the rest of the day. The same would be true for days to follow as our bodies slowly and painfully adjusted to this abrupt new lifestyle.

We met two well-toned, stoic-looking northbounders resting at the Hurd Brook Lean-to not far from the northern edge of the Wilderness. Less than a day's stroll separated them from Katahdin. They would arrive in half the time it took us and with twice as much vigor left over. Caribou and Cannonball, though intimidating at first glance, openly chatted with us. New to this lifestyle, we were eager for any breadcrumbs of advice on how to sustain ourselves and see the whole trail through. Caribou, eyes dancing with the bouncing limbs of the trees, succinctly summed up what was in store for every thru-hiker, "Monday may be bad, but that doesn't mean Wednesday won't be great… It's a roller coaster out here." Hilary, along with many other seasoned travelers, has made the same important observation that during travel, there are often many highs but many lows, and that going on great adventures doesn't mean you're going to be living in a state of euphoria all the time. One must be willing to accept a greater range of uncertainty and discomfort than their normal daily routine. Gritty adventures like this don't just offer us opportunities to learn resilience; they force us to be resilient. It is nonoptional.

For me, one of the most salient things about doing something like this was to take advantage of this expanse of time to reflect more on the significant aspects of our lives. Who do I want to be in this world? How do I want to spend my time? What is my role in contributing to improving the world? The structure of modern society doesn't easily grant us such opportunities in the normalcy of our everyday, expedient lives. Time on the trail tended to take on a very different meaning and dimension. Our minds mimicked our feet and often trailed off in meditative wonderment for many hours.

There was something powerful, even visceral, in what we were doing, and it can be difficult to explain in words. Each day on the trail feels born anew. So fresh and vibrant are its happenings that the days don't quite collide in the same fashion as in one's typical routine lifestyle. It may be Friday, yet it is no Friday comparable to last week's Friday. So much tends to change, so much distance is covered, and so much is unexpected. Common life seems far more predictable and monotonous. Much like the wavering effects of being on a hallucinogenic drug, time dilates and nearly becomes senseless. Time seems to shift in a new way, and the memory of the preceding days is enhanced and falls into a new system of chronicling events in one's mind. Weeks seem to become months and months, years. In a way, it feels as though you've stepped outside of time.

The landscape morphed into endless mosquito-infested bogs of muddy black sludge and fallen timbers slowly being pounded into a pulp by the occasional trail-goer. The path remained ungraded and decorated with obstacles. Roots weaved in the manner of a snake orgy, and rocks with a minimum weight requirement of a hundred pounds were strewn carelessly about our way, coercing our eyes to constantly survey the ground. It was a path unlike any I had ever hiked, and it was not the path I once imagined. It was as if those who'd originally blazed this section of trail were in a hapless fury to get out as quickly as possible. I could certainly sympathize at that moment.

The forest seemed to have a frequent tradeoff between hardwoods and conifers as if some unjust law of segregation prohibited their mingling. The pattern was nothing more than the natural dictating forces of the rise and fall of elevation, along with the favorable conditions of sun and soil, temperature, and moisture. Plentiful rivers and streams laced through the topography. The Hundred Mile-Wilderness was the only section of the trail we felt comfortable enough drinking directly out of springs and streams due to its remoteness and also because our poorly chosen water-treatment method, i.e., iodine tablets, a) quickly ran out and b) made our water brown and disgusting. Like dropping a coin in a pocket, another lesson was gained.

The most invigorating moment occurred on day seven when we summited White Cap Mountain, the highest point in the Wilderness. The mixture of sunshine and breeze felt divine. The views were the best we'd witnessed since Katahdin: splotches of lakes embedded below rolling, bulging mounds of greenery scattered for miles in every direction, and a hazy white mist faintly blanketing all of it. The time was uplifting. For a moment, we forgot the anguished groans we'd let out on account of our aching bodies all the preceding mornings as we attempted to claw our way out of our sleeping bags, the tent, and up yet another hill or mountain. There were three things I'd found to rejuvenate my mind and body while on this excursion: percolated coffee in the early morning, a dip in a cool lake or stream in the evening, and standing on top of a mountain, pensive and peering out over the landscape. What is in our nature that causes us to pause and stare from atop mountains? I took it as a great reward and felt that maybe the most beautiful places on earth ought to be those hardest to reach.

In a rare moment of clarity, I knew exactly why we were there on the trail and why we all, deep down, might yearn for adventure. This cuts to the very core of what we all so desperately need to understand, not only as a single country but as a global species. The type of industrialized world we are unwittingly cast into when we are born is a very new phenomenon for humans. Naturally, we are adapting, as humans do, but not without a whole slew of chronic problems related to diet and lifestyle change commonly referred to as "diseases of civilization." It remains to be seen whether the trade-offs we are making when we opt for greater dependency on societies with advanced technologies that radically transform our habits and behaviors are conducive to human physiology and well-being in the long run or not, but a price is being paid. In what ways and to what degree will be borne out in time.

Nevertheless, it seems apparent that we are living within the confines of an increasingly claustrophobic, restless, and fearful society. It can be hard to breathe, much less think, sometimes, especially when it comes to the things that truly matter to us. There is a toxic brew of arrogance and ignorance churning in there. We live with such technological prowess, entitled abundance, and egotistical freedom, but why do we feel so vehemently entitled, and in what sense are we truly free? Free from what and free to do what? What is it really that we have that is so abundant? Time certainly doesn't feel like one of those things that are abundant and free.

Out in the forests and the mountains, one is quickly humbled by the realization that we are entitled to nothing, we are greatly vulnerable, and society's "abundance" is illusory, relative, and ephemeral. There are fine lessons too easily neglected because we are undeniably shrouded in a culture of entitlement, fear, anxiety, and unbalanced abundance. At the same time, we're incredibly well-insulated by an unprecedented level of security living in the United States, and that includes this trail. If we never step outside the confirming echoes of our coveted social circles to find ourselves challenged from time to time, we'll never realize our fortune and our privilege. A core lesson you learn studying anthropology is that you never really come to understand your own culture until you've been immersed in others. The same is true for adventures that carry us far and wide.

There are risks to leading a highly sedentary life. For one, we are less exposed to other landscapes, cultures, and other ways of doing things. Whether we realize it or not, these things are existential. We may fail to learn valuable information about who we are and what we are capable of. We may lend ourselves to illusory perspectives of grandeur, and we may shamelessly take for granted and lose the sense of what so many have done before us to grant us such prosperity and well-being. Rarely do we make the time and personal space to reflect on what we truly want to create for ourselves and others living in a society full of immense distractions. Things tend to snap into sharper focus when given proper time to wander.

I later came to realize that this journey was just as much about studying and understanding our wider society and culture as it was about learning something about the people and culture of the Appalachian Trail. From the perspective of the trail, one is granted a unique opportunity to look outward at our wider culture and question it more. There were bound to exist countless lessons to be drawn from this experience, insights that might very well be of benefit to our society in some capacity, if not on a collective level, then at least on a personal one.

○

Fresh out of college with degrees in anthropology, Hilary and I didn't want to let all our recently accumulated knowledge rot in our brains, so we thought we'd be clever and put it to some creative use. We eventually came up with the idea to share our journey and observations of the people of the trail on a blog, *Those Who Wander*. Deciding to wander along the Appalachian Trail wasn't random either. We both loved to hike, camp, and explore. We also both loved the endless ways anthropology taught us to see the world in all its eclecticism. For me, anthropology is less of a vocation and more of a way of conceptualizing or framing the world. As anthropologists are well-equipped to study groups, we imagined those drawn to the Appalachian Trail as a subset of people within a subculture little explored through an anthropological lens. The months spent on the AT provided an exceptional opportunity to interact with a fantastic sampling of people who originated from various parts of the United States, along with some we encountered from Germany, Switzerland, France, Australia, Ireland, Japan, and China. From many parts of the globe, a relatively small group, some several thousand determined folks, make the pilgrimage every year, only a fraction of whom complete the entire thru-hike. Since the trail's official completion in 1937, over 20,000 people have successfully finished the full trek.[39]

Wonderful arrays of people trudge along this dirt corridor every year. Those who wander this trail come with innumerable backgrounds and experiences, ages, ethnicities, occupations, religious, cultural, and political beliefs, and different socioeconomic upbringings. Despite the wide differences, there's a tremendous recurring and lasting sense of camaraderie and oneness: that we're all intimately experiencing and sharing in something special together. Other well-known accounts of the trail, such as David Brill's *As Far As the Eye Can See,* have made similar observations and ascribed the trail as a "linear community" that is "predicated on trust, fellowship, and sharing—values that too often seemed lacking in the more 'civilized' society we had left behind."[40] It is an astonishing and overwhelming feeling to confront living through such a communal atmosphere, especially at a time like now, when the cynicism and corrosiveness of contemporary politics and other societal malaise have us feeling as though we share nothing in common. What we came to discover was that our experiences with the trail and those who wander provided us with some important lessons to share with our highly restless and fearful society.

○

AN ANTHROPOLOGY OF WANDERING

Extensive travel and adventure tend to create rare types of humans—the restless few. Indeed, there is something peculiar to be found in the minds and characters of those who wander—the world's travelers, cosmopolitans, explorers, adventurers, pilgrims, mountaineers, old merchant traders, nomadic herders, hunter-gatherers, thrill seekers, vagabonds, drifters, those who climb the highest peaks and swim in the deepest depths, and of course, the AT thru-hikers, all-inclusive, the historical and contemporary ones. This subset of humanity keeps alive the continuity of adventure in our species, like survivalists or shamans, religiously doctoring embers for a future fire. Irrespective of the amount of money they have or don't have in their pockets, they are all fascinating and inspiring because of one thing: they willingly cast themselves into a quest of unnecessary risk and unknown danger; how much easier it would be to just stay put like everyone else. What fascinating behavior!

These outliers have had and still have much to tell us, perhaps more today than ever in a society obsessively bothered by change and unrest. I have imbued those who wander with a certain mystique in my mind. There is something often vibrant and uplifting, yet well-reserved, almost sage-like, in their demeanor. It is as if they possess many of the answers to humanity's long-standing questions surrounding philosophical inquiries into meaning and being. They tend to walk the earth with a poise of great contentment and resolve, though in no way is it pretentious—well, perhaps sometimes it is. I know, I am embellishing greatly here and have romanticized and caricatured these figures time and again, raising them to mythical status. I admit that I am envious, but this stems from a wish to see and partially understand where others have gone, what they have seen, what they have learned, and what they have done throughout the vastness of time and space while on our pale blue dot of a planet. Ultimately, that might well be one of the universal dreams and drives *we all share* as a species. Perhaps that explains why so many of us are transfixed with the lives of celebrities and royals, epic drama series, science fiction, fantasy novels, video game entertainment, social media, and the bulk of our everyday gossip transpiring around the lives of others. We can only ever know what it is like to be one individual being with our time here. Human stories then serve as our most vital attempts at understanding others and seeing life through wildly differing eyes.

○

A sensible starting point for studying adventure in anthropology can begin with a reflection on human origins, more specifically, human movement and settlement across the globe. Asking ourselves the perennial question of where we come from gets to the heart of who we are. Our ancient narrative as a species is perhaps the grandest tale of adventure. Archaeological and linguistic evidence has long confirmed the evidence for human movements across the globe stretching back millennia, but it was a mystery as to how much people were isolated and how frequently they moved. More recently—within the last 15 years—new genetic evidence in the form of ancient DNA has demonstrated how incredibly mixed human populations are in their ancestry, which is all the result of human interactions over vast distances and time. As famed geneticist David Reich recently wrote on the extraordinary revelations of ancient DNA in his book *Who We Are and How We Got Here: Ancient DNA and the New Science of the Human Past*:

> Prior to the genome revolution, I, like most others, had assumed that the big genetic clusters of populations we see today reflect deep splits of the past. But in fact the big clusters today are themselves the result of mixtures of very different populations that existed earlier...There was never a single trunk population in the human past. It has been mixtures all the way down.[41]

What much of this new genetic data reveals is that humans have not been as nearly isolated in the deep past as once thought, but have been fervently wandering and exploring the globe for far longer and more frequently than we realized.

In highly condensed form, our ancient narrative goes something like this: From parched African soils, various groups of former hominins gradually ventured over many years across vast open landscapes. We found our way into the depths of long wintered fire-lit caves and rock shelters, crossed scorching wind-torn deserts, set our sights on soaring and endless snow-draped mountain ranges, and followed endless stretches of roaring waters that plummeted into deathly gripping canyons and engorged rivers that wound through thickly humid tropics. Some of us eventually settled along the fertile veins of Mesopotamia, Egypt, the Indus Valley, and China due to the attractive and plentiful game, soil, and water found there. We diverged and pushed through the centuries, the millennia, to greater distances back and forth like an undulating pendulum along the Eurasian steppes and outward toward Australia, Polynesia, Oceania, up into Siberia.

Onward we trudged into the Americas over the now-submerged land known as Beringia, which once connected Asia to America when the Ice Age reigned. We found our way into ever more intoxicating forests, deserts, mountains, plains, woodlands, and marshlands through corridors of ice and down limitless rocky, sandy coasts to the southern tip of South America, the "land of fire," an enduring namesake for the many campsites aglow along the coast from indigenous fires spotted by the 16th-century Portuguese explorer Ferdinand Magellan and crew as they circumnavigated the globe: a unifying moment of exploration's vast and often enigmatic history.

Restless and insatiable, our appetites seemed only to have thrived for the voyage. During the deep time when numerous divergent hominins shared a vast tract of space, adventure and life seemed inextricably intertwined. The concept of 'adventure' was not just something of a commercialized recreation as it has become in our modern world, but a way of life. Defiant, though keenly aware of the hazards and perils of the journey ahead, we humans couldn't help but move, explore, and let the mind blossom with an endless labyrinth of myths and tales of the world beyond the horizons and the stars.

With continents continually being traversed and trade networks coming into and out of existence, small vessels and ships were crafted and forged to set sail and sights on those barely visible islands over the horizon, sprinkled like irresistible sugar-laced breadcrumbs across a still inconceivable planet. Ceaseless movements of human activity and interaction gave way to crossing oceans, building empires, unearthing, and forging minerals. We devised industries to continue that involuntary motion and to seal once firmly beaten dirt paths with roaring concrete and steel, which remains to be beaten and pounded by the occasional modern tramps that buck our trend in stale sedentism and continue the peripatetic spirit of our wandering forebears. Because of our industriousness and restlessness, we've now stamped human feet into the surface of the Moon, preserved not unlike the 3.7-million-year-old hominin footprints preserved in volcanic ash at the archaeological site of Laetoli in Tanzania; footprints that serve as powerful symbols that urge us, again and again, to reflect on time, space, and the thrill to move!

Anthropologists and historians of the mid-20th century were well aware by then that ancient travel and migration routes by sea and land across the globe were a testament to some of the most remarkable accomplishments of our species.[42] The Silk Road—what is now increasingly being referred to as the Silk Routes—was an ancient network of prominent trade and travel corridors. Beginning in the 2nd century BCE and lasting until the middle of the 15th century CE, these routes once connected numerous cultures, spreading ideas, food, and items of trade, and bringing about untold growth and prosperity to many eastern and western regions throughout Eurasia and Africa for more than 1500 years. Likewise, seafaring peoples ventured across remarkably vast stretches of the Indian and Pacific oceans. The anthropologist Ralph Linton noted the incredible wandering achievements of the people of Southeast Asia and Oceania:

> The migrations of the Malayo-Polynesian speaking peoples from their homeland in Southeast Asia and the adjoining islands present one of the most amazing phenomena in history. In spite of their atomistic political patterns, which made it impossible for them to organize large communal projects, and their late acquisition of metal, they were able to encircle *a full third of the globe* in their voyages of exploration and to establish permanent settlements at points as remote as the island

of Madagascar, only 250 miles off the East African coast, and Easter Island, only 2200 miles from the coast of South America and nearly due south of Denver, U.S.A.[43]

The anthropologist Bronislaw Malinowski, writing over a century ago, famously observed and documented the *Kula* exchange system and impressive long-distance expeditions of the seafaring Trobriand peoples of Papua New Guinea in the southwestern Pacific Ocean. Malinowski commented on the motivation for adventure that the landscape and planning for such excursions surely inspired for centuries:

> The open sea now lies before the fleet with the high, distant peaks of the d'Entrecasteaux mountains floating above the haze. In very clear weather the nearer Ampheletts can be seen—small steep rocks, scattered over the horizon, misty, but more material against the faint blue of the distant land. These far-off views must have inspired generation after generation of Kiriwinian sailors with zest for adventure, wonder and desire to see the much-praised marvels of foreign lands, with awe and with superstitious fear. Mixed with it all—associated in the native mind with the allurement of the distant *koya* (mountains)—there was the ambition to return with plenty of *vaygu'a* (valuables). In myths, in traditional legends, in real stories and in songs, *Kula* expeditions were and are described and praised and there is a definite complex of *Kula* tradition and mythology, governed perhaps by two dominating emotions: the desire to obtain the *vaygu'a* and the dread of the dangers to be encountered.[44]

When we return to the present and reflect on our adventures with more sobering eyes, this romantic or idealistic vision of adventure and human origins can be shortsighted. There is a disconnect between how we envision adventure and what it sincerely entails. This feeling of wanderlust, we may notice, often only occurs before and after our adventure, and rarely ever during our experience. The paths we travel, one comes to find, are as perilous, tedious, and mundane as they are pleasant and rewarding. True adventures do not often resemble dramatically embellished films and novels after all. It is this ironic clash between our ideals and reality that forces us to ask ourselves, often in moments of deep exasperation as we struggle up another mountain, "Why the hell are we even doing this!?" That's not to say that having a romantic or idealistic mentality doesn't serve a particular function, because it certainly does. It serves the "before" role of prodding and activating our inborn desire, ambition, and motivation for the journey ahead because we cannot fully anticipate what is yet to come. This romanticism serves to overcome the anxiety, fear, and self-doubt we often feel under such inconceivable pressure. In a sense, adventurers *need* to be naïve and idealistic, at least at first. After all, rational people don't strap a sixty-pound pack on their back, forego career opportunities, blow through what little money they have, and set off to tramp in the woods for months "just for the fun of it." As the German sociologist and philosopher Georg Simmel wrote in his essay *The Adventure*, "...to the sober person adventurous conduct often seems insanity."[45] In other words, you need to be a little idealistic if you're going to be adventurous.

After the adventure, the act of sensationalizing particular moments of "what *really* happened" is not so much to mislead our listeners or readers but is possibly due to the framing of vivid memories in our minds so that we can later engage in humanity's most ancient of traditions—the social art of storytelling where we share and intimately relate our experiences with others hoping to inspire someone else to venture off and continue the wandering ethos. We want, no, *need* to inspire others to be courageous and find the will to break out of our highly individuated comfort zones and the social bubbles that rob us of genuine human connection and stronger, more intimate relationships. *That* is what adventure affords us.

O

While on the AT, we quickly came to see that nearly everyone we encountered took an immediate interest in others and their stories. Time often feels endless in the woods; there are far fewer reasons to rush about. Small talk typically vanishes within the first couple of minutes and leads to a lengthy conversation with someone you'd regard more as a friend than a stranger by the end of your exchange. As one of our wandering comrades who went by the trail name Left Field put it, "The most important things out here are kindness, food, and where you're going to sleep tonight." Another trail companion by the name Forester Gump, a second-time AT hiker, eloquently summed, "The trail is really about people. It's about sharing *a common struggle*. And what is remarkable is that all barriers are stripped away out here. No one is concerned about where you come from, your politics, your religion, your creed. All the petty things are brushed away, and what's left is what's important." What is also remarkable is the staying power of the trail and the community it replenishes over time. David Brill, writing about his experiences hiking the trail in the late 1970s, comments more or less along the same lines as Forester Gump that the trail served as a "great equalizer" and "what truly counted was your worth as a companion and an enriching presence among the men and women of the trail community."[46] Many on the AT would agree that that is the essence of this remarkable trail and community that continues to remind us that adventure is still available to us if we are only willing to take the opportunity and risks to experience it.

We seemed to have stepped into a distinct alternative realm of existence, a world that held a mirror up to recast a light on things about our previous existence we never thought to question. This seemingly harmonic atmosphere appeared to contrast and clash with our discordant wider society: a society increasingly out of touch with the world beyond bickering television and computer screens, and cities and towns overloaded with a million other distractions. What was it about this experience of this trail or these particular folks that made it different from "normal" life? The pace quickly became unencumbered. The forests and all the other features of the landscape brought comfort and comprehension. The people we met were animated and revealing. Amid a secluded wilderness upon crossing a glossy bark-stripped pine beam over a stream, we met a couple at one of the many three-sided bucolic log shelters that dot the AT every ten to fifteen miles. A man wearing a red handkerchief wrapped loosely around his neck stood tall and slim. Well-toned, gray-haired, and evenly bearded, Bypass was perhaps at the midpoint of his sixties. He was accompanied by his wife Songbird, appearing younger, but not by much, with a welcoming, well-spoken voice, smooth-toned bronze skin, shortly cropped brown hair, and a smile that stood out.

Absent mass communication and most modern technology, word spread along the trail in a simple traditional way from one being to another via word of mouth or journal entries found in shelters and hiker hostels. Northbound hikers tramping toward Katahdin relay what's in store for the southbounders up ahead, and the southbounders reciprocate with their information: whether the upcoming spring is dry, how difficult it is to hitch a ride into the upcoming town, how far until the next road crossing, how high the rivers are, how close to the next campsite or shelter, and if they came across their friends in the last couple of days. Thus, we already knew the adopted trail names of some of those we hadn't met, including Bypass and Songbird. "We were speculating about what your trail name might mean," I said to Bypass to get our conversation going. "I had triple bypass surgery three months before we began the trail." My eyebrows lifted, and I was briefly stunned into silence. After the AT, they had plans to set off to an island south of the Philippines to scuba dive, then on to the Camino del Norte, a trail running along the coastline of Spain, then to Panama for six more months. Fresh into retirement and the new lease on life, a scare like that is surely bound to inspire, who wouldn't become a globetrotter? Then again, I also don't know many with the energy, determination, and wanderlust to set out on such an adventurous retirement. We're unlikely to do so in any earlier stage of our lives, either. Most of us seem content kicking back in the warm air with a beer and nachos and baking in the sun over the years as our stomachs swell like rising loaves of bread in the oven.

What became apparent to us fairly quickly was that the Appalachian Trail was a diverse transient community where people entered as strangers and exited with deeply personal relationships with the landscape, other people, and themselves. Jon Krakauer observed among the climbing and mountaineering community in *Into Thin Air*, "Climbing provided a sense of community...to become a climber was to join a self-contained, rabidly idealistic society, largely unnoticed and surprisingly uncorrupted by the world at large."[47] The same ethos encapsulated this group of wanderers as I'm sure the same is true for numerous other contemporary outdoor subcultures. In his book *On Trails: An Exploration*, journalist and AT thru-hiker Robert Moor makes similar observations about the trail and its culture about "how remarkably humane a space the AT has become." Moor remarks on and captures the envisioning words of Benton MacKaye, the sole inspirer, and originator of the AT writing, "His original intention was not just to give people an escape from urban environments; he wanted to set aside a space where people could unite around the common effort of living outdoors, a place where 'cooperation replaces antagonism, trust replaces suspicion, [and] emulation replaces competition.'"[48] MacKaye's vision, nearly a century in the making, seems to be thriving and may have even exceeded his expectations. We've even heard of people meeting for the first time on the trail and then getting engaged upon arriving at Mt. Springer or Katahdin.

One of the central anthropological questions we hoped to answer was this: what explained the emergent solidarity found among this widely diverse assemblage of people that stretches along a route spanning nearly 2,200 miles? Though a seemingly deep and mysterious question, the answer was right before us. We were walking on it. The trail itself *was* a character in this plot, a force, an agent, influencing us and funneling us together in a single shared experience. The trail provided the crucial classic elements that typically bind human groups together: community, identity, structure, and purpose. The *structure* consisted of trail lingo, trail names, the gear, the types of hiker cuisine, the nearby trail towns, the huts, lean-to shelters, the features of the landscape, the southern and northern termini, the seasons, the stories people shared, and so many other components. The *common struggle* to endure the trek and finish was the *purpose* that linked everyone together because of the love-hate relationship we all shared with the trail. We could all relate to one another as a *community* of fellow hikers at the mercy of it all. And each one of us crafted our unique sense of self under the banner of our "trail names" and varied personalities to form our new *identities*. Once more, Brill poignantly echoes this sentiment:

> We climbed the same mountains; we plodded through the same rainstorms; we suffered the same aches and pains as our bodies adapted to the physical challenge of fifteen-to-twenty-mile days; we drank from the same springs; we stopped at the same towns to resupply; we experienced the same insatiable hunger—which I termed "hiker's disease"—as our bodies metabolized as many as six thousand calories a day. We carried the same equipment; we swatted the same mosquitoes; we slept in the same three-sided, rough-hewn shelters. And we shared the same quest.[49]

We live in a society more and more divided along political, social, and economic lines, cutting each other off from experiences that are not shared and not so obvious. More and more, we hear, "I don't understand why *they* do x or y," and nor do we seem to want to understand one another anymore. Becoming more individualized or, to be more precise here, individuated in society comes with severe social costs: ennui, alienation, anomie, apathy, conflict, tribalism, violence. This can leave many of us feeling distant, hollow, and unable to relate to one another. Pure, raw engagement in such settings may be the substantial thing we're lacking. This is one reason why adventure can be a unifying force for society and a way for us to renew our faith in humanity. We have to venture out to discover that not all is lost.

I've been using the term 'wandering' up to this point as a general synonym for adventure, exploring, or journeying. But the term should be considered more distinct. Whereas adventure is a fairly broad term, *wandering* can be more exclusively viewed as a non-commercialized, non-programmed adventure, unconstrained by time, with an ability to freely explore a landscape or cityscape at one's discretion. This isn't meant to imply that commercialized or pre-scheduled experiences, such as a one-week rafting vacation, can't be an exhilarating, meaningful, or empowering adventure, but the very nature of those experiences can potentially limit the power and curiosity of someone to move and think in a way they may have otherwise chosen. Though we're never ultimately free of responsibilities and time constraints, wandering experiences are meant to be as liberating as possible for an individual to choreograph and chart their path. This is what makes something like the Appalachian Trail and a growing list of other long-distance trails incredibly unique and so important for us to experience. Having this designated space for people to escape our time-crazed modern lifestyles for a change is one of the most wonderful life-altering experiences that we ought to take advantage of.

Some places and experiences are like therapy, and the Appalachian Trail serves that role for many. The author Alain de Botton observed in *The Art of Travel* that

> Even if we allow how beneficial contact with nature may be, we recognize that its effects must surely be of limited duration. Three days in nature can scarcely be expected to work a psychological effect lasting longer than a few hours.[50]

I view a lot of special places like the Appalachian Trail in the same vein as great works of art or films. One wouldn't go to an art gallery for ten minutes or only watch a half hour of a renowned film and report that they were nourished by that experience. It would feel rushed and disappointing—an insult to both ourselves and those who designed and choreographed this artwork to be appreciated in a moment of timelessness. We must invest plenty of time in wandering to reap the benefits on offer.

That said, let it also be known that the trail is no utopia either and that it would be incredibly naïve and irresponsible to promote such a thing. Of course, bad things have happened and will *occasionally* continue to happen. The truth is, people have become lost out here for good. A number have died, either from exposure, murder, or suicide. Violent acts, though rare, do happen. We should always remember that any adventure—and life in general—will always be fraught with risks and varying degrees of hardship. Indeed, risk and hardship are some of the defining characteristics of adventure and travel. That is the reality, and that is what can be and should be expected when contemplating one's risks. But what is also true of contemporary life, albeit counterintuitive to the constant news headlines, is that the good things do often tend to far outweigh the bad things if only we lend ourselves to seeing them and remembering this trite fact. This is especially the case on the trail. We'll discover more about the origins of our contemporary fears in the upcoming chapters when discussing the role of our media and our evolution.

The interesting wording of the Appalachian Trail Conservancy safety tips from their website, though largely optimistic, disclaims "No matter how much kindness, friendship, sanctuary, and beauty the trail may show you, remember that the trail is not insulated against the problems of larger society."[51] This is a pretty telling statement that reflects the overall ethos of what the trail is about. It also hints at the apparent contrast between adventurous-type communities and "larger society." Where exactly does one even draw the line between a subset of society and a "larger society?" Nevertheless, the uninsulated "problems of larger society" certainly are anomalies along the trail.

The values, qualities, and actions of many of the people encountered and witnessed along the trail (and what we can envision of many of the world's historic and contemporary travelers) reveal something very important about the human condition. It may be wise for more of us to lend an ear to them in these times of great societal distress. This thing we've titled 'adventure' is both a cultural idea and an integral behavioral impulse. It can even come to be a perspective or philosophy of life for many. If it is indeed a human impulse, then it is a trait that we all share. Not all of us respond to this adventurous impulse, and when we do, we don't all respond in the same way. There are numerous ways to express and respond to our adventurous "calling" in our culture. For many of us, it is rather in a passive form, such as watching a movie about climbing K2, while for others, there is a greater desire to actively attempt to climb K2. Yet in such active adventures, from hiking a long-distance trail to climbing mountains, to kayaking down a river, when we compare the numbers of people in the active category compared to those in the passive category, we see that far more people fall into the passive category. What explains this imbalance of those who wander from those who do not? Why are there only a restless few wanderers amongst us? In later chapters, we will explore how media, the structure of society, and our own brains prevent us from indulging in more travel and leading a more adventurous life.

O

The eye-opening experiences and hard-fought lessons from those who wander are as diverse as they are fascinating. One of the more interesting things about them is that they dare to face a challenge despite the risk. Their voices ought to be embodied much more in our familiar society. They are the kind of people that should be representative of our communities and society, not anomalous or strange, especially so when society is confronted with danger. After all, when's the last time one of our political officials could relate an actual adventurous tale that didn't involve an extramarital affair in Buenos Aires?[52] Often, those who wander are the individuals most adept at dealing with danger and adversity. It should not be a rare or incredible thing to find someone who's hiked the Appalachian Trail (non-euphemistically), backpacked Europe for half a year, attempted a summit of Everest, lived abroad for a year, or took part in whatever other adventures one can imagine. The small numbers of adventurers reflect not so much a lack of opportunity or means, but more a lack of value for adventure in our society and culture. Everyone ought to be encouraged to have had at least one of these kinds of experiences in their lives, and hopefully even more than that. This sentiment is perfectly captured from one of Primo Levi's more famous quotes, "...the sea's only gifts are harsh blows and, occasionally, the chance to feel strong...how important it is in life not necessarily to be strong but to feel strong, to measure yourself at least once, to find yourself at least once in the most ancient of human conditions, facing blind, deaf stone alone, with nothing to help you but your own hands and your own head." Travel and adventure are vitally important, and we must do more to recognize that fact and learn how to better incorporate it into the structure of our lives and society.

The contrast of behaviors between someone on an adventure and someone operating in their normal habits of life deserves attention. It's not clear if the experiences obtained while on the trail, or any adventure for that matter, have had this humility-inducing effect on people or if other previous circumstances have given them such predispositions. Nonetheless, those who wander are a naturally curious bunch. Because most have the opportunity to more freely express themselves in an environment less socially constrained, their thoughts and ideas are provoking, refreshing, and at times, unsettling. Those who wander reveal themselves to be passionate, sentimental, and caring, contemplating much, and living through much. There's exceptional eagerness for life in their eyes. Self-reliance becomes one of their most enviable virtues. Having been to places and seen things we've only dreamed or read about gives them their praiseworthy status because it becomes evident that they understand some of the complexity and depth life begets from *standing from so many vantage points*. Their laughs are hearty and honest. There is a shared understanding of the importance of personal relationships, as well as the consolation of solitude.

The anthropological lesson about the relationship between the individual and the community rings true even among a widely varied group with no previous interaction or dependency on each other: how we relate to others is subtle, yet crucial to the underpinnings and proper functioning of a constructive and progressive society because it relates directly to our well-being in an almost Karma-like way. Above all else, those who wander appear far less fearful, less anxious, and purpose-driven. Although I can't say for sure why this is, I suspect it is in part because they are embedded within an environment with a shared experience and sense of belonging that has a clearly defined goal with visibly defined identities and roles. In other words, when people are placed in uncomfortable, but encouraging situations, they are motivated to act and interact with others often in much more uplifting, cordial ways. And these experiences can't help but bring out some of the most incredible versions of ourselves.

Now, is everything just perfect with all these people? Of course not. They're average people like you and me. But there lies the remarkable thing—they are *average* people doing something extraordinary. Interestingly, many we met were suffering from a great deal of grief, misfortune, and personal struggle. One of the notable ways in which people use the trail is for therapy and healing: a radical or unsettling shift in one's life, a spiritual crisis, chronic illness or devastating injury, the recent loss of a loved one, a crippling divorce or faltering marriage, or recovering from the tragedies of war. One of the trail's more famous and inspirational characters was Earl V. Shaffer, who, upon becoming the first officially documented "thru-hiker" in 1948, set out on his quest to "walk the army out of my system, both mentally and physically".[53] "To walk off the war" has been adopted as the official slogan of the Warrior Hike, a program that aids combat veterans transitioning back into civilian life from their military service.[54]

Not everyone is out to bond or make nice with everyone, either. Personal space and solitude are highly valued by many, too. We once encountered an individual who seemed pretty frustrated and annoyed with the arrival of new hikers at a campsite, and while moving his tent away from everyone, he unwittingly placed his tent on a cat hole (human scat burial). Before he started anchoring his tent down, I notified him of the unwanted package (and no, it wasn't mine) lurking beneath him, which only seemed to perturb him more, but he managed to keep his cool. Another hiker, a veteran, explained how much he enjoyed the group of people he was traveling with, but at times needed to disband and be alone "for his and others' sake." And not everyone retains the humble traveler ethos upon reentering society. Some can become extremely abrasive, cynical, and sanctimonious toward others, feeling as though their "epic" experiences justify their sense of superiority and status, vanquishing so many long-distance trails. Thus, adventures do not automatically endow us with mystical powers of enlightenment and guru-like calm and poise, so they shouldn't be treated as such. But more often than not, people change for the better, often radically so.

Then there are those who, contrary to the idea that people seek solitude during such adventures, are the folks who often link up with others. Here they are called "trail families." Even if they begin their journey alone and expect to be alone, a fair number of them seek companionship just as much, if not more, than solitude. Many of these relationships remain strong long after the completion of the trail. David Brill's book *As Far As the Eye Can See* highlights this extensively for those interested in knowing more about group solidarity on the trail. One such trail family meeting up in Shenandoah National Park in Virginia for a one-year reunion of their successful thru-hike generously granted us some southern hospitality one evening, providing us with a feast with their family, a warm shower, a bed, and a whiskey tour the following day. Even a lot of those who remain solo hikers the whole trail through often are eager to link up with others and are quite chatty, hinting at desperation for human contact and the ability to share their stories. We are social creatures after all.

One of the more striking elements of our experience was coming to realize how transparent and willingly vulnerable many people were. People spoke of their struggles and trauma in arresting detail with such comfort and ease out here, that it really baffled me at first and honestly made me a little uneasy. I wasn't accustomed to such openness, especially to such powerful and personal details of one's life. Terry, an older woman with short straight graying hair, sitting solemnly alone at a shelter, perhaps in her mid-sixties, told us about how she and her late husband had hiked the trail decades before. With a stare of despair in her eyes and the tranced gaze of someone with a compelling story to tell, she openly recounted the time she met him. She'd been solo hiking in the Adirondacks when she came upon a man with a broken ankle. Fortunately, she was an EMT and couldn't simply leave him out there to fend for himself. Upon finding an unhelpful ranger who concluded with some backward logic that since he had food and shelter, he could eventually find his way out just fine, she left her pack at the ranger station and returned to carry his pack and help him walk out. A year later, they were married and hiked the Appalachian Trail for their honeymoon.

Many years later, Terry lost her sight temporarily for several years. During this time, her husband had come down with a serious illness, gradually withering away, but due to her condition, she was unable to detect anything wrong with him from auditory cues alone. By the time she had recovered most of her eyesight and it became apparent to her of his failing in health, it was too late, and he passed away within the following year. Encountering similar touching stories eventually became the norm on the AT, but this made me wonder why we appear more guarded in our "larger society." We sadly tend to close ourselves off from such intimate kinds of conversation, given the fact that virtually every one of us is facing something difficult in our lives on one level or another. The fact that the rapid-paced nature and demands of modern society often prevent or limit a lot of such meaningful time and interaction could have something to do with it.

○

Travelers and adventurers throughout time and space provide us with some important questions and invaluable thoughts to reflect on. What are the initial causes that provoke an individual to snap out of their lethargic state of being and leap into the woods for a few semi-solitary months? Why would someone climb on a freight train just to see where it goes? Why is it rare or taboo for a high school girl to dismiss the societal pressures to remain for one's final months of high school and instead explore a foreign culture all on their own?

Are there just a select restless few of us somehow inherently drawn to confront the unknown? More broadly put, why do we want to seek adventure in the first place?

There are a myriad number of plausible reasons. Collectively, they have a lot to do with curiosity, challenge, transition, and personal growth. Psychologically, it has something to do with the freshness of beginning something new that brightens our moods, hooked by the pursuit of serendipity. These experiences transform and alter a person's perceptions of themselves, the world, and others. Some might do it for feelings of simplicity and renewal because they find themselves disgusted by modernity's lingering obsession with material acquisition and disillusioned with the way things are in contemporary society.

Others may seek adventure for the sake of optimal experiences and what famed psychologist Mihaly Csikszentmihalyi coined as reaching a "flow" state in which "people are so involved in an activity that nothing else seems to matter; the experience itself is so enjoyable that people will do it at great cost, for the sheer sake of doing it."[55] Some seek adventure "to rebel against the inevitability of aging" as Taz, a 71-year-old Alabama man, smirkingly put it in his aged southern drawl. Others do it to escape from and eschew social responsibilities as well as to reflect on who we are and how we relate to the world. Adventure can also be done for the sake of doing something vastly different and making an attempt to change one's life. We can do it to fill a spiritual void with purpose and meaning, perhaps by sojourning on a pilgrimage. And we do it to revolt against those who are fearful and say it cannot be done—to *prove* that it can be done—as was the case with Joshua Slocum, the first man to sail alone around the world from 1895 to 1898, "I was aware that no other vessel had sailed in this manner around the globe, but would have been loath to say another could not do it…I was greatly amused, therefore, by the flat assertions of an expert that it could not be done."[56]

For me, the adventure of backpacking the Appalachian Trail was initially about self-reliance and a personal challenge, but it became much more than that. After spending nearly four months in a tent with Hilary, I realized that this experience had solidified our relationship significantly, permanently in fact. I knew that an incredible bond had grown between us, and it was as if we had stepped into an alternate time dimension where those four months were the equivalent of a decade spent together. Thus, the meaning of adventure also morphs in time.

○

We see that many reasons provoke an individual and inspire their adventures. There are many lessons to be drawn from such experiences, lessons for our "larger society" to consider. But even though most of us do have many reasons and a great desire to experience the thrills of an adventurous life, many of us would not think of ourselves as leading such a life. Many of us use the idiom of wanting to "see the world" when we become cognizant of the larger world as adolescents and young adults or want to do so in our later years of retirement, yet how many of us take the bold initiative to choreograph those quests? Why do we partition adventure as a category of life, something we partake in on occasion? How do we learn to structure adventure into our lives in a modern context? I believe the answer to this can be answered first by asking ourselves if we value adventure, or why we should. Can we foresee that there is something to be gained from indulging in adventure? Do any of the above-listed reasons why people seek adventures resonate? If so, then the process of building (or reaffirming) travel and adventure into our personal lives has already begun. The next set of questions to examine are: what is the significance of adventure for our wider culture and society, what are we seeking when we say we want to "see the world," and, most importantly, what's stopping us?

CHAPTER 3
Perspectives through Adventure:
Grappling with Change and Continuity

"[A] favorite spot in the hills or the woods...can give often forms so vivid, that for the time shall seem real, and society the illusion."
—Ralph Waldo Emerson

"The real voyage of discovery consists not in seeking new landscapes, but in having new eyes."
—Marcel Proust

What is there to be gained from exploration in our modern age? Hasn't all our technology and entertainment made contemporary adventures obsolete, or worse, slow and dull? What's the point of sauntering in the woods for months when the internet provides us with instant, ceaseless excitement? From things like Google Maps, Zoom, Netflix, and boundless social media apps, we're granted unprecedented levels of communication, navigation, information, and entertainment. An emergent digital economy has appeared seemingly overnight that fortuitously transfixes our minds to screens and keeps our bodies planted in place. Though technology promises to augment reality in an incredibly transformative way, it remains to be seen whether humans will prefer it exclusively over the real thing in the long run. There is real concern on the horizon that our minds and social skills are atrophying as we outsource our time, attention, and critical thinking to machines.

What many of those who wander ultimately wish to gain in their experiences is the perspective of physically being somewhere very different from where they've been. The art of wandering is much more focused on the idea of physical and mental renewal of one's environment. We're drawn to unknown places because, not surprisingly, we want to know not only what a place looks and sounds like, but *what a place feels like*. We want to see how much a place matches up to how we pictured it in our minds (and on our screens), and almost every time the response is, "It's nothing like I imagined it would be."

Despite the onset of many mind-blowing modern techno-communications, one of the more impactful, albeit traditional, ways to acquire new ideas remains direct physical engagement with diverse environments, which often entails an adventure in one form or another. But what exactly do we mean by labeling something as an *adventure,* and who qualifies as an *adventurer*? Over time, adventure has meant many things to many people. This indicates that it's largely subjective and weighs on the authority of the individual to define in their own terms. However, there are some crucial details as to what an adventure is and what it isn't.

The term *adventure* is often highly packaged and vague. Take Google's definition of adventure: "An unusual and exciting, typically hazardous, experience or activity." By that measure, just about anything can be deemed an adventure, be it taking meth, having sex with strangers, or throwing bricks through someone's shop window. So then are the dope fiends, nymphomaniacs, and self-righteous anarchists all considered "adventurers"? I'll let you decide.

Consider the goal of a sculptor or architect completing the design of something in three dimensions. For the viewer to grasp the essence of Michelangelo's David or a cathedral, they are required to circle the object, probe the intricate details, and stand from many vantage points, thus gathering a perspective and a feeling that taps into multiple senses. Likewise, the heart of what people look to gain or often gain by default from an adventure is all about perspective. And a broad perspective is a very important trait for humans to acquire. The mind lacking perspective is like the body lacking proper nutrition. Although the human body is exceptionally resilient—one can fathom, for instance, the occasional modern medical mystery of how some humans seem to live many years primarily on Mountain Dew, bologna, and cigarettes—it is normally common sense to say that a diversity of nutritional foods in one's diet is what enhances a person's mind and body. The same can be true when individuals cultivate a diversity of experiences in different cultural and natural environments.

Adventure is and has always been an integral human behavior, both ingrained in us culturally and biologically. It can mean many things for many different people, but generally speaking, it is often described as a perspective, a mindset, a philosophy of life, and a way of experiencing the world. The German sociologist and philosopher Georg Simmel describes adventure in his 1911 essay *Das Abenteuer* (translated as *The Adventure* or *The Adventurer*) not in terms of the content or sequence of events but as a "form of experiencing" or what is going on experientially within our minds. The adventure is ultimately a fresh experience that challenges an individual to actively engage with new environments and systems of being and thinking. The adventurer, then, is a person who takes a risk and attempts to see beyond their initial apprehensions and likely perils they may face as they chart their path into the unknown. They become captivated by the significance, benefits, and insights a given journey will inevitably bring. Being adventurous is not easily acquired nor is it easily kept, but it is readily accessible to nearly all of us if we are daring enough to see it and work to structure it into our lives.

From the literature on the anthropology of adventure, Robert J. Gordon at the University of Vermont sums up, "An 'adventurer' is not only 'one who seeks adventures,' but also …one who lives by his wits." Adventures "are fueled in the imagination but grounded in perceived and real risk that, were it not for the adventure, could be avoided… one has to be prepared, momentarily at least, *to let go of a controlled situation and accept one's fate.*"[57] Gordon further illuminates a more scientific standpoint that suggests adventure is not only cultural but also innate to our behavior:

> In Western cultural contexts, adventure is often communicated and understood through a biochemical idiom, as the pursuit of the 'adrenaline rush' and the 'endorphin high.' Recent research does indeed show that risk-taking can have a drug-like effect on people because it releases dopamine, the chemical transmitter that pushes the neurological levers marked 'gratification' in the mesolimbic reward system…what differentiates humanity from our genetically close cousins is the synergy of three otherwise ordinary evolutionary vectors, namely the de-

velopment of the opposable thumb, a slight alteration in vocal-cord anatomy which allowed for a broad range of sounds, and the rapid accretion of neurons in the brain's cortex, all of which fueled a 'taste' for searching, analyzing, and exploring. In short, questing. Indeed, some psychologists see evolutionary advantage in gratuitous risk-taking, in that it promotes both physical and cultural exploration and growth.[58]

The logic goes that there is a lot that can be considered adventurous, and all humans seem biologically primed to explore and grow. Thus, it is not required that someone necessarily be a Hemingway running with the bulls in Pamplona, a Roosevelt stalking lions on the African savanna, or a John Muir tramping barefoot in the Sierra Nevada to qualify as adventurous. All one needs is the imagination and the willingness to keep pushing themselves into unknown and yet-to-be-experienced realms of life. Adventures need not be elaborate or exotic, distant or remote, life-threatening or foolhardy. Neither are adventures necessarily something solely entitled to the extreme risk-takers of the world or the well-to-do elites. They can simply be in the backyard, your hometown, the next county over, a neighboring state, or virtually anywhere that changes our perceptions. As Thoreau once wrote, "It's not what you look at that matters, it's what you *see*." Maintaining one's wanderlust has to do with being aware of what opportunities are available to us and our willingness to be creative and receptive to those opportunities.

Adventure is all about doing something bold or something we might be nervous or afraid to do: beginning a new workout routine; training a new martial art; visiting a museum never explored before; wandering around a state forest; taking a walk down the railroad tracks to see where it leads; making the effort to spontaneously hop in the car for a road trip to visit old friends that have moved out of state; devising an entirely new "scenic" route to work; living a week without a personal vehicle or phone to experience other ways of navigating a town or city; going for a long walk on a snowy day; kayaking or canoeing a local river we've never thought about exploring; or simply letting ourselves become lost in a new landscape. Adventures ultimately lie on a spectrum of risk and imagination and can simply be doing something on a whim with little or no planning, letting our day simply unfold as we engage with it, "living in the present," as we say.

Being proactive in renewing the freshness of our experiences will keep that childish impulse of discovery and creativity afire, even if it means being a little mindless in seeing where and how far our feet can take us. I once spent the entire day walking aimlessly in cheap sandals from my home into town. Tramping the railroad tracks, I followed the river, down back streets, into an old bookstore, and back up the highway, which ended up totaling 16 miles at the day's end. It was the farthest I'd ever walked, and it never occurred to me that I could walk so far in a single day. All I did was let the world pull me along and follow what grabbed my attention, akin to what the French have termed being a *flâneur*. All of this was done on a whim, and I couldn't explain why I did it, but the day ended up being incredibly fulfilling, though my feet were utterly crippled afterward. I saw a boring town I'd visited hundreds of times in a completely new way. The experience was quite an epiphany and had a profound impact on me. I ended up doing something like this every chance I got and still never came close to seeing everything there was to see in my relatively unexciting small rural Indiana town. These experiences made me realize just how vast and arguably infinite our planet is, and that we are the arbiters of our adventures. Allowing *the world to pull us along and follow what grabs our attention* is all that is required to completely reorient how we become intrigued by what is already happening around us. It is remarkably powerful and yet so simple as that.

○

Though this book is themed largely around adventures oriented toward exploring our natural world in more detail, the intention is not meant to neglect the cityscape. Most humans live in cities after all, and cities are not exempt from the wandering ethos. A former version of my self viewed cities in an undeserved, hostile light, growing up in the country. I viewed them as places that were overcrowded and polluted, and I couldn't understand why anyone wanted to live there. As I've found myself in more contact with many cities over the years, I've come to see the appeal of the many manifestations of city culture. Ironically, one of the most memorable moments from our time on the Appalachian Trail was the time we decided to take a train into New York City to visit some friends for a few days. At first, we experienced sensory overload going straight from the quietude of the woods to the overwhelming towers of skyscrapers and bustling, noisy city life. But I quickly became enthralled with the endless activity of the cityscape. As we wandered through Central Park, we witnessed all kinds of bustling human activity, from dancing to yoga to musicians touting various instruments. We moved onward into the American Museum of Natural History and Hayden Planetarium, where all I wanted to do was lay down my tent for the next month outside the door so I could explore every square inch of the place. Our evenings were spent in the late-night bars where sleepless conversations carried on, and we frequented the never-ending restaurants and delis that supplied inexhaustible food selections from every conceivable corner of the world. I began to understand and appreciate why so many fall in love with cities, and especially NYC.

Wandering certain areas of a city can be just as alluring, enchanting, and adventurous as exploring any natural setting. However, with the vast majority of people living in urban areas, it is easy to remain planted and content, thus unwittingly limiting our experiences of other rural and natural settings. As of 2014, four *billion* people lived in urban areas. Predictive trends estimate that another 2.5 billion will move to urban settings, putting two-thirds of the world's population living in cities by 2050.[59] The takeaway is that for those consumed with city living, it may be wise to venture beyond the everyday hustle and bustle and escape to more natural environments from time to time to renew our perspectives. Likewise, for those living outside the concrete jungle with apprehensions about the city and the people living there, we ought to dare a little more to acquire the perspectives of an adventure within the cityscape.

○

While I strongly believe that daily life can be full of adventure, with the right mindset, there are also times in our lives when we should consider investing in some grander adventures. Removing ourselves from the entire routine and familiarity of a place is unsettling, but an important exercise, and could be envisioned as a rite of passage for our youth. Traveling abroad or taking an extensive backpacking trip, cross-country road trip, meditation retreat, or whatever similar adventure that suits a person can have a vital impact on their well-being and outlook on life. Immersing ourselves in a completely new environment is initially daunting and filled with anxiety. However, adventure is all about facing the unexpected and doing so as fearlessly as we can muster. Again, adventure, or more specifically, the art of *wandering*, is not just some activity we go and participate in a few times in our lives: it's an entire creative mindset that one becomes completely absorbed with and allows oneself the liberty to be pulled into new and unexpected experiences. It is akin to modern forms of mindfulness and meditation practice, where one learns to steady the mind on the present moment and absorb everything in front of us.

The art of wandering begins by waking up in the morning and asking, "What's something new I could do and learn today? Where haven't I been before? How much power do I possess to get there? Can I make it happen?" We too easily let ourselves get constrained and trapped in the mire of routine, complacency, and social convention. We invent excuses to justify our inaction or procrastination. None of us is immune to this.[60] Like being gradually constricted by a snake, we nonchalantly allow mounting responsibilities to encroach on our impulses to venture and, before we know it, our "life is flying by." This could prove potentially fatal to our creativity and sense of self-discovery. Our perception of time, and hence our lives, seems to rapidly speed up when we repeat yesterday. In psychology, there is a form of learning known as "habituation," where environmental stimuli we repeatedly encounter without experiencing any positive or negative consequences fade from our attention over time. This explains why morning commutes to work and eventually, entire weeks become nearly indistinguishable from one another. It's no surprise then how 40 years of repeating the same uneventful weeks "fly by." When things become monotonous and routine, our perception of time condenses. The opposite seems to be the case during an adventure; our perception of time almost seems to expand.

How many times have we driven our cars down the same street? After a while, that street has naturally become an unconscious distance without anything noticeably different. If there isn't a car or building on fire, we're likely not going to notice much along the street. Now, how many times have we taken a walk or ridden a bike down the very same street? Try this sometime and consciously study the experience. It can be quite startling how different the experience becomes despite covering that same distance numerous times in our vehicles. It can feel like an entirely different road with completely new surroundings. We may notice dozens of houses and probably run into people we'd passed hundreds of times who were there all along but ended up being scrunched together in a speeding haze of detachment. Thoreau captured this phenomenon by observing, "An absolutely new prospect is a great happiness, and I can still get this any afternoon. Two or three hours' walking will carry me to as strange a country as I expect ever to see. A single farmhouse, which I had not seen before, is sometimes as good as the dominions of the King of Dahomey." Things miraculously slow down and enhance their resolution as we naturally take in many other features of the landscape.

The challenge for us, therefore, lies in the fact that slowing down isn't in our nature anymore because the inherent design of our society rarely allows for it. All our institutions, from the cradle to the grave, threaten us with a tardy slip, unemployment, or missed meals if we don't make it to school or work or the retirement cafeteria on time. This is what some of us mean by society feeling oppressive. Towns, once small and manageable on foot, have evolved to their present state of concrete and steel edifices stretching for lengthy miles that require mass transit systems to bolt us quickly to our destinations, abolishing everything in between. Let's return to the trail for a moment to unpack this more.

○

On the trail, Hilary's pace was thwarted by her plantar fasciitis. It took a while for me to learn patience and sympathize with a pain I hadn't experienced. I was frustrated by how slow we were going, thinking it was all the fault of her defective feet, but it wasn't. What the hell was I rushing for anyway? I had the thought that maybe the emotional anxiety and impatience I felt might very well stem from the fast-paced lunacy I'd spent my entire life absorbed and conditioned by. I took responsibility for this impatience because I had upset her, and I started to focus on slowing down and meditating on the sources of my anxiety. As the days continued to unfold, the anxiety started to diminish. I breathed a little deeper, and my appreciation for slowing down increased. It then occurred to me that the Appalachian Trail may be one of the few remaining places where people could wander in such an unencumbered way; a unique place where people could actively choose the pace of their day without the oppressive weight of society breathing down their necks.

The late futurist and writer Alvin Toffler essentially devised an entire lexicon throughout his esteemed career to help us conceptualize and explain the impact of how technology affects our behaviors, cultures, and societies worldwide. His thesis examined how rapid changes in society affect our psychology and well-being. He identified five key interrelated yet transient relationships we now have with people, places, things, ideas, and organizations as a result of increasing technological advancements. Most known as a businessman and the writer of the nonfiction trilogy *Future Shock, The Third Wave,* and *Powershift,* Toffler went to great lengths to show how the rate of change enveloping us is still speeding up at an alarming pace, resulting in what he called a "disease of change." He explained that in the wake of such rapid change, many are left disoriented and alienated in modern life. With each passing generation, products, services, and occupations come in and out of existence ever more rapidly. Transportation whisks us around the globe at an unprecedented speed. Buildings, relationships, and institutions alike, once more permanent, have been transformed into ever more temporary states of existence and have become as easily disposable and replaceable as our consumer products. When things constantly change all around us without our input, it's inevitable to be frustrated.

Toffler goes on to point out that we have created a "throw-away society" inhabited by "modular men" burdened by an "overchoice" of dispensable products and people. Increasingly prescient today, he observed in 1970,

> Never in history has distance meant less. Never have man's relationships with place been more numerous, fragile, and

temporary...commuting, traveling, and regularly relocating one's family have become second nature. Figuratively, we 'use up' places and dispose of them in much the same way that we dispose of Kleenex or beer cans. We are witnessing a historic decline in the significance of place to human life.[61]

Recall from Chapter 1 that although we have surprisingly adapted more or less to this onslaught of quickening changes, all of us collectively traveling trillions of miles each year, the *quality* of that travel is becoming increasingly more sullied and meaningless because the essential ingredients of adventure are all about *distance*, *time*, and *place*. Typically, these three components are exclusively removed from most modern travel.

That said, there are positives we must acknowledge as well. Consider the last century and many of the sudden societal changes in perceptions in response to those technological and scientific changes. The way we now look at our world, and indeed the cosmos, has altered so swiftly and so dramatically due to scientific and technological advances that we've hardly had time to blink and give it a second thought. The eminent author, psychologist, and linguist Steven Pinker notes the enormity of this intellectual impact, summarizing, "There *has* been an intellectual renaissance in recent decades, perhaps not in culture but certainly in science and technology." Pinker directs us to the observation that in various avenues of the sciences, ranging from cosmology and quantum physics to neuroscience, genetics, and many more fields:

> [V]ertiginous leaps in understanding [have been made], while technology has given us secular miracles such as re-

placeable body parts, routine genome scans, stunning photographs of outer planets and distant galaxies, and tiny gadgets that allow one to chat with billions of people, take photographs, pinpoint one's location on the globe, listen to vast music collections, read from vast libraries, and access the wonders of the World Wide Web...we are now living in a period of extraordinary brainpower."[62]

These advances have undoubtedly improved human well-being, granting us a great deal more comfort and leisure. They have inspired a system of remarkable innovation, efficiency, and an appreciation for humanity's capacity to improve its circumstances and eliminate drudgery. We must acknowledge that these are net gains for humanity, even if we still have a long way to go for more of us to benefit from them. One thing to be curious about, however, is how these new understandings and consequential technologies are affecting our psychology, things like our sense of adventure, perceptions of space and time, self-exploration, self-fulfillment, and *meaning*. Are the consequences all positive? Assuredly, no. Some drawbacks inevitably stalk the pros in nearly all cases of large-scale changes to society.

What, then, are the negative attributes of such heightened levels of luxury and convenience? Might we be too coddled by this womb of technological advancements? How do such advancements in things like artificial intelligence and automation influence our decision-making and our skill sets? There is a genuine concern about the balance between "amplifying humans and making them redundant," as noted historian Yuval Noah Harari cautioned in a Q&A in the March 2017 issue of *Wired*.[63] "Take Google Maps or Waze. On the one hand, they amplify human ability—you are able to reach your destination faster and more easily. But at the same time, you are shifting the authority to the algorithm and losing your ability to find your own way...we become less important, perhaps irrelevant." It's debatable whether advancements in technology make us more or less independent, more or less relevant. A case can be made that every leap in technology that replaces one's developed understanding of a skill or activity comes at the cost of greater dependency on such technology. But from there, it becomes less clear whether that dependency will play out to be good, bad, or neutral. If technology changes so swiftly, as Toffler demonstrated, what happens if we become too dependent on technology just in time to see it become obsolete? Many of us already experience this in the workplace when we have turnover in some software or a change in an organization—it often feels like the rug is continuously being swept out from under us. Nevertheless, with extraordinary brainpower comes extraordinary responsibility; a premium is placed on utilizing our foresight. It is a moral imperative that we remain cognizant of our trade-offs: with every gain, typically comes a loss (A loss doesn't necessarily imply something bad, and a gain doesn't necessarily imply something good).

Forceful criticism of the cons of our rapidly changing world and what Rebecca Solnit has titled "Calvinist technology" comes from her book *Wanderlust: A History of Walking*. She begins one polemical chapter by stating, "Freedom to walk is not much use without someplace to go."[64] As a consequence of industrialization, we've spawned a world that "accommodates the automobilized and suburbanized mind" with the "privatization of space" where previous public spaces in cities and towns that were once much more densely integrated and had naturally evolved for walking—allowing for the free flow of people to wander, to interact, to exchange ideas, to democratically assemble and protest with much ease—have been dramatically altered and eliminated to make way for suburbs, highways, and other infrastructure for driving and expediting consumerism.[65] This has had a tremendous effect on the ways we perceive and experience space and time. Then again, it must also be pointed out that the amount of Earth's land surface that has been protected like national parks and wildlife reserves has also increased from 0.03% to nearly 15% since 1900.[66] A good portion of that land is available to citizens and foreign visitors alike in the United States, as our vast national parks and other public lands have enormous networks of trails where no single individual could ever reasonably complain of having "no freedom to walk." Then again, we often have to drive to national parks to walk. Again, seeing things in terms of trade-offs lends nuance to these debates.

Solnit briefly chronicles the advent and history of fast-moving transportation and the impact such ways of moving changed perceptions by citing German historian Wolfgang Schivelbusch's work *The Railway Journey: The Industrialization of Time and Space* where he states, "The train was experienced as a projectile, and traveling on it as being shot through the landscape—thus losing control of one's senses…the traveler who sat inside that projectile ceased to be a traveler and became, as noted in a popular metaphor of the century, a parcel." Long before becoming a celebrated general and president, Ulysses S. Grant feverishly wrote in his memoirs before his death, reflecting on his first trip on a train when he was headed to West Point. Full steam ahead at 18 mph, the trip seemed as though it was "annihilating space."[67] This mode of transportation ushered in a revolutionary way of perceiving (or perhaps not perceiving) the world.

Though today we've kept the all-encompassing term "traveler" to refer to anyone who travels by any kind of means, whether it be via trains, planes, or automobiles, recall that this is distinct from the type of traveler we're categorizing as an adventurer or wanderer. Any modern method of mechanized traveling typically excludes us, the traveler, from *distance*, *time*, and *place*. Solnit draws this out by noting how "speed did not make travel more interesting…but duller; like the suburb, it put its inhabitants in a kind of spatial limbo. People began to read on the train, to sleep, to knit, to complain of boredom. Cars and airplanes have vastly augmented this transformation, and watching a movie on a jetliner 35,000 feet above the earth may be the ultimate disconnection of space, time, and experience."[68] In other words, our bodies and minds do not feel or experience the true distance, time, and places that would normally have impacted us in otherwise dramatic and meaningful ways.

Our bodies have evolved to function in a world completely unlike the world we now inhabit, and as a result, Solnit worries, "that body has begun to atrophy as both a muscular and a sensory organism." This sudden phenomenon of technology supplanting the functioning of the human body, leading to a lack of movement, may help explain rampant health problems in society such as obesity, stroke, high blood pressure, and osteoporosis along with such marketable niches of gyms, dietary supplements, surgeries, and tenuous gadgets and other modern charlatanism promising to make you perfectly fit in 30 days or less. The physical effects are just the beginning. *How* we think individually and collectively is also transformed as technology coopts our bodies and minds in unpredictable ways. As the journalist and globetrotter Paul Salopek poignantly reflects on his ongoing 21,000-mile journey from Africa to South America:

> When you traverse continents on foot, [what] becomes painfully obvious [is] the utter subjugation of the human landscape to the rubber wheel, to our automobiles...Space is parsed, diced, scissored, and torn into unnaturally straight lines (highways) and into right angles (streets). We lose track of the truly vast scale of our homes—our towns, our provinces, our countries—because our brains have atrophied, grown flabby, through unearned speed. (Twitch your right ankle muscle, and the accelerator pedal underfoot annihilates miles, hours.) Even more unnerving: The oldest, most natural, form of locomotion in the human experience—walking—often elicits suspicion in motorized societies. To be a walker on a planet conquered by cars is to be an outsider, a marginal figure, and a potential source of trouble.[69]

Since the debut of the railroad and the subsequent developments of all fast-moving machines, we have unconsciously raised our level of standards and expectations to match the pace of our machines. Consequently, we get an anxious sense of how inadequate our bodies are and become disgusted by their devastatingly slow speed. We thus become heavily dependent on our machines because they appear to liberate us and allow us more free time. But, as Solnit once more observes, this may just be another illusion:

> Like most 'time-saving' technologies, mechanized transit more often produces changed expectations than free time; and modern Americans have significantly less time than they did three decades ago.[70] To put it another way, just as the increased

speed of transportation binds people to more diffuse locales rather than liberating them from travel time (many Californians, for example, now spend three or four hours driving to and from work each day). The decline of walking is about the lack of space in which to walk, but it is also about the lack of time—the disappearance of that musing, unstructured space in which so much thinking, courting, daydreaming, and seeing has transpired. Machines have sped up, and lives have kept pace with them.[71]

Thus, the urgency I felt when first stepping on the Appalachian Trail and the idea that I needed to get more and more miles covered each day could very well have been a bad habit inherited from a society predicated on getting to a destination as quickly as possible, not on appreciating the journey along the way.

○

In what other ways have our perspectives changed over time? Let's revisit some history and dwell on frontiers for a moment. What comes to mind when we hear the term *frontier*? Since this book largely targets an American audience, we'll assume the context of American history for a moment. Many of us probably think of the frontiers of bygone adventurous eras like that of the 15th, 16th, and 17th century's Ages of Discovery and Exploration; the 18th and 19th centuries, where manifest destiny was prophesized and subsequently "fulfilled" and the West "closed" and "tamed"; or as our current century's resurging trend in space exploration, the "space frontier." We think of Alaska as the "final land frontier." We view places abroad like the Amazon, parts of India and Africa, and the Indonesian islands as the last bastions of indigenous or more humorously "lost" tribes (as if they've been wantonly wandering the forests like zombies desperate for global contact and attention).

Something quite extraordinary has occurred very recently in human history. For thousands of years (and millions if we include our extinct hominin cousins), our minds have looked beyond the horizon from a perspective that found comfort in the knowledge that there would always be new lands to discover and explore, be it for the game, resources, or maybe the sheer thrill of a quest. When land became exhausted and devoid of its natural wealth, we could rest assured that somewhere "out there" we could search, find, and settle more greener pastures. Even as recently as the mid-nineteenth century, people feeling constrained by the crowd could find solace by echoing the favorable, albeit male-centric, slogan of westward expansion, "Go west, young man!"

The term *frontier* implies a divide between known and unknown, but this has come to an abrupt end, except in the case of the eternal space frontier. The terrain and seas on the maps of Earth today no longer read *terra incognita* or *mare incognitum*, Latin for "unknown land" and "unknown sea" respectively. This isn't to imply that these lands were truly unknown, given how long many indigenous peoples inhabited these regions for millennia before cultures with cartography showed up on the scene. Nevertheless, we've come to a time where we have categorized and given a name to every tract of land, waterway, and ant hill on the planet. In addition, it has become international custom, under United Nations initiatives, to "freeze" borders in a laudable attempt to curb the most common and long-running source of conflict and violence: territorial disputes. So in some sense, we've become bitterly accustomed to viewing the world as wholly known and inactive in terms of future exploration and discovery. Those of us newly on the scene and filled with wanderlust may lament as Sir Arthur Conan Doyle's Professor Challenger in *The Lost World,* "I'm afraid the day for this sort of thing is rather past...The big blank spaces in the map are all being filled in, and there's no room for romance anywhere." The same was true for the aspirations of Joseph Conrad's Charles Marlow in *Heart of Darkness,* where his idolized "blank spaces...had got filled since my boyhood with rivers and lakes and names. It had ceased to be a blank space of delightful mystery—a white patch for a boy to dream gloriously over. It had become a place of darkness."

Many of us have acquired the notion that our world has been circumnavigated and explored extensively in the past. The land has been meticulously chopped out and squared by our surveys for centuries, and the enterprise of private property heavily restricts our mobility to wander. We now must compete with our dollars to gain a smidgen of land to call our own. The United States Geological Survey (USGS), in its victorious war against blank spaces, has an endless supply of topographic maps that we are free to purchase or download[72] so we can know the exact contour at any location and any resolution of the earth's formations and every point, line, and polygon that are the scars of our civilization.

For those of us burning with a desire for an adventure into the unknown, we gain an unfortunate and dismaying sense that Earth today is already discovered, staked, and claimed—although the remaining two-thirds of the planet is water and remains largely unexplored. But to be fair, we are primates, land creatures who enjoy our air, and the crushing weight of miles of the ocean makes it understandable why most of us like to keep our heads above the water. We know footprints have already patterned the dead lunar surface. We know satellites clutter and circle our globe like sleepless sentinels. We know that several unmanned space probes like the Voyager spacecraft are now doing our bidding in interplanetary and even interstellar space. The disquieting end of this depressing view is that we know the vast majority of us are likely bound to our modest little rock in space for many centuries to come (pending Elon Musk's Red Planet migration attempts). What's more, population trends and land regulations seem to be stifling our ability to move. The world is metaphorically shrinking on us, and it can feel oppressively claustrophobic at times, as global population density has skyrocketed in recent history.

Our culture occasionally attempts to uplift us. When we become entranced by movies, listen to, or read the eloquent words of those passionate about the vision of our future, the effects are often exciting and uplifting. Many of us are deeply inspired by scenes from epic movies and poetic musings by Carl Sagan, Neil DeGrasse Tyson, and so many other brilliant scientists who deliver beautiful discoveries and insights through TED talks, podcasts, and documentaries. But what happens to us, their captivated audience, after the closing credits end and the clapping hands, jubilant voices, and stimulating music subside and fall to silence? Where does that leave the viewer after his or her catharsis? What happens to all that initial inspiration and motivation instilled in us? Do we immediately pack our bags and head out for our dream adventures or act on that inspiration? A few of us may very well be able to retain that adventurous feeling and finally push ourselves out into the world to live out our envisioned journey. But this is rare. Very few become engaged and enabled this way.

Many of us are unfortunately quickly swept up and ensnared by the pessimism also prevalent in our culture that works to diminish our enthusiasm and wanderlust. The harsh reality quickly sets in: unending work won't allow such a trip; the money isn't there; surmounting bills leave us distraught; there's not enough time to get in shape; there's social unrest "over there." We may even get the sorrowful feeling that it won't be *me* who places my foot on the moon first, it won't be *me* who makes the voyage, those days are long gone, and my only attempt to feel such emotions and thrill is indirectly through films and novels, so why bother, why not forget about it? There is much in this world that washes in and cripples our grandest dreams and desires. It happens to all of us. Cynicism and nihilism are all but too frequent in our media and culture. The weight can seem unbearable. So for most of us, we return to the theater or the novel or to the TED talk or another podcast to reclaim this supplemental feeling of adventure, only to repeat the process all over again.

How often have we succumbed to this kind of complacent and pessimistic attitude? Doesn't having this outlook give the misguided impression that the world is changeless? Is something tainted or taken away from us if someone else has already been somewhere and done something we desire to do? This is fully understandable. I, too, felt discouraged when first thinking about hiking the Appalachian Trail. I asked myself, "Why even do this? So many others have already done this. What's the point?" Same with even writing this book, "There are dozens of books on the Appalachian Trail and adventure out there already, who's going to bother reading this?" But

I, fortunately, came to realize just how narrow-minded, unimaginative, and defeatist that attitude was.

The trail and all of life are so incredibly dynamic and variable. There's an old saying, certainly well-worn by now, attributed to the pre-Socratic philosopher Heraclitus, that one cannot step foot in the same river twice. This is a concept that applies not only to the trail but to all areas of time and place. Rivers, trails, and life are equally fluid and actively changing. We are ever so slowly moving through time, but it moves so slowly that we fail to notice all the subtle changes occurring around us. To be fair, particles shifting at the atomic scale aren't exactly intuitive nor all that interesting to most of us. Nevertheless, we too easily become absorbed into the humdrum normalcy of life. It's difficult to see sometimes that every detail of existence we experience today will be in some form, either subtly or dramatically, altered tomorrow. We're all fundamentally aware that things change, and much is unpredictable. We wouldn't look both ways to cross the street if we weren't that way.

To be sucked in by the poor nihilistic logic that tells us that nothing is new and that it's been done before is demotivating and debasing one's creativity. After all, "Creativity," as the anthropologist and well-rounded explorer Wade Davis deems, "is not the spark of action, it's a consequence of action." We become more creative in the aftermath of our initial plunge into the unknown. We can't afford to sit around and wait for creativity to tap us on the shoulder to get us going. The trick is making the first leap. That someone else has done something you desire to do means very little because *you* haven't experienced it yourself. And once we experience something remarkable that others have also experienced, we become *more* relatable to others: we experience a particular rite of passage in that particular niche of adventure. We become a part of a unique fraternity of like-minded adventurers. It is as essential now as it always has been for us as a species to continue exploring because there is always something our minds have yet to encounter. That will always be the case. When framed this way, adventure is not a thing of the past after all, but a thing of the present and future. Experiences and knowledge are the true infinite resources we can never fully exploit, and we live at an extraordinary time with extraordinary means of wandering. Take advantage of it. No matter how trodden the beaten path may seem, it still hasn't seen your footprints.

○

The value of adventure in society is a fairly recent phenomenon, and I suspect it may clash with much older values in society, particularly the concept of work, which I will turn to in a moment. We first have to come to value adventure more and work to make it a larger part of our lives if we wish to reap the benefits of what it has to offer. This change in thinking and acting requires a rerouting of our behaviors to a certain extent, namely, how we spend our money and time, and learning more about those who wander and their lifestyle changes. Also, we must work to move beyond certain prejudices or stereotypes we have lodged in our heads. For example, a plausible holdover from the cultural revolution of the '60s and '70s, with the generations of bohemians, hippies, and social deviants, has left a bad taste in people's mouths. Many, unfortunately, automatically identify people with overly burdened backpacks and thumbs in the air as intrinsic freeloaders. These emotions and prejudices are deeply ingrained in our culture and likely contribute to the devaluing of adventure. So where do we begin reconceptualizing and prioritizing adventure in our society? Perhaps we can begin with how adventures have been thought about at a cultural and historical level.

Adventures are not freestanding events, separate from our identities, but very much a part of our identities. They have been integral to human behavior and have found expression in numerous cultures since time immemorial. One important clue to gauging and charting how we have perceived adventure can be found throughout our literature about adventures and "cultural myths." As Paul Zweig has shown in *The Adventurer: The Fate of Adventure in the Western World*:

> Our modern disregard for adventure reveals how thoroughly domesticated is the view we have come to take of our human, and cultural limits. Man, *we have decided*, is the laboring animal whose ability to create values depends upon his infinite capacity to buy and sell: his time, his work, his very life. From this point of view, adventure is, at best, a recreation. Yet other civilizations have thought differently about adventure, as becomes abundantly clear when we enlarge our perspective to include the literature of ancient Greece and the Middle East, the narrative tradition of tribal cultures in Africa and, in general, of any of the non-Western, non-Christian cultures we know. When we do so, we make an interesting discovery. For adventure then appears to be the oldest, most persistent subject matter in the world.[73]

In reading Zweig's soaring prose and insightful literary analysis, there seems to be a back-and-forth between optimism and pessimism in his view of the current state and fate of adventure in our society. But the message emerges that perceptions of adventure can and do change, that we have a great deal of choice or *agency* in the matter, and that action, not idleness, is the central key required to becoming an adventurer. Zweig's criticism of modern culture is not necessarily one of disapproval or hostility. It is one of boldly accepting a challenge. Though we have become a "domestically inclined culture...the possibility of adventure lies within our grasp. Perhaps not the exploits of Odysseus in the magic countries, but the irruptive, dazzling intensities of risk and inner venture which flit by us in the margins of our lives. We need only *value them* and take them with high seriousness, to possess them, and to be possessed by them."[74] Thus, the fate of adventure as a feature of our culture lies in whether we decide to value it and *act* or be idle and passive in the world. But why *should* we value adventure? Perhaps before answering this, we might first ask why we *don't* already value adventure all that much in today's society.

O

We do not view adventures in our society as a particularly important cultural element. As Americans, we typically have our traditional one or two weeks of vacation time each year that we may or may not use. Adventure and travel thus largely have served a role essentially as a timeout from work: a time allotted to relax and recharge before getting back to work, and it usually comes in the form of the annual vacation. Often, we might very well end up staying home just to relax, e.g., the new trend of "staycations." We put off the "big" vacations for later in life when we expect to retire and can afford the time away and the financial burden. Some of us share in the belief that there are specific people who do adventurous things, but can we all not find meaningful ways to incorporate adventures more into our daily, monthly, and annual routines?

Much of how we feel about adventure and adventurers, I suspect, has something to do with our *work ethic* and the history of our country's values. We have an interesting way in which we view things like "labor", "action", and "idleness" that have been more or less constant since Protestant Europeans came to the shores of the Americas. Not only did they bring their guns, germs, and steel, but also certain values and religious principles. Because the idea of adventure is often placed within the category of a leisurely activity or something seen as "not work," it can, therefore, be viewed by some as idleness. Many of us are incredibly uneasy with idleness, and work, after all, is the lifeblood of our reputations and the source of income to sustain our lives.

We know this as the American work ethic today. The famous German sociologist and economist Max Weber wrote extensively about the Protestant work ethic and its relation to modern capitalism in *The Protestant Ethic and the Spirit of Capitalism*. This Puritan value ethic originated within the Protestant community, particularly among the Calvinists, and other sects that dotted the coastline and spread from the North American eastern shores to the interior beginning in the early 17th century. Ultimately, this concept of humans being required to work and "gain your bread by the sweat of your brow" is rooted in the Book of Genesis in the Bible where, as a form of punishment for defying God and eating the fruit from the tree of knowledge of good and evil, mankind is no longer free to leisurely stroll in the Garden of Eden and is therefore condemned to a life of toil for his disobedience.

A plausible source of this distinction between "action" and "idleness" comes from may have deep roots in our culture that can be traced back to early American society in the days of the American Revolution. The historian Gordon S. Wood, in *The Radicalism of the American Revolution,* details the transformation of American society, culture, and politics during this period. Studying Wood's analysis of early American society, one explanation emerges as to why some might perceive adventure and adventurers as frivolous, futile, or crazy. Wood suggests this is due to a deeply ingrained idea in American culture and history, with heavy roots anchored within the Protestant community, which viewed idleness as a sin. In short, if leisure equates to idleness and if one is not working or seeking work in some fashion, one is not contributing their labor, which is viewed highly as a duty, to the good of the community or society, and ultimately an affront against God and a threat to one's salvation.

This idea was vehemently challenged during the days of the American Revolution, when the entire social structure was uprooted. The upper-class gentry and their ideal of freedom were to reach a status where they no longer had to labor to live and survive and could thus dedicate their life to decadence and leisurely activities like cricket, picnicking on manicured lawns, and tea drinking. Once they climbed the social ladder and obtained a level of wealth and land with servants or slaves to do all their bidding, no more effort was required. That was the game they were playing. What's more, some never even had to climb the ladder, and this was largely seen with envy and respect at this time, rather than resentment as it is today. Many "gentlemen" simply inherited the wealth of their progenitors and, by natural right, were born a more worthy ape than those miserable ones struggling to feed themselves. This is why many have contempt for the "nepo babies" of today, who get an easy ride in their career paths because they ride coattails of their parents with minimal struggle. Class distinctions carried over from Britain were very clear in those days. Everyone knew and accepted their lot in life. The ensuing revolution didn't just shatter relations between America and Great Britain; it also shook up social relations within America and soon placed pressure and scorn on such elite behavior.

After the Revolution, the family and social structure were no longer modeled in a monarchical and aristocratic way. The husband in the family and the gentleman strolling down the street became equalized within the historical context with the wife and children in the household and with the "vulgar" or common people in the marketplace. Together they morphed, in time, into a middling class where finely distinguished upper- and lower-class lines dissolved into one class more or less:

> By absorbing the gentility of the aristocracy and the work of the working class, the middling sorts gained a powerful moral hegemony over the whole society. The aristocracy lost its monopoly of civility and politeness and the working class lost its exclusive claim to labor. *Leisure became idleness*, work became respectable, and nearly every adult white male became a gentleman. It happened nowhere else in the Western world quite like this.[75]

Leisure became idleness. What is ironic about all this is that adventure, as Paul Zweig firmly noted, is all about *action*, yet if one is not making money for themselves or others or doing something to benefit the community and society as a whole in some direct form, it is not considered worthy or respectable action by the creed of the Protestant work ethic. Indeed, it might even be observed as disrespectful and insulting to the community, deserving of resentment and ridicule. Over time, humans have come to accept this fate and now even take great pride in work as a revered act of discipline and frugality. Many of us view holding a job as highly dignified and central to our identity. One of the first things we inquire about a person when we first meet is what kind of work they are involved with, and one immediately detects the shame in someone's sheepish response if they are "out of work" or unemployed. It is an indisputable and well-known fact that hard work is highly prized in American society and culture and has been for a long time. Being skilled, diligent, and knowledgeable in some trade or craft creates inherent meaning for a lot of us. This is a praiseworthy trait for any society that wants to function and grow.

These ideas aren't exclusive to the American mentality and likely have far deeper roots in human history, which makes a lot of sense. Not everyone can lavishly soak themselves in a hot tub, consuming caviar and wine until the end of their days. Someone's got to keep the lights on and keep society running. Thus, humans have constructed and relied upon various methods of coercion, religion, ideologies, and value systems to market principles that inspire and convince us of the nobility of things like work. Even in classical Greece, Hesiod's *Works and Days* praised honest labor and condemned idleness. He argued that laboring together is what maximizes wealth, "More hands mean more work and more increase...If your heart within you desires wealth, do these things and work with work upon work." Among gods and men alike, the idle are despised. Then again, the Romans had an "idle class" of nobles where idleness was perceived as a *virtue*.[76] Thus, what is perceived as virtue or vice changes over time. Nevertheless, adventure is in a state today where it is not prohibited outright, but it is not promoted as an acceptable thing to do for a long time, either, or perhaps until one earns the right after 40 years of laboring.

Adventure is thus in a sort of gray area for us. Consider the contemporary tensions of how public land should be used in our country: some desire to use these places for recreational adventures and preservation, while others want the land for locals to develop, mine, graze, or "work" the land for profit. The reality is that some compromise is typically sought. However, it can be pointed out that those in the "utilize the resources camp" have an attitude that resembles the early colonists, who viewed Native Americans with contempt for not "working" their land and therefore justified its theft on these grounds.

We hold an interesting form of cognitive dissonance about adventure. It seems perfectly okay when we fantasize and glorify our exploratory protagonists when we get our vicarious kicks from adventure films, novels, and magazines. We valorize historical icons like Lewis and Clark, Davy Crockett, and Daniel Boone for their adventurous spirit. Yet at the same time, it is not exactly seen as a legitimate way to spend a couple of years venturing around the continent or globe if our protagonist exists in the real world and is not somehow turning a profit or committing one's labor to the service of their country, state, or community. Thus, most of us still seem to hold a pretty strong attitude about work as a measure of our worth.

As I write, it's become a common meme that "No one wants to work anymore!" However, some minor positive trends are on the scene. The idea of the gap year, long popular in many other Western countries where students take a year off between high school and college to visit foreign countries, is becoming more acceptable within the United States. Maybe it's all about the marketing and presentation of how we word our prospective adventure to others. Hilary and I joked that had we told our parents, "Hey we're going to take some time off after college and live in the woods a bit, ramble to and fro, and spend all of our money on granola bars, peanut butter, and ramen" they probably wouldn't have been so supportive even though that was essentially what we were doing. Only under the guise of a temporary splurge in adventure on *the* Appalachian Trail did it sound somewhat acceptable and respectable. The art of framing is everything nowadays.

However, the harsh attitude some of has have toward adventure is still implicitly strong in our society as well. Many still undoubtedly perceive those trying to invent a way to limit their need to work as a lifestyle choice disdainful and perhaps equivalent to living the pitiful life of a "bum," a "hippie," a "bohemian," a "drifter", and squandering one's life away, as "cheats" in society. Here, then, it becomes clear why the grungy backpacker on the side of the road with his thumb in the air is still largely scorned as no more than a parasite or freeloader from a materialistic and consumer-saturated society, enamored with work. Perhaps this lends some explanation as to why so many of us fail to lead more adventurous lives: we fear being judged and ostracized and hearing the jab "Get a job hippie!"

Then again, if we take a closer look, we'll see that there are many parallels between adventurers and the principles of the Protestant ethic. Anthropologists studying the culture of modern mountain climbers reveal that such activities "mirror the essential ingredient of the Protestant ethic for which the habits of self-scrutiny, self-discipline, and deferred gratification ideally transcend spontaneous pursuits of the moment in favor of higher goals and values."[77] A plethora of activities, such as kayaking, hiking, climbing, cross-country biking, and many other outdoor activities and subcultures, largely attract people wanting to push themselves to greater heights, literally and metaphorically, and *not* because they are attempting to see how they can best cheat society. Many of these people are seeking personal growth, exploiting their inner desire for adventure.

The Dutch historian Johan Huizinga drafted an interesting thesis in his book *Homo Ludens: A Study of the Play Element in Culture*. *Homo ludens* translates to "man the player," and the book is a classic anthropological text that poses an interesting question of whether the defining feature of culture, and ultimately who we are as a species, is how actively we pursue play. Play permeates virtually all aspects of human society and culture. Perhaps we have always been "working for the weekend" with work only a means to reach our true desire of playing and enjoying our free time. He defined play as,

> [A] free activity standing quite consciously outside "ordinary" life as being "not serious", but at the same time absorbing the player intensely and utterly. It is an activity connected with no material interest, and no profit can be gained by it. It proceeds within its own proper boundaries of time and space according to fixed rules and in an orderly manner. It promotes the formation of social groupings which tend to surround themselves

with secrecy and to stress their difference from the common world by disguise or other means.[78]

This is also how I would describe adventure. I often described the experience of backpacking the Appalachian Trail in my journals as something "outside our normal routine" or something "separate from everyday life." And yet, is adventure even a form of "play"? Backpacking the AT felt neither like work nor play, but something unique and distinct that is difficult to articulate. Thus, the experience of our adventures does not seem to fit neatly into a category of work or play, but something in between or perhaps something that stands all on its own. The famous British philosopher Bertrand Russell had a well-balanced view when it came to the relationship between work and leisure, one we should consider adopting.

> A certain amount of work is not a thing to complain of; indeed, in nine cases out of ten, it makes a man happier than complete idleness. But the amount and kind of work that most people have to do at present is a grave evil: especially bad is the lifelong bondage to routine. Life should not be too closely regulated or too methodical; our impulses, when not positively destructive or injurious to others, ought, if possible, to have free play; there should be room for adventure.[79]

For those of us who grew up in a society heavily dependent on rigid manual labor and a whole set of skills and knowledge that are simply not around anymore due to the rapidly changing effects brought about by science and technology, it can be difficult to see these activities on the same value level of skill, hard work, and determination as their jobs. Indeed, older generations typically scoff at the lifestyle choices of younger generations as being spoiled. But this is likely just an age-old phenomenon repeating itself. The old will always castigate the young as lazy. We need only consider how we've transitioned very quickly from a highly industrial manufacturing economy that demanded strict discipline and unerring obedience to a service economy that now allows greater spontaneity and nonconformity to flourish. The moral of the story is that times and values change, some stay the same, and tradeoffs are always taking place. It will be wise for contemporary generations to understand and anticipate other radical changes that may take place in the coming decades and not be so quick to make such snap judgments of the attitudes and behaviors of the future youth as they mimic the economic, political, and social systems of their time. In other words, never abandon perspective and don't be so harsh and puritanical toward the modern adventurers: they might just end up being the ones to save you when you do decide to take the plunge into the backcountry canyons and forests and find yourself lost in need of their rescue.

○

As we trudged deeper into the seclusion of the Hundred-Mile Wilderness, we encountered a motley crew of characters. One was Tumbleweed. A thin, jovial young guy with patchy facial hair, he was nearly finished with the entire length of the trail, an accomplishment for which we congratulated him. Nonchalantly, he replied, "Yeah, I've been looking at Katahdin a couple of days now, and I've been saying,

'I'm coming for you bitch!" We asked him if he had any wisdom for two newbies like ourselves. With a smirk, he counseled, "Make sure you have plenty of food through the wilderness. I've already given half of mine away to people who have run out. I met a couple who were eating tree bark and another guy who looked like he was about ready to eat his dog." Suspecting (and hoping) he was only kidding, I jokingly said we'd try not to eat each other then. "Nah," he casually rebuked, "eat a northbounder, you'll gain all their miles!"

We can opt to see the world as the sarcastic and cynical character of Karl Pilkington sees it in the brilliant comedic British travel documentary series *An Idiot Abroad*: as a "grim" and "dangerous" world, not knowing what Louis Armstrong was going on about in 'What a Wonderful World.'" *Or* we have the option to take the world for what it is with a dose of humility and humor, appreciate the tremendous progress we have made so far, and marvel at how infinitely diverse the natural and cultural world is. Upon doing that, we'll find ourselves more centered and prepared to cope with the unforeseeable future. As a species already endowed with an innate desire to venture, all we have left is to understand the forces that keep us in place, frightened, confused, and jaded.

CHAPTER 4
A Nation Suffering from OSD (Obsessive Safety Disorder):
Context for Our Brave New World

> *"As one becomes aware of the decline of violence, the world begins to look different. The past seems less innocent; the present less sinister...We can obsess not just over what we have been doing wrong but also over what we have been doing right. Because we HAVE been doing something right, and it would be good to know what, exactly, it is."*
> —Steven Pinker, *The Better Angels of Our Nature*

Nothing motivated us to move from the cradling womb of our shelter. The morning sky, dark and dreary, was still weeping with rain, loudly pattering the corrugated metal roofing atop the three-sided lean-to like marbles clanking around in a washing machine. We eventually gathered our strength and willpower and left after a while, perhaps stimulated only by the fact that we had only one more night's worth of food and the town of Monson was at least a day's trek away. Lonely thru-hikers also march on empty stomachs.

We had no idea what was in store for us. All the rain blowing in from the purported hurricane working up the east coast over the past few days had the rivers gushing pure white with rapids in many places, including those dreadful areas we needed to cross. Unbeknownst to us, it was something we hadn't even thought about until we reached the first of our four river crossings for the day. Alas, another unanticipated obstacle, with no choice but to *adapt* and deal with it.

Scuttling down the path toward the river, we found a thoroughly built northbound hiker white-knuckle gripping a hand-rope strung across the river. He'd lost his tent poles and rain fly cover in the process, but the glint in his eyes suggested that he was glad that's all he'd lost. Our eyes were of a different hue; wide with hearts pounding, and not because of cheerful excitement this time. Considering we were novices and our strength was yet to be sculpted by the trail, unlike all these chiseled Roman statues known as northbounders gliding effortlessly over the terrain, it didn't seem wise to keep our cumbersome packs on while crossing something like this. We sat back and put our minds to the test. It took us an hour to muster up our courage and devise a semi-secure way to get across. We'd rigged up our packs with para-cord and strapped them to the rope. I made the first crossing with Hilary's pack cord in hand and mine in my pocket. The water was relentless and ripped the cord from my pocket just after crossing, infuriating me in the process. I regained my nerve and pulled Hilary's pack across.

Worried her petite stature wouldn't be enough to battle the torrents, Hilary secured my pack on the line, grabbed the cord I'd dropped, and bravely grappled across the rope ninja-like with her legs wrapped tightly around the rope. I based myself, hoisting the rope up on my shoulder out of fear that the line might slump low enough with the weight of her body to cause her to be torn off by the thundering rapids. As she grappled, her hands became numb as she pulled her body across. She heard me yell something and quickly looked around, only to find that she, too, had accidentally let go of the cord; it now dangled and bobbed in the water on the other side, along with my pack hovering motionless above the stream. She made it safely across. Out of frustration, I used this surge of anger to ford back, grab the cord, and carefully make my way back again, pulling my pack across on the hand rope.

Now islanded between the forked stream, we faced the second half of the first river, which proved to be less technical, yet still physically taxing. My reaction to the whole situation was voiced in frustration, then followed by a moment of euphoria after we'd managed to get across. Hilary was still shaken, both from the cold and the distress, unwilling to yet congratulate herself on the victory. Nearly ten days isolated in the wilderness had us completely beaten down by exhaustion, and we teetered on the edge of desperation.

During the second crossing, we luckily found an oak tree that had recently fallen across, providing us with what we gratefully thought was a perfect bridge, though in reality still required great patience and balance as it resembled more of a stripped slanted telephone pole coated in newly applied lube. Scant patches of furrowed bark remained for some traction. The third crossing was much slower-moving and much easier to ford, and only required the bottom half of our bodies to be submerged momentarily in the placid water.

The fourth and final "stream" was a spirit crusher. The decaying moose carcass just on the shore next to the hand-rope was an ominous sign. Gazing at this abnormally bloated river truly put fear in us. Nevertheless, I tried stepping in to gauge the depth, my hands tightly clenching onto the dirty, faded white rope that stretched approximately 80 feet across like a circus performer's tightrope. Within seconds, my body was nearly swallowed as the river tugged and threatened to take me downstream in the rapids. The muscles in my arms were stinging. With our bodies utterly depleted of energy, I felt sure that if we attempted to cross, it just might mean serious injury or the drowning of one or both of us. Tired and beaten, we searched for more tree-fallen bridges to no avail. Out of options and forced to turn back and find an alternate route, we were devastated. Being only ten miles from Monson, how could we not finish one of the trail's most secluded and beautiful sections? At this point, we were determined purists, believing we had to cover every square inch of the trail for it to count as an authentic "thru-hike."

Our day turned into an unexpected journey as we had no map or compass to aid us. All we had at our disposal were our heads and a survival instinct to keep going. We carefully reasoned that the river gave us a rough north and south direction, and the late afternoon sun in the west sparked an ancestral sense of pride in us upon gaining our natural bearings. As anthropologists, we took an inordinate amount of pleasure in feeling this surge of innate adaptability overcoming us despite how harrowing our situation could likely become. This was a salient moment for us because it began an in-depth discussion that Hilary and I would have for the rest of the trail and years to come about the contrast between *perceived fears* and *actual risks* in our world: we wondered how often people allow their perceived fears to rule their lives unaware that the more likely fears come in the form of tough obstacles like flooded rivers rather than men in ski masks wanting to

A NATION SUFFERING FROM OSD (OBSESSIVE SAFETY DISORDER)

hold us hostage for cash.

Surely there are many of us nowadays missing out on some pretty spectacular adventures due to how consumed our culture is with safety, risk, and overblown fears. Little do most of us know just how deeply wired by evolution we are and how well-equipped our minds are to steer us from danger when confronted with a barrier that prevents us from reaching food, water, shelter, and our social and cultural enclaves. The paradox is that we have to be amid some adventurous peril to better appreciate and understand what we're truly capable of.

We'd passed some railroad tracks that paralleled the river less than half a mile back, so we reluctantly turned around and headed up the hill. We followed the tracks north momentarily in hopes of discovering a bridge, road, or cell service. We abandoned the idea soon after, turned around, and followed the tracks south as we knew roughly that this was our direction to Monson.

A road came upon us, which led us to another road where Hilary attempted to make a call to Shaws, the hostel we intended to stay in Monson. We knew they provided shuttle service, and we were approximately ten miles from the town. The signal was weak, and it didn't seem they understood us, so we decided to just start walking and perhaps hitch a ride into town if need be.

As we crossed the bridge that painlessly carried us over our spirit crusher, there stood a doppelganger of Charles Bukowski, the same swollen face and unkempt, greasy hair in a hippie's long-sleeved, baggy blue woolen shirt, smoking a cigarette and staring at the flooded river below. He was jovial and familiar with the area and trail. The man clued us in on a way to get back that would place us directly on the other side of the river. We smiled, our spirits resurging and soaring now, and we were off, destined to find the trail and finish as we had originally intended. The purist ideal would not be abandoned today! We had no choice but to take his word in good faith, and his advice proved sound.

After another hour and a half, we intersected the trail and walked until we couldn't walk anymore, which was about nine-thirty at night. The sun had already set, and our headlamps artificially replaced the light for the night. Not including the unforeseen detour, we covered about twelve miles of the AT. The detour added another five cumbersome miles. It was the most miles we'd covered so far on the trail. Our two great reliefs of this exhausting and bewildering day were the trail magic of bagels, crackers, raisins, and grits we'd found shortly after intersecting the trail and the end of the day itself. We both collapsed into a deep sleep within minutes of stuffing our faces with our fortunate finds.

○

We all find ourselves momentarily facing flooded rivers throughout our lives; some literal, but mostly metaphorical. In our experience, these were real rivers but for most of us, these represent a physical or mental obstacle that might seem daunting and insurmountable at first: the risks and worries of moving out of state or the country; the decision to have a child; determination to get in better shape and eat healthier; giving a public lecture; going to school, returning to school, or changing career paths; or taking the adventure we've been longing for. These can all be frightening, anxious endeavors where we more often narrowly focus on the imminent rising waters—the startling aspects that shock us into inactivity—instead of what might be obtained

A NATION SUFFERING FROM OSD (OBSESSIVE SAFETY DISORDER)

on the other side once we've overcome the barriers and distress.

By nature, we are primed to be cautious. It's difficult to forecast the future. Uncertainty leaves us all fearful and doubting ourselves much of the time. It's well known that psychological stress arises primarily from experiences where we lack both control and predictability.[80] This might help explain why many of us steer clear of adventures because those are the key elements that define an adventure: uncertainty and lack of control. That said, we also tend not to give ourselves enough credit for our ability to adapt and reason our way through seemingly inescapable dilemmas. A problem is that most of us are not challenged experientially—to see and feel—how adaptable and resilient we truly are because we live in a society obsessed with safety, all the while consuming endless media that scares the hell out of us all the time. An analysis of our media's effects on us will be discussed in Chapter 6. For now, we are going to focus on the context of our culture here in the early 21st century.

A keen lesson drawn from our experiences on the Appalachian Trail was how surprisingly composed we became at handling periodic distressing situations. There were a few meltdowns, to be sure, but they were manageable. Reflecting on these days, our tale on the surface might appear harrowing and, to some ears, extraordinary. As flattering as that sounds, it wasn't all that extraordinary. In reality, every one of us has an innate capacity to face the flooded rivers of our lives. We're incredibly adaptable and creative in crafting ways to overcome challenges, especially when we are dropped face-to-face with real challenges. Adaptability is one thing we can, fortunately, find in the toolkit of humanity. The challenge that remains for us is to recognize how adaptable and resilient we truly are, even in a world that appears dangerous and forlorn. It is in our best interest as a society to overcome our greatest anxieties and fears by emboldening ourselves through our most aspiring adventures. But how exactly do we overcome these fears when are entire culture is awash in them?

○

There are many reasons few of us might dare to adventure nowadays. Adventures come with a host of inherent risks and challenges. They can be too burdensome financially, socially irresponsible to our relationships, families, and careers, and physically and mentally a potential threat to, or at least a strain on, our health and well-being. When considering travel to foreign countries, learning languages, unfamiliar social and cultural norms, currency exchange rates, and navigation can be a tedious and intimidating process. These seem like fair enough reasons to avoid something that, on the surface, doesn't appear to have an immediate or substantial return on investment or obvious benefits to an individual, or society, for that matter.

As we begin to plan a trip or adventure, we can default into 'what if' mode. Our minds race as we contemplate all the potential risks. This is a completely natural response to have. Travel and adventure *are* stressful and do warrant *reasonable* concern. But we should also know that *we are capable, adaptable, and resourceful*. These things are nestled within us, whether we realize it or not. We can begin an exercise by asking ourselves why we are nervous and where those fears and anxieties might be coming from in the first place.

We can be confident that we are resilient creatures because we

A NATION SUFFERING FROM OSD (OBSESSIVE SAFETY DISORDER)

come from an incredibly long evolutionary line of ancestors who have already experienced a gauntlet of unspeakable pain and suffering. Through both biological and cultural developments, our species has been granted a far safer and better-prepared world to cope with our remaining, but manageable fears and problems. We possess an incredible organ that has faithfully navigated our ancestors through the course of vast millennia into our present time, our brains. But as wonderful as it is, the brain still has many quirks and biases that are colliding with our modern, brave new world. And that's just the biological side of things. So many more symbols and ideas buzz around like locusts in the air in our cultural environments that also poke and prod at our still-developing brains. This is a tricky business because we are emergent biological machines bundled in cultural wombs. Biology and culture, then, fuse in both subtle and dramatic ways that influence the ways we fear, make decisions, and perceive our world.

Let us first examine our brave new world—the context of our culture and its obsession with safety—from a bird's eye view to see how the structure of our society influences our culture of fear. In the next three chapters, we will reveal the roles our minds, the media, and we, as individual agents, have in influencing our fears and decision-making. As we will see, our evolved brains, other people, and we, as individuals, form a triad of interacting causes that impact the lack of adventure in our lives.

○

We have a finicky, unhealthy, and imbalanced obsession and relationship with safety and risk in modern American society. Every television commercial, product, and service comes with volumes of mind-numbing warning labels and waivers to sign to highlight the endless safety hazards surrounding us. Politicians sweep through each passing election, bolstering a fresh fear campaign of hyperbolic proportions. Every institution we work for or visit has endless literature to consult on every conceivable issue we might face once stepping onto the premises; most hanging and dripping with bold red ink in the office lobby or break room, imploring us to *beware!* Because we are immersed in a culture of fear, we tend to overinflate certain dreads, misplace our worries, lash out at others in unreasonable ways, and prevent ourselves from taking any meaningful risks throughout our lives—adventures that might prove to have the capacity to *relieve* some of those misbegotten fears and worries. But why would we even consider taking an adventure when the majority of us, around 60%, believe the world to be getting worse?[81] Aren't there more important things to do, like build a doomsday shelter?

Many of us have access to great educational and healthcare institutions (though outrageously costly, at least we can be grateful they exist and are available to train and treat us). The last reported case of smallpox was in 1977.[82] Innumerable catastrophic diseases like smallpox,[83] measles, mumps, and many other appalling diseases have been nearly all eradicated (pending anti-vaccination trends). This effort alone has saved more than five billion lives, quite possibly you and me included.[84] Our defense spending is absurdly astronomical—the average American household spends $700 per month accrued from taxes that go toward the ever-towering sum of around $700 billion a year in military expenditure.[85] The second runner-up country is

A NATION SUFFERING FROM OSD (OBSESSIVE SAFETY DISORDER)

China, but we in the United States spend $450 billion more than that! The amount we pay for security is so unprecedented, yet paradoxically, we're nonchalant about this, yet also feel we are headed for imminent ruin. This is puzzling behavior. We've reached a stage in history where we are so smothered by security, and yet many of us feel we still need to build literal walls around our borders and continue to spend even more on security. This is a sign of great unease, but is it justified? Are things that bad? Or are we all steadily just losing our minds and grip on reality?

O

The term "risk", which comes to us from the Italian word *risicare*, meaning "to dare"[86], in a colloquial sense, has a completely negative undertone in contemporary conversations and often now means "to court social disapproval."[87] If something is "risky", it's often something to be avoided or for the activities of our foolish youth to take part in as a learning curve, but something to eventually grow out of when we enter the "real world" as parents love to patronize their children. Consider the ongoing heated debates between "free range" and "helicopter" parenting; in some parts of the country can apparently now be arrested and jailed for "child endangerment" for having their children simply walk a half-mile home.[88] A person who takes inordinate risks is often viewed by many in society as being careless and neglecting social responsibilities. Think of the harsh criticism mountaineers of Everest or skydivers, or climbers receive in condescending remarks of how "selfish and irresponsible" they were, or, even more sinister, how "they had it coming" and somehow deserved their fates for being so reckless when their deaths are broadcast to the world. These stereotypes and prejudices are one small element of our culture that stifles people into not taking meaningful risks. We fear being judged and ostracized by our communities.

These social pressures to conform come in very subtle ways. I recall a story my wife and mother-in-law told me about when Hilary was considering traveling to South America years ago. At the end of high school, her aptitude and performance allowed her to graduate early. Determined to travel to Peru, she chose to spend her remaining months of high school tramping around a country she had fallen in love with. She knew all about rural Indiana and wasn't going to have anyone convince her that lengthening a few more months of her high school experience was preferable to seeing another country. This was bold for a young woman still in her teens to do alone, especially coming from a small town where many were perplexed by such a decision. For some, she had violated some unwritten taboo. Some in the community spoke of her parents as being irresponsible to allow her to do such a thing on her own. "Wasn't she going to regret missing out on her last days of high school?" some wondered. Her response was one of amusement at such a commonplace question. She brazenly fired back, "Weren't they going to regret not seeing the world?" She had the attitude and foresight of one who wasn't going to be deterred by the social conventions and fears that everyone else let themselves fall victim to. People are right to be concerned for one another, but how often do our concerns encourage us to remain in place rather than "see the world," and what may be the risks of not taking risks?

In its original form, 'risk' signaled a chance to display courage and

A NATION SUFFERING FROM OSD (OBSESSIVE SAFETY DISORDER)

boldness, to live up to a challenge. Indeed, "at various times, risk-taking was represented as an admirable enterprise."[89] The coveted classic American myths and symbols of the Mayflower, the Lewis and Clark Expedition, Theodore Roosevelt and his Rough Riders, the endless migrations into the West, and the Moon landing once powerfully energized generations of risk-taking adventurers. Today, however, the opposite seems true. Even the most thrilling adventure our species has yet devised, humans venturing to Mars, still has not seemed to have captured the same level of awe and wonder in our imaginations as so many previous human expeditions once did. Avoiding risks and ramping up security has become our noble pursuit instead. The same plot unfolds in every primetime TV crime drama: a human-made disaster puts a city on lockdown as a flawless band of patriotic law enforcement officials clad in chivalric SWAT gear protect the weak and helpless citizens and save the day from terroristic and psychopathic destruction. Time and again, citizens are portrayed as passive victims lacking agency, awaiting the arrival of someone else to save them.

We breathe meaning into these terms of "risk" and "adventure" in the subtle ways we decide to speak and act. In characterizing "adventure," anthropologist Robert J. Gordon notes, "It is…not a fate, but a choice that will depend on how much knowledge one has and how free one is to exercise options. Risk is…a cultural construction that is the result of active agency, not some passive reaction."[90] In other words, we all make the conscious decision to live boldly or cowardly with risk. Again, our opportunities for adventure are dependent "on how much knowledge one has and how free one is to exercise options." The fact of the matter is, information about nearly anything anywhere in the world is readily accessible to the vast majority of us. Endless online maps, blog posts, guides, and limitless other information about our world abounds, nearly all free of charge at our fingertips. If we want to travel to another country, chances are the resources are readily available to us to know what parts to explore and what parts to avoid. We are virtually drowning in information and technology. Technology has even granted us near wizardry in our ability to plan and foresee the journey to come: the weather, the time zone, the duration of flights, available cuisine, safe places to visit and stay, and on and on. We can even take virtual tours of the street and enter buildings all from our computer screens. In addition, we possess unprecedented liberty of choice and security as Americans. But something contagion-like has affected our society in recent years, and it's not COVID-19, although that has likely exacerbated things.

Anthropology and other behavioral sciences tell us that, being social creatures, we often mimic others, seeking behavioral advice on how to properly think and act. A lot of this happens subconsciously and regardless of how independent or nonconformist we think we are. If a majority of us act or feel a certain way—say, being overly unnerved and cautious all the time—this will have a powerful sociological effect on others, and it will spread like a subtle yawn. Collectively, we appear to be suffering from a pathological case of what I've termed *obsessive safety disorder (OSD)*: a stubborn conviction that things are becoming increasingly unsafe and out of control, with unrealistic expectations to foresee and prevent any and every tragedy that might befall us. In Chapter 1, we saw how little Americans travel and, of the places they do go, the geography and cultural exposure are not that diverse. Given the fact that we are some of the wealthiest people to ever exist and have many opportunities to explore, could a culture of fear and OSD have

A NATION SUFFERING FROM OSD (OBSESSIVE SAFETY DISORDER)

anything to do with our lack of adventure?

○

A Moorish proverb reads, "He who does not travel does not know the value of men." Without the knowledge that comes from long exposure to vast areas of the world's landscapes and peoples, we are only left with the inflated fears we build up in our minds and hear in hyperbolic out-of-context media snippets: parents panic over pedophiles that supposedly cache themselves in bushes and paneled vans on every conceivable route our children might wander. Psychopaths, drug cartels, illegal criminal immigrants, and terrorists seem to be reproducing *en masse*. Crime rates in cities only seem to skyrocket. And when tragedy strikes, we are outraged that someone wasn't Nostradamus and didn't foresee it coming, and so we propose radical policy changes before our heads have had a chance to cool. The late Christopher Hitchens once proposed in the context of his discussions on the writings of George Orwell, "I would only amend the constitution, which I think is a perfectly good document the way it stands, in one way, which is to say, that Congress shall make no law in six months of any act of violence because all the worst legislation in our history has always come as the result of panic."[91]

One side of our political spectrum leans toward overly ramping up security and surveillance on every conceivable block and back alley, pushing us closer to an Orwellian police state. The other side wants guns in the hands of every man, woman, and child, ready at a moment's notice for a Wild West takedown of the bad guy—though our approaches may differ, deep down we all share an underlying assumption that society is unsafe and that someone is to be blamed and punished. Even for minor infractions (spilling hot coffee on ourselves or someone accidentally cutting us off in traffic, for example), some of us can't seem to help but vilify another person and assume the worst—we immediately fill up with rage, morphing like a werewolf out for blood. We abandon our sense of agency, being swayed by negative emotions, and nothing is ever *our* fault. The pointing finger never seems to find its way back around, as our nerves are left continuously on edge. Our outlook on our world and other people has become quite grim, to say the least.

Sociologist and author of *Culture of Fear: Revisited,* Frank Furedi, has highlighted that our attitudes are skewed in the direction of "a fatalistic perspective towards uncertainty. This sense of fatalism continually counsels us to avoid risks, to take measures that can promote safety...our culture of fear discourages people from taking risks. It is a culture that continually promotes precaution as a virtue and fosters a climate where risk-taking is equated with irresponsible behaviour."[92] Interestingly, Furedi further points out how defining "risk" can be difficult to identify, because "the usage of the term is changing all the time, it is important that it is considered in relation to specific societies and contexts. Ideas and values about society and its future that prevail at any one time influence the way in which risk is perceived."[93] This means that we can change our perception of risk if we choose to think about it and frame it more constructively. And we should, because taking risks can be beneficial.

Calculated risks are what allow us to overcome adversity and face our fears. Adventures lie on a spectrum. Those on the left end of the scale are easier, more accessible thrills like taking up a new hobby, kayaking around a lake, or wandering around a state park. Eventu-

A NATION SUFFERING FROM OSD (OBSESSIVE SAFETY DISORDER)

ally, we ease our way up the scale by ratcheting up the intensity to more daring adventures. The skateboarder doesn't begin their career careening and flipping their board in chaotic directions down the first ten steps of stairs they see and hope to land a spectacular trick. He starts with one or two cautious steps and, over time, works his way up, incorporating more difficult and riskier tricks as his body acclimates to gravity and other obstacles in the environment. Likewise, we don't just plunge into the Alaskan forests inexperienced and hope to have a thrilling adventure. It takes time to build up adequate skill and knowledge to be adventurous, just like any trade or hobby. We start with some small backpacking trips and work our way up. However, this "fatalistic perspective of uncertainty" Furedi talks about keeps us all narrowly focused on dreadful 'what if' scenarios, the rising waters, that only end in tragedy in our minds, never epiphany and self-discovery. The insights into taking risks only come after we take a daring chance. Sadly, many of us expect to live in an unrealistic world, one devoid of danger and risk. Collectively, we appear to be waiting for some utopia to arrive. We're expecting a world that never was and never will be. This all begs an important question: *What is the risk of not taking risks?*

○

One of the most common surprises hikers report when on an adventure like the Appalachian Trail is how amazed they are to find so many kind and humble people along the way willing to assist them at a moment's notice. This isn't something we can learn and fully appreciate through our televisions and computer screens. We have to *be* in other places to learn this. This was another striking element we quickly became aware of while on the trail, especially when it came to hitchhiking, something we originally had a lot of anxiety about. Before life on the AT, my brain was conditioned to never hitchhike. Unquestionable! Such a thing was *risky*, I was always told. But when participating in an adventure like a long-distance hike, one comes to find out how much *you will have to rely on the goodwill of others*. After 44 days of being on the trail, I noted:

> I no longer feel timid or nervous about hitchhiking as I did before our journey. I'm not all that certain why I was nervous, to begin with. I just never had the experience. Most of the things that we are uncertain about or have no experience with tend to be given negative impressions in our culture. They are too easily perceived as risky or dangerous, and we are often naively warned and influenced by those who also have no experience in the matter, but have only maybe heard of just a few bad instances via the news or rumored word-of-mouth hysteria. The "evil" we hear of is what most easily imprints and stays in our minds. How often have we avoided harmless interaction with others or taken a loss of an otherwise great experience due to worrisome impressions stoked by the flames of ignorance and inexperience? This is a great shame in my mind. I recall a fitting quote from Emerson that states, "What it does not see, what it does not live, it will not know."

How can we ever expect to learn anything vital about this world if we

A NATION SUFFERING FROM OSD (OBSESSIVE SAFETY DISORDER)

rarely physically immerse ourselves in it?

Historically, our previous perceptions of hitchhiking as a society weren't always as grim and paranoid as they are today. In the 1940s and '50s, hitchhiking witnessed a "Golden Age" and an "era of good feeling" which has likely been most popularized by the writings of Jack Kerouac and several other 'beatniks' and countercultural writers. Hitchhiking has a bad stigma in public perception nowadays, probably thanks in some part to Hollywood's creation of the psychopathic hitchhiker and/or driver. But a more mundane economic explanation shows that "perhaps the largest factor in the demise of hitching was the rise in car ownership across the nation. Starting in 1960, the percentage of households that didn't have cars began to fall, from about 20 percent to less than 10 percent in 2010. Nearly everyone had a driver's license, and Eisenhower's Interstate Highway System in 1956 made traveling by car even more ubiquitous. Traveling at faster speeds made picking up a hitcher much more difficult than when people were slowly driving around smaller towns."[94] In addition, along the many "freeways," it is now illegal to walk due to the not unreasonable safety concerns. Six states, Utah, Nevada, Wyoming, New Jersey, New York, and Pennsylvania, even ban hitchhiking (but this doesn't deter the thru-hikers trekking through those last three states). Undoubtedly, there are real-life cases of hitchhiking going wrong, and there have indeed been heinous crimes committed by hitchhikers and drivers picking up hitchhikers, but again, the perception of it being unquestionably dangerous in any location or situation is likely overblown, one of the many byproducts of our society's OSD.[95]

○

One of the major overshadowing sources of our current climate of fear has a lot to do with the recent events of the early 21st century and the effects it has had on our society. And so this context is important in framing our following three chapters. A fog of fear still lies thick and has failed to dissipate over two long decades and a half after September 11th, 2001. The smoldering remnants of the two trade towers amidst a backdrop of an immense opaque cloud of dust and the instantaneous transformation of two other planes into rubble and fuming debris, as they struck the Pentagon and a Pennsylvania field, remain vivid in all of our minds. We may not comprehend exactly *what* changed, but we all sense *something* changed. Many now argue that our political class has even exacerbated it. Any administration seems ill-equipped to ease the ceaseless insecurity so many of us feel, and our time is still heavily laden and plagued by unwarranted fears, paranoia, confusion, and restlessness. Some of our worries can surely be justified, but a fair amount of it is undoubtedly irrational and threaten the very core of our liberties and sympathies we have for others, both domestically and abroad.

Many throughout history have made the forewarning observation that those who fear will gladly surrender their liberties in exchange for security. This seesawing between liberty and security has been one of the defining features of our history—one can argue it's the central focus of most human societies throughout time. What's more is that we pay an exorbitant amount financially for that security. In 2024, the U.S. nearly hit $1 trillion in defense spending.[96] These staggering figures are far more than any current or past society.[97] Despite such over-

A NATION SUFFERING FROM OSD (OBSESSIVE SAFETY DISORDER)

whelming investment in security, however, we are still miraculously absorbed by this infectious "culture of fear." It doesn't appear that any amount of spending on defense is going to quell such restlessness and distress. So what will?

From *The Culture of Fear*, sociologist Barry Glassner exemplifies the impactful role the phrase 'the war on terror' has played in exciting societies' fears by quoting former National Security Advisor Zbigniew Brzezinski, "Constant reference to a 'war on terror' did accomplish one major objective: It stimulated the emergence of a culture of fear. Fear obscures reason, intensifies emotions, and makes it easier for demagogic politicians to mobilize the public on behalf of the policies they want to pursue."[98] Glassner elaborates on how fear further infiltrates various avenues of our society,

> Fear-driven legislation is good for politicians looking to arouse voters, for advocacy groups looking to attract donations, for ratings-hungry media, and for social scientists, attorneys, and other professionals who choose to cash in on them. Taxpayers foot the bill. And there is another, unintended consequence of fear-based legislation for the public: rather than reassure us, these laws further underscore the already overhyped danger.[99]

Perhaps the rapid passage of the controversial Patriot Act in 2001 is what most readily comes to many American minds as one of the more alarming assaults on civil liberties. Even the most well-intentioned politicians and officials can inadvertently create panic due to the not unreasonable conclusion "that if they warn us to be afraid about some impending catastrophe, they will protect themselves from accusations of irresponsibility."[100] Since 9/11, it's not a hard case to make that a culture of fear has only intensified.

War, tragedy, and crisis are what we're most conscious of collectively, and maybe rightly so. These events are critical to remember so that we may prevent similar disasters in the future. That is logical enough. However, it is the frequency with which we are reminded of terrible events that forces us to ruminate incessantly over them. War memorials are popular monuments dotting our landscape. Even along the quaint rustic scenes of the Appalachian Trail, one can't escape the persistent thoughts of past bloodshed. In Massachusetts, a weathered and tilted monolith commemorating the location of the last battle of Shay's Rebellion that took place on February 27th, 1787, stands in a quiet field. Atop the highest point in Massachusetts, Mt. Greylock is a structure erected in 1931 as a "Beacon Standing for Peace" to honor those men and women lost in the First World War. Passing through Harper's Ferry, West Virginia, one can't help but first recall and dwell on abolitionist John Brown's raid on the armory in 1859.

War and conflict make up the bulk of our history classes, news headlines, and political gossip. It's the hearty substance that sells films, books, and music records. And it's what we assume will always be the inevitable dominant side of our nature and the common thread of our existence. All of these elements and more encapsulate our current culture of fear. We ought to consider how the constant rumination on negativity could be related to a lot of the unease and suspicions we have toward one another. It may not be all that healthy. Think of the enormity of such dreadful information saturating and gestating in the minds of millions over generations. It's little surprise then that we look toward the future with dispirited eyes.

A NATION SUFFERING FROM OSD (OBSESSIVE SAFETY DISORDER)

O

Our entrance into the 21st century has coincided with the labeling of our time as living in a post-9/11 "Age of Terror." Although we witness depraved and catastrophic instances of violence and terrorism nearly every day in the media repeated *ad nauseam*, we fail to recognize how rare these things are, what repetition of the same event does to our minds, and how unlikely they are to happen in the United States, and indeed throughout much of the world. If you were to guess, how many people do you think have been killed in terrorist attacks on U.S. soil over in the more than 50 years, from 1970 to 2021? Pause before reading the next line and make a guess. Including the September 11th casualties, there were 3,952 U.S. fatalities (including the perpetrators.[101] Excluding the casualties and perpetrators of September 11th (3,014), that makes 938 over the course of the last half-century. Most terrorist attacks are taking place in zones of civil war throughout Iraq, Afghanistan, Libya, Pakistan, Nigeria, and Syria, whereas in the U.S. and Western Europe in 2015, one-half of one percent of the deaths were from terrorism.[102] No one is suggesting we stop taking active measures to prevent such heinous acts, but at what point does reason transform into an obsession?

As Harvard cognitive psychologist Steven Pinker recently opined, "As states try to carry out the impossible mandate of protecting their citizens from all political violence everywhere and all the time, they are tempted to respond with theater of their own. The most damaging effect of terrorism is countries' *overreaction* to it, the case in point being the American-led invasions of Afghanistan and Iraq following 9/11."[103]

According to the *Diagnostic and Statistical Manual* (DSM), generally speaking, something becomes a detrimental obsession when adverse effects begin to plague an individual's life and well-being. For the amount of money, time, and blood poured into this project of extinguishing terrorism, shouldn't the outcome be making the world feel safer, more stable, and more peaceful? Would we say that is where we are after a quarter-century since 9/11, more stable and peaceful? Unfortunately, there is no DSM equivalent to diagnose a collective society for sociological disorders. If there were, perhaps OSD could be included, and we could begin to properly measure all the ways our obsessive safety disorder has impacted our society and culture, and perhaps made things worse.

What might be some of the adverse outcomes of OSD? We only have so much money and time to spend, and when we throw time and money into one area, we may be skimping on other desperate institutions of our society. By comparison, motor vehicle deaths since 2001 have exceeded 800,000 lives.[104] That is a figure over 200 times more deaths than terrorist fatalities since 1970, and averages roughly 30,000 per year. Oddly, we don't seem to consider this figure and similar statistics on other preventable life activities that cause far larger body counts, quite in the same light as terrorism. An estimated 300,000 people were gunned down in America by their fellow gun-toting citizens over a single decade from 2005 to 2015.[105] In the last twenty years, 1.4 million (63,000 per year) died from alcohol, and the risk of ourselves or a loved one being killed by a drunk person is 50 times higher than the risk of being killed by a terrorist.[106] Nearly 46,000 citizens take their own lives every year.[107] Medical errors (many of which are attributable to simply failing to properly wash hands) resulting in 250,000 deaths each year rank number three on the leading causes of death in the United States, next to heart disease and

A NATION SUFFERING FROM OSD (OBSESSIVE SAFETY DISORDER)

cancer.[108] In the developed world, the United States has the worst record for women dying from pregnancy or childbirth-related causes, averaging 700-900 deaths per year, with some 65,000 nearly dying.[109] We even execute a good deal more of our citizens per year than most other developed countries.[110] At least we get to say that China, Iran, Pakistan, and Saudi Arabia are ahead of us in this regard.

In addition to these fatalities, such ailments as cancer, stroke, heart disease, diabetes, obesity, arthritis, and the flu impact people and the economy inconceivably more than any cluster of heinous crimes we can imagine.[111] Then there are quite mundane activities and poor habits or decisions, some we even laugh about on televised viewings of home videos (now TikTok videos), that can cause deaths with much greater odds of dying (OOD). This means that for the given number of incidents, a death will likely result. For example, for every 802 motorcycle crashes, a death will likely result. If we consider the average length of one's life and how frequently we engage in such activities, these numbers are a little too close for comfort, yet most of us would hardly detect these things as threatening or at least very unlikely to happen to *us*; such things as heatstroke, hypothermia, falling from a building (OOD: 1 in 6,115), firearm discharge (OOD: 1 in 5,981), choking on food (OOD: 1 in 4,404), bike accident, ATV accident, motorcycle accident (OOD: 1 in 802), assault by firearm (OOD: 1 in 300), poisoning or drug overdose (OOD: 1 in 139.)[112]

Many more of these statistics abound, but the point is hopefully made. As the author of the *Science of Fear: How the Culture of Fear Manipulates Your Brain*, Daniel Gardner laments:

> These risks are not new or darkly glamorous. They're not even

terribly complicated or little-known. We have made enormous advances in human health, but so much more could be done if we tackled them with proven strategies that would cost little compared to the benefits to be reaped. And yet we're not doing it. We are, however, spending gargantuan sums of money to deal with the risk of terrorism—a risk that, by any measure, is no more than a scuttling beetle next to the elephant of disease. As a direct result of this misallocation of resources, countless lives will be lost for no good reason. That's what happens when our judgments about risk go out of whack. There are deadly consequences. So that's why it's important to understand why we so often get risk wrong.[113]

Every one of us engages unwittingly in activities daily that are statistically much more dangerous and likely to kill us than whatever dark menace is chilling our spines on a given week.

The arguments typically heard about why terrorism requires more attention and resources to solve are that it causes greater devastation to both the economy and the lives of those it affects due to the gruesome nature of their death, its unpredictability, and the innocence of bystanders. But surely the 30,000 deaths that will be tolled by the year's end in motor vehicle accidents are comparably as gruesome, unpredictable, innocent, socially tragic to families, and economically damaging. In fact, might the social and economic repercussions be far *worse* in magnitude? And doesn't this logic apply to many of the other ailments listed above? Many things about human behavior we call "unpredictable" and "senseless" are quite predictable, in fact, and do make sense, especially when it comes to violent behavior. Author and

A NATION SUFFERING FROM OSD (OBSESSIVE SAFETY DISORDER)

security specialist Gavin de Becker has spent his life doing such work and notes, "People don't just 'snap.' There is a process as observable and often predictable as water coming to a boil."[114] Assuming things remain the same, the above-mentioned statistics will predictably play out to roughly the same annual figures by each year's end. This should give us pause.

The only reasonable argument for why terrorists are high on the list of civilizational threats is due to their potential to obtain nuclear, biological, or chemical weapons and thus truly inflict mass casualties. On the surface, then, maybe it is justified to spend $100 million a day to maintain and protect nuclear arsenals, as we do.[115] But with a little more digging, this argument becomes slightly more untenable, though not completely. What about terrorists obtaining the materials to build a nuclear weapon? After all, the information is readily accessible, and it's not the most sophisticated or challenging thing to construct *given the appropriate materials*: it turns out obtaining the necessary raw materials, infrastructure, and technology required to properly construct a viable nuclear weapon is extremely costly, logistically challenging, and exceedingly dangerous; something only a nation-state can pull off. Hell, it's taken North Korea decades of almost exclusive focus on building a viable nuclear program at the expense of starving its entire population and leaving them literally in the dark. Just take a look at the satellite images from space to see the stark contrast between the infrastructure of North and South Korea if you haven't seen those already.

A nuclear holocaust is one of those high-risk, low-probability scenarios like asteroids and supervolcanoes, something so incredible and so alarmingly potent enough to keep us repetitively unnerved. So it does make sense to be concerned about states that sponsor terrorism or states vulnerable to being taken over by extremist groups, and for us to keep putting pressure on governments to keep reducing and, hopefully, one day, eliminating nuclear arsenals. Until that day arrives, is it worth all of us upsetting our lives and obsessing over it? After all, isn't the whole objective of terrorism to terrorize, psychologically paralyze, and subdue its victims, to get them to the point of irrational decision-making and self-destructive behavior? Are we still terrorism's fearful victims? If we abandoned such lingering fear, wouldn't this strip terrorists of their power? For how long does the Age of Terror persist? Who determines when it's over?

○

Contrary to popular opinion and some social scientists' beliefs, the violence portrayed in culture is not an accurate representation of the reality of violence in our society. Steven Pinker has stimulated an important debate in recent years about violence in society. In *The Better Angels of Our Nature,* he notes something curious about popular culture and violence:

> Many of the popular musicians in recent genres such as punk, metal, goth, grunge, gangsta, and hip-hop make the Rolling Stones look like the Women's Christian Temperance Union. Hollywood movies are bloodier than ever, unlimited pornography is a mouse-click away, and an entirely new form of violent entertainment, video games, has become a major pastime.

A NATION SUFFERING FROM OSD (OBSESSIVE SAFETY DISORDER)

Yet as these signs of decadence proliferated in the culture, violence went down in real life.[116]

Though many of us remain enamored with violence in these various media forms almost daily, there is a compelling argument and a lot of data to support the notion that nearly all trends in violence have been on the decline for some time.[117] However, in recent years, shootings and gun deaths may be the exception as they sadly appear to be rising. Nevertheless, Pinker's data and the general thesis make for a very useful and accessible jumping-off point for public discourse because American society is saturated with content about violence and safety.

One of the more startling accusations about downward trends includes war. In 1996, anthropologist Lawrence Keeley released an important text titled *War Before Civilization: The Myth of the Peaceful Savage* that compiled extensive data cross-culturally and across time to demonstrate that not only are modern wars less frequent, but they even affect a smaller percentage of the population when compared to prehistoric figures on violence and warfare.[118] Intuitively, this doesn't seem to make much sense if we pay attention to the news. A couple of things we fail to take into account when synthesizing violent reports are the incredible bursts of the human population witnessed since the Industrial Revolution, amidst an ever-growing trend in mass surveillance to capture any act of social deviance. Another researcher studying trends in violence is Joshua S. Goldstein, who points out,

> If the world feels like a more violent place than it actually is, that's because there's more information about wars—not more wars themselves. Once-remote battles and war crimes now regularly make it onto our TV and computer screens and in

more or less real-time. Cell-phone cameras have turned citizens into reporters in many war zones. Armed conflict hasn't vanished, and today, anyone with a mobile phone can broadcast the bloodshed. But our impressions of the prevalence of war, stoked by these images, can be misleading. Only objective numbers can identify the trends.[119]

Any person with a working knowledge of human history knows that if we could time-travel to earlier times, armed with iPhones to capture the brutality and depravity of a lot of events in the past, we'd probably be shaken with so much terror we'd lose all nostalgia for the "good ol' days" in a heartbeat. The strangest thing about the obscene amount of violent content circulating throughout our media is that hardly anyone disputes it or attempts to put it into a more favorable context. A lot of this has become incredibly politicized. Media attention seems exceptionally skewed toward coverage of the worst human behaviors to the point where it is universally accepted as conventional wisdom that war, conflict, and violence are proliferating and getting worse.

Most of us fail to realize just how much we'd be trading away the further back in time we go. Keeley asks us to further reflect, "What is morally wrong with longer life; lower infant mortality; wider knowledge of the universe; water and food cleansed of parasites and pathogens; photography; Western literature, art, and music; or larger numbers of humans living on less land with fewer premature deaths, including violent ones?"[120] Our perspectives on the supposed poor state of contemporary society might be due to our inability to envision the past and accurately compare it to today. We often take enormous pleasure in mythologizing past times and wrongly think that the "good old days" were somehow

A NATION SUFFERING FROM OSD (OBSESSIVE SAFETY DISORDER)

far more glamorous and peaceful. This isn't necessarily the case. Keeley further challenges our nostalgia by interestingly pointing out,

> Cynics have observed that those who have benefited the most from "progress" –the citizens of the First World –are the people most inclined to disdain it. The privileged few who eat better, lead longer and more stimulating lives because of modern agriculture, medicine, education, mass communications, and travel, and are most cushioned from physical discomfort and inconvenience by industrial technology are the most nostalgic about the primitive world. This attitude is more difficult to find among the real "victims of progress" in the Third World except among members of these nations' Western-educated elites…the current Western distaste for progress may be just another luxury Westerners enjoy. But a less cynical gloss is that civilization inevitably looks grimmer to those intimately familiar with its thousand discontents, whereas its streets seem paved with gold in the eyes of those farthest from its citadel.[121]

It is rather strange that some of us remain nostalgic for the days when public sanitation wasn't a thing and people didn't bathe or brush their teeth *ever*. Gavin de Becker adds to this observation by commenting on a poll that shows 90 percent of Americans feel less safe today than in the supposed "safer" world of their youth:

> [I]t was a world without air bags or mandatory seat belts, before the decrease in smoking, before early detection of cancer, before

911 systems showed dispatchers the addresses of people in distress. You remember those carefree fifties before CAT scans, ultrasounds, organ transplants, amniocentesis, and coronary bypass surgery. (Admittedly, there was no AIDS back then, but there was polio.) You remember those oh-so-safe sixties when angry world powers planned nuclear attack, and schoolchildren practiced regular air raid drills.[122]

We've unwittingly been granted far more time and opportunity to sit around and pinpoint scrupulously the "thousand discontents" of society while neglecting the thousand substantial improvements and other positive developments that have gone unnoticed or underappreciated. Historical context, like probability, eludes us. Again, we focus on the fear, while failing to value the fortune.

Thus, if the data turns out to be accurate in showing that we have improved many things over time and rates of violence have declined substantially, then a great many of us have a very jaded and misinformed view of the world and, thus, of ourselves and the future of our world. Some major consequences are in store for us if that is the case. If we accept at face value and without question that the world is falling apart, we're more likely to abandon hope and less likely to take actions to prevent it from happening. As Pinker reiterates,

> [T]he greatest danger of all: that reasonable people will think, as a 2016 *New York Times* article put it, 'These grim facts should lead any reasonable person to conclude that humanity is screwed.' If humanity is screwed, why sacrifice anything to reduce potential risks? Why forgo the convenience of fossil

A NATION SUFFERING FROM OSD (OBSESSIVE SAFETY DISORDER)

fuels or exhort governments to rethink their nuclear weapons policies? Eat, drink, and be merry, for tomorrow we die![123]

Adopting a fatalistic mindset could turn our situation into a self-fulfilling prophecy. This would be akin to complaining throughout the day, convinced that we are going to miss our flight, thus dawdling around, blaming traffic and our mother for holding us up, instead of focusing on getting to the airport. In the end, we eventually make it to the airport and indeed do miss our flight, proclaiming, "Aha! See. I told you we wouldn't make it!" In reality, we might have made it had we had the appropriate attitude and determination to do so. By complaining that all is lost, accepting our tragic fate, and doing nothing about it, we not only commit ourselves to a self-fulfilling prophecy but add insult to injury by uncoupling everything that contributed to the betterment of our world.

○

I do hope that none of this is read as a callous dismissal or indifference toward terrorism, or any other acts of violence, for that matter. What's important is to recognize a clear distinction between the fears provoked by terrorism and other forms of violence and the actual probability of becoming a victim of a terrorist act and other low-probability events. The discrepancy is quite large and doesn't appear to be discussed with much nuance. Terrorism *is* a problem and a tragedy that has irreparably damaged too many lives and changed the course of history. That is especially true when we turn our gaze to the latest crises in Syria, Libya, Israel, Iraq, Afghanistan, and their neighboring states throughout the Middle East, living day in and day out with the horrors of war and terrorism literally at their doorsteps. It would be tremendously heartless and naïve to argue that since things are relatively good here, there is little to worry about. That is not the argument. The suggestion is to reevaluate what some of our greatest fears and anxieties are as a society, and if our ethics, policies, and life decisions are in line with the evidence and reality, because the consequences we make for unjustified or invalid fears may, in the end, do more harm than good.

Also, there is certainly nothing wrong with being upset about a tragedy and wanting to be proactive in learning from problems and trying to fix them. What is unreasonable and irresponsible is to create a culture that attempts to stamp out every conceivable risk and reach a point where we can no longer even calculate risks in any meaningful way when we do try to take them. When we live in a world where we perceive highly improbable misfortunes as likely to happen to us and we fear the wrong things, our sense of risk goes completely awry, and many of us, along with our important social institutions, unwittingly suffer because of it. We simply *must* be more clear-headed about these things going forward.

Our ultimate subconscious wish seems to cater to the desire for a benign Big Brother utopia where every jagged edge of society has a pillow securely fashioned to it, where superheroes with lightning speed can swoop in just in time to save the day, and where every risk we take, we demand safety nets be deployed to catch us when we fall. Rather than freedom *of* choice, we want to trade in for freedom *from* choice, freedom from risk. With delusion in our minds, we fatally crave pre-

A NATION SUFFERING FROM OSD (OBSESSIVE SAFETY DISORDER)

dictability in an unpredictable world. There is a mantra among those involved in the field of risk assessment that states *that one can always make things safer, but never safe.* It might be wise for us to savor those words from time to time.

○

Our society suffers from many problems. However, what history beckons to tell us is that more and more of us have been afforded a lot of fortunes, privileges, and longevity, but we're not listening to all the good that has happened and understanding what this means for the continued improvement of our well-being. Like fish in water, it's difficult to grasp the context in which we're living and all the social forces that influence our thoughts and behaviors. Many of us are convinced that society and culture are crumbling and the apocalypse will soon commence. This is a devastating thing to believe. It probably won't, but it sure feels like it. I sympathize with this. It's difficult to follow the news with a level head and not to become a little jaded, fearful, or misanthropic. If there's any good modern indicator for the crazed addiction to cynicism, alarmism, and lost hope in humanity today, it can be found in pathologically perusing social media threads and the evening news (more on the influence of our media in Chapter 6). We're sadly committing ourselves more and more to political tribalism and constant slandering on social media. Is this the best use of our time on this planet? Even if we do believe in the imminent destruction of the world, why not get out there and see it all before the bombs drop? We might be pleasantly surprised that the fear-mongering doesn't quite match up with the distorted views circling on social media.

My concern is that the social and cultural context in which we live substantially restrains a lot of people's enthusiasm for adventure and experiencing the real world. There are risks from not taking risks, and self-isolating and avoiding the world are some of the worst decisions one can make. Too many are succumbing to fear in this way. Thus, we must not forget that facing challenges awakens us to who we are and what we're capable of. In response to someone asking him the awkwardly sarcastic question of why he went up Mount Everest to die, the Italian mountaineer Reinhold Messner famously responded, "I didn't go up there to die. I went up there to live!" By not venturing, we gain no reference points for our innate creativity and resiliency. After all, we don't *become* resilient. We *are* resilient. We need only wander and ford some streams of our own to discover that fact.

There is no equation or cost-benefit analysis for adventure, and asking what the practicality of doing something with no immediate or obvious gains ends up being a futile question because we're demanding a looking glass into our future. All that can be answered by my own experiences in adventuring is that anxiety and apprehension of the future nearly vanish. I *always* encounter the overwhelming goodness in people while traveling and often feel more connected to humanity when I do. I find myself feeling incredibly healthy and alive. The days extend their length and feel timeless while immersed in an unhabituated environment where mundane things strike me suddenly as extraordinary. I become less concerned with all that could go wrong as I gain greater confidence in my abilities to adapt to changing circumstances. The bulk of the responsibility lies with us to become daring enough to break away from the context of our fearful culture, test the waters of our limited existence, and discover what the world "out

A NATION SUFFERING FROM OSD (OBSESSIVE SAFETY DISORDER)

there" is ultimately like. It is only in the aftermath of such an experience that a person can truly come to appreciate what they have learned and accomplished—to see what it is they gained because the nature of their experience will be far too varied and unpredictable.

What will certainly happen as we come to interact with the real world, its landscapes, animals, and people in particular, with all senses present, will tell our brains something quite different about landscapes, animals, and people. We'll be told that landscapes are incredibly beautiful, diverse, and worth protecting. We'll be told that most animals are shyer and far more harmless than we are. And we will certainly find people are far more generous and hospitable than we could ever imagine. Do people perish in the harshness of the wild? Yes. Are people mauled by bears? Yes. Can people be depraved and hostile? Yes. But overwhelmingly, those are rare, isolated events and shouldn't deter a person from experiencing something truly wonderful and stimulating about their world. Ironically, the cure for overcoming our OSD might just be doing something we've always been afraid to do. Next, however, we'll need to understand something about our ancient brains and how they are clashing with our media-saturated world.

CHAPTER 5
Our Ancient Brains Meet the Brave New World:
Evolutionary Baggage and Cognitive Bias

"There's no room for facts when our minds are occupied by fear."
—Hans Rosling, *Factfulness*

"Today's intellectual pessimism and cultural disorientation serves to distract the human imagination from confronting the challenges that lie ahead. Alarmist accounts about human survival expresses a crisis of belief in humanity. That is why the real question at stake is not whether humanity will survive, but whether or not our belief in humanity can survive the twenty-first century."
— Frank Furedi, *Culture of Fear Revisited*

A formerly unknown mix of emotions, ranging from ecstatic relief to a new sense of victory and pride came over us as we exited the Hundred Mile Wilderness. Our muddied boots pounded along the damp dirt path onto the quaint, orderly streets of Monson, Maine. We survived!

The pointed steeple of a white-clad church poked through the pines on the outskirts of the town. A few small shops full of baked goods and souvenirs adorned the streets. One of the effects of being in the woods for a prolonged time is that the nose familiarizes itself with the earthy scents of pine needles, pollen, and many other natural scents. Many hikers contend that smells become enhanced. Curiously, though, the nose seems to neglect the stench emitted from days and even weeks-old body odor absorbed into their crusty clothes and battered gear. The wafting air shuffling down the main street of Monson carried the scent of breakfast food, and I was immediately hooked and hauled by the aromas into Pete's Place, a general store and restaurant full of comfort foods. Breakfast foods and diners are my weak spots, and it was the perfect occasion to celebrate Hilary's birthday. I think we ordered nearly everything on the menu: a plentiful feast of flapjacks, grits, a cinnamon roll, a donut, eggs, ham, toast, orange juice, and coffee. The hiker's stomach grows just as much as the nose deepens its sense.

The evening arrived as we relaxed with our beers on the shores of a lake with newfound friends at a pub, listening to a folk duo strum their acoustic guitars. The sun went down behind the steeple of the white-clad church. The buzz from the beer evoked warm feelings as we recalled the vivid scenes and lessons the trail had taught us so far. Despite rigorous planning, we failed to anticipate many challenges. We both underestimated how physically and psychologically demanding the trail would be. Another memorable lesson was observed during this time: many of us often forget about our indifference to nature. Our culture, a lot of the time, romanticizes "man's relationship with nature." But it is neither kind nor cruel, and it can be difficult to understand and accept that lesson.

We were ecstatic to have made it through safe and sound through some of the toughest terrain the trail had to offer. The experience was an eye-opener. Being completely isolated, save for the few other hikers we encountered, it was both a frightening and encouraging moment to realize all a person has with them are their own hands, feet, minds, and meager essentials to suit them through unpredictable obstacles. Even all the planning and research won't guarantee you'll be mistake-free. I jotted down the top ten mistakes we made so far: 1) Ran out of iodine tablets (also there are much better options for purifying water as we quickly came to learn), 2) Hilary using her old boots that were too small causing painful blisters on day two, 3) Took a wrong turn multiple times, 4) Ran out of water on top of a mountain and had to walk four hours in the rain dehydrated, 5) Prolonged hunger, 6) Left phone light on which killed the battery, 7) Brought harmonica, don't know how to play, 8) Gave Hilary too much pack weight, 9) Failed to bring camp shoes, 10) Miscalculated the number of days it would take to get from Katahdin to Monsen which explains number 5. We made many mistakes, but we were at least prepared to adapt and we did so successfully. For the southbounders, the Hundred Mile Wilderness serves as a litmus test, a gauge to measure whether you can make it the rest of the way or not. We were confident now that we could.

O

A growing body of evidence and recent literature argues that, collectively, we are living longer, healthier, wiser, more comfortable, less violent, and safer lives than ever before.[124] Logic would seem to indicate that we ought to be one of the most *fearless* and content societies populated by healthy, active people, more than eager to engage and fulfill our childhood dreams of "seeing the world." Despite so many of these positive developments and improvements to our lives, American public perceptions and behavior do not seem to reflect it. And if all this amounting data and our prim and proper academics can't convince us of this supposed near utopia we're inhabiting, what can? Has our exposure to too much television and social media hijacked our brains and radically disoriented our perception of reality? Are elite academics like the Swedish physician Hans Rosling and Harvard psychologist Steven Pinker, who have laid out a plethora of optimistic trends in the development of humanity just too pollyannaish and shortsighted as their critics allege?

By now, most of us see that an alarming number of us, regardless of our political affinities, are fatally attracted to some rather unseemingly and consequential human behaviors—tribalism, populism, cynicism, nihilism, consecutive weekly trips to Chick-fil-A. All of our collective apprehensions and fears suggest that a lot of us have adopted a rather sinister outlook on human nature and our potential future as a society. This phenomenon is bannered the "culture of fear" by another cohort of researchers who attempt to explain this sociologically.[125] If the data on human progress is accurate, then how is it possible that so many of us feel restless and disoriented after centuries of societal and technological transformations that have radically improved our material conditions and standards of living? Why is our gaze often directed toward the pessimistic side of things, while the optimists are perpetually scolded and shamed as being naïve or utopian? Is this truly such a dangerous and forsaken time to be alive as the vastness of media sources and popular culture would have us believe? Is there perhaps a way of circumventing, reframing, and alleviating some of these problems?

OUR ANCIENT BRAINS MEET THE BRAVE NEW WORLD

○

Many of the people I come across nowadays are quite jaded and apprehensive about the state of modern affairs. It almost seems taboo to be optimistic or point out anything hinting at progress, especially if we've just been gawking at the news that is curiously always "breaking." Since our tenure on the Appalachian Trail, I've had the fortunate opportunity to spend a lot of time living, traveling, and working throughout the southeastern and western United States as an archaeologist. Interactions and conversations often abound over a beer in a motel parking lot these days as an archaeologist in the United States. Archaeologists are often situated in remote areas and have the privilege of talking to a wide variety of people across the American landscape. The anthropologist in me has also developed a fly-on-the-wall eavesdropper approach, tuning in to many conversations that hint at our modern unrest and taking notes on how we express our anxiety, especially when it comes to travel. My ears have become antennas for the many words of worry when it comes to travel and adventure. As we saw in the last chapter, things like money, language, careers, community, family, and friends can compel us to stay home, opting out of adventures. However, even wealthy people with the means and desire to travel are often afraid to do so. And the things they say also suggest that my hypothesis that there is a link between fear and a lack of adventure seems all the more plausible.

As an example, I once found myself doing an archaeological survey in eastern North Carolina on private farmland that produced a variety of crops throughout the year, from cotton and soybeans to corn and peanuts. The fields would soon be converted to a solar farm, hence our survey work. An inquisitive man approached every other day to ask how we were progressing and if we had found anything "interesting." This translates to the archaeologist's ear as, "Did you find anything that is going to hinder the development of our project and prevent me from getting my money?" Nevertheless, he was still interested in archaeology on some conceptual level. It became clear his family was well-off financially, and he was in decent physical shape as far as I could tell. Our crew told him the nature of the work we did and how we had all worked throughout the country, and the conversation eventually led to travel abroad. The man had a glimmer of envy, maybe even disbelief, in his eyes as we relayed our stories of travel. He then remarked how anxious he was to see the pyramids of Egypt and Mexico, but how he couldn't find anyone who wanted to go with him (I've noted people typically want others to go with them on their travels and use that as their excuse for not traveling somewhere themselves). We all told him he should just go and gave him tips and resources he could consult on the Internet, as he was somewhat older and perhaps not as keen online as we millennials. In a smooth southern drawl, he then pointedly asked, "But aren't ya'll scared considering how dangerous things are today?" In listening to countless exchanges like this, I often wonder, "Dangerous compared to what or when?" I have yet to meet someone equipped with statistics and history of their desired destination to justify their anxiety about not going somewhere. It's always just some vague gut feeling we have. The consensus agrees that we live in dangerous times, but what makes us so convinced of this belief?

OUR ANCIENT BRAINS MEET THE BRAVE NEW WORLD

○

Human psychology plays a critical role in making choices in our contemporary world, and it has a lot of relevance to travel and adventure. The interplay between internal and external fears can often undermine our decision-making when it comes to evaluating risks, especially when contemplating an adventure. What makes an extensive adventure so demanding for our brains is the incredible amount of foresight we have to invest in forecasting so many scenarios we might have to deal with. It's not like a prepackaged vacation destination like a resort where the place we end up will likely have everything we could want and need in the event we forget something. Civilization comfortably cradles us in an artificial womb, shielding us from having to think much about life's necessities on a day-to-day basis. An adventure, on the other hand, requires vigilant planning. And somewhere amid all that thinking and planning, we inevitably begin to ponder all the dark "what-if" scenarios—our minds naturally veer toward compounding risks and anxieties. In addition to the last chapter's assessment of the context of our culture, we also need to examine this internal combustion taking place within our minds if we want to better understand how to live a less fearful, reasonable, and more self-fulfilled, adventurous life.

Researchers have recorded over a hundred cognitive biases and commented extensively on their implications.[126] Much like learning grammar or rules of the road, learning about our psychological biases and how we fear can be taxing, but unsuspectingly helpful for our lives. We certainly won't be fully immune from biases or cognitive distortions in the way we won't be flawless grammarians or drivers, but we will be poised to have an improved and more balanced relationship with our fears, and thus can better assess our risks in our world and our adventures. Barry Glassner, sociologist and author of *The Culture of Fear: Why Americans Are Afraid of the Wrong Things*, distinguishes the two faces of fear for us to differentiate and bear in mind, "We had better learn to doubt our *inflated fears* before they destroy us. *Valid fears* have their place; they cue us to danger. False and overdrawn fears only cause hardship."[127] Living in such a media-saturated culture full of endless contradictions, the lines between reasonable fears and outlandish ones are severely blurred, and it will take some time to translate what's bullshit and what's worth worrying about.

Another expert at keenly deciphering patterns related to fear and violence in our everyday lives is Gavin de Becker. In his National Bestseller, *The Gift of Fear*, he demonstrates the power of our intuition to raise the alarm on the valid fears in our *immediate* environments and how we can learn to distinguish them from the sensationalized fears we're often distracted by from media, popular culture, moral panics, and other hysterical gossip. He chides,

> The strange way people evaluate risk sheds some light on why we often choose not to avoid danger. We tend to give our full attention to risks that are beyond our control (air crashes, nuclear-plant disasters) while ignoring those we feel in charge of (dying from smoking, poor diet, car accidents), even though the latter is far more likely to harm us...Many Americans who wouldn't travel to see the pyramids for fear of being killed in Egypt stay home, where that danger is twenty times greater.[128]

When these two types of fears are blended, we can become confused: Either 1) we fail to see the actual dangers right in front of us, or 2) we accept that rare scenarios are likely and thus cause us to behave irrationally, obsessing over highly unlikely scenarios. The first type is more consequential, say, downplaying the pushy guy at the bar that makes you feel uneasy when he tries to walk you to your car, but being more concerned about being seen as rude or discriminatory rather than politely telling him to get lost. De Becker strongly encourages us to heed the unsettling warning signs despite any social faux pas or taboos. They are a gift given to us from long and tedious iterations of evolutionary development in a dangerous world. What's more, it logically follows that being wrong and rude is far better than being nice and ending up in serious trouble. The second type of misplaced fear might cause us to avoid adventurous opportunities because we listened to too much hysterical information that scared us into idleness and complacency. "Better safe than sorry" will always have its appeal.

Furthermore, de Becker challenges us not to simply put these things out of our minds, but actively confront and learn something valuable about violence and fear in our society. Violence is an obvious problem in our society, and we should not shy away from its reality. We must become more vigilant and informed citizens. He remarks, "We don't need to learn about violence, many feel, because the police will handle it, the criminal justice system will handle it, experts will handle it. Though it touches us all and belongs to us all, and though we each have something profound to contribute to the solution, we have left this critical inquiry to people who tell us that violence cannot be predicted, that risk is a game of odds, and that anxiety is an unavoidable part of life. Not one of these conventional 'wisdoms' is true."[129] In coming to appreciate the sources of our modern unrest, we will be better prepared to deal with the myths and truths of things like violence and fear in our society. With this practice, then, we may also come to lead a more fearless and adventurous life.

○

We possess two broad psychological blunders that most of us are already aware of, and they contribute to us reaching a wrong-headed conclusion in the contemporary world: 1) our memories are devastatingly unreliable, and 2) we are terrible with numbers. Science and mathematics do not come naturally to us. The long patterns of history and statistics are not the easiest things for humans to pick up on or keep in our heads for very long. This is why having a cohort of dedicated experts who spend their lives studying this stuff is still critical. We need trustworthy experts to lean on. These subjects require rigid focus and often repetitive analysis. Why? A very brief revisit of our evolutionary history of the brain will show that our limbic system or paleo-mammalian brain comprises primarily the alien-sounding components known as the amygdala, hippocampus, hypothalamus, olfactory bulbs, cingulate gyrus, and various other areas. These are where emotions (especially aggression, rage, and fear), memory, sense perception, and motivation, among other functions, are located and regulated. This system was developed many millions of years before the furrowed reasoning parts of our brain in a world that needed to be well-equipped to deal with direct risks at a moment's notice. In short, little to no thinking was occurring, just responding and acting. For millennia, our ancestors were simple reactionaries.

Summoning emotions and being able to remember and parse out immediate threats was, for a *very* long time, crucial for our ancestors' survival. There was a lot at stake in those days. This nascent brain encountered *more threats more frequently* because our ancestors were prey rather than predators, situated much lower on the food chain.

As a student, I volunteered in an archaeology lab at Indiana University, where a small glass cabinet just outside in the hallway housed numerous skeletons of small to medium-sized mammals. A placard drew attention to the placement of the eye sockets, which turns out to be a clear indication of where a creature broadly lies on the food chain. A small mnemonic rhyme noted "Eyes on the side, the animal hides. Eyes in the front, the animal hunts." Many of the earliest mammals from which we descended were small scurrying critters for many millions of years using their side-eyes to avoid being stomped on or eaten by colossal reptiles.

Much later, when proto-humans and our species evolved and became nestled higher up on the food chain, our brains still had to take a firm mental note of where the lion's den was and where water might be unsafe to drink. There was still much in our environment that could easily maim, sicken, or kill us, and we relied heavily on our guts. In *The Science of Fear,* Daniel Gardner explains the context of how our system of reasoning and system of intuition/feelings were shaped during this evolutionary phase:

> The problem is that System One [limbic system/emotions/feeling/our gut] wasn't created for the world we live in. For almost the entire history of our species and those that came before, our ancestors lived in small nomadic bands that survived by

hunting animals and gathering plants. It was in that long-ago era that evolution shaped and molded System One. Having been forged by that environment, System One works quite well in it. But today, very few human beings spend their day stalking antelope and avoiding lions. We live in a world transformed by technology—a world in which risks are measured in microns and parts-per-million and we are bombarded with images and information from all over the planet. [130]

Psychologically, when living in an environment like that of our ancestors, where threats were far more direct and imminent, it would be highly beneficial to have a heightened sense of awareness each time we were cued to something potentially dangerous. And it's still useful when in direct contact with danger. However, today these cues of some danger that keep us perpetually asking "What is wrong with the world?" are rarely in our immediate vicinity, yet they still generate the same unnerving emotions within us by viewing so many harrowing images. More simply put, we possess brains that are still trying to catch up with the ever-accelerating modern world and our subjective calculation of risks.

Things are much different today, though the hardware in our heads remains largely unchanged. As an expert on human decision-making and the evaluation of risks, the late psychologist Daniel Kahneman succinctly points out in his popular book *Thinking Fast and Slow* why our minds are skewed toward the negative,

> [T]he brains of humans and other animals contain a mechanism [the amygdala, i.e., the 'threat center'] that is designed to give priority to bad news. By shaving a few hundredths of a

second from the time needed to detect a predator, this circuit improves the animal's odds of living long enough to reproduce…no comparably rapid mechanism for recognizing good news has been detected.[131]

And the detection of danger also carries over to "purely symbolic threats" in the forms of words and images.[132] With incessant 24-hour news coverage and the repetitive nature of that coverage, it's hardly surprising that images of masked men with malicious eyes and words like "terrorism," "war," "9/11," and "ISIS" flashing endlessly across screens evoke immediate visceral responses in us, namely fear, anger, anxiety, and disgust. These deep sighs, expanded pupils, flexed muscles, gritted teeth, and increased heart rates, subsequently triggered by shocking news segments, have deep evolutionary roots. These signals, being ever more prompted to prepare to fight or fly, tell our brains to be on guard. As Gavin de Becker neatly puts it, "Though we live in space-age times, we still have Stone-Age minds."[133] That said, many significant changes and environmental pressures have also taken place since those Stone Age times, some ten thousand years ago, and some evidence suggests that as much as 10% of our genome has undergone recent selective pressure, and changes to the brain may have occurred at a faster rate than previously assumed.[134] So yes, we are still evolving and adapting, but to what extent is challenging to know at the moment. However, we aren't going to evolve our way out of this modern dilemma any time soon.

The takeaway and consequence to this transformation of our world from millennia of Stone Age wandering to agrarian village dwelling to the information-saturated age of today is a phenomenon remarkably new and highlighted by Furedi in *The Culture of Fear: Revisited:*

Our personal experiences shape the imagination and our fears. However, today, many of our fears are not based on personal experience. They are often shaped by television programs...or by alarmist media accounts of avian flu in Asia, the Ebola virus in Africa, or of desperate Middle Eastern terrorists plotting our downfall. These are threats that do not necessarily emerge out of our immediate personal experience. We can neither fight them nor flee from them. They are about dangers that we cannot directly confront, but simply fear passively.[135]

Thus, we are transfixed by the highly visual warnings of our media culture, and the emotional parts of our brains cause many of us to err on the side of caution, not realizing our brains are misguiding us and likely influencing our decisions in extremely subtle ways. One of those subtle ways could well be something like not taking a long-distance trip, all because of some frightful content the news just spewed at us for twenty minutes, causing our primitive system of hormones and brain structures to err on the side of caution. Nonetheless, understanding a little bit about the inner workings of our brains helps us see how the makeup of our brains contributes to our unrest. But what are some of the more specific instances of the brain's errors, the cognitive illusions or biases that disrupt our view of the world and our humanity?

Though the human brain is an extraordinary three-pound, highly efficient organ that is the root of all we are, it is still not without its flaws and evolutionary baggage as we've begun to see. Even the healthiest and most intelligent of brains can be susceptible to various psychological "tricks," so we need not be ashamed. Instead, we can be humble about. As the late Hans Rosling wryly put it, "Knowing that most people are deluded means you don't need to be embarrassed. Instead, you can be curious: how does the illusion work?"[136] Again, reframing how we see things can work wonders. It is in our interest to familiarize ourselves with some of these biases because they dramatically influence our ideas, behavior, and perceptions of the world. Once we have a grasp on some of these cognitive biases and have more control over our reactions, we'll be better equipped to transcend our current culture of fear and OSD in society. Perhaps a new version of us, one more calm, collective, and informed, can begin wandering a more adventurous path.

O

One psychological mechanism briefly mentioned in the third chapter, "habituation," causes us to subconsciously ignore stimuli that have no positive or negative impacts on us, and also has a side effect in today's world. Traditionally, habituation allowed (still allows) us to cope and organize what things posed a threat and what didn't. It allows the mind to calm down once threats are assessed and no longer apparent. It would be evolutionarily impossible to survive on a Jason Bourne-style alert system always calculating trivial data. If we were able to go back 30,000 years, transport, and plop one of our Stone-Age Cro-Magnon forebears of the Ice Age down in the center of Manhattan, we would be able to witness habituation in real time. At first, he would be incredibly on edge, trying to take on the overwhelming foreign stimuli. After a while, however, his nerves would eventually calm down as he habituated to the new environment and ruled out the things that were unlikely to injure or kill him. Perhaps our fellow caveman could eventually learn to make a decent living making GEICO commercials.

Habituation is a good thing to have overall. However, once we've become habituated to a given environment, everything that was once fresh and nuanced fades into the background, and what remains are the exciting things. Where is the most exciting thing happening in your home, the place you probably spend a lot of time? It's typically the television or computer screen. This is where content has been designed to grip our attention and fill our minds with ever-changing stories, where a lot of it is more often than not sensational, provocative, alarmist, and inflammatory.

The problem arises because habituation seems to occur within the emotional parts of our brain, areas that are the first to react to new stimuli, and there also remains a plethora of unintuitive things that the brain isn't naturally adept at to counter or mediate these immediate emotions; things like science, mathematics, statistics, and history. These things help establish context and are essential tools for making some sense out of the chaotic image-crazed and video clip world of today. The part of the brain that can deal with these things is the neocortex, but it can be slow, and our limbic system is the first to naturally react to the world. Gardner puts this into our modern perspective:

> Habituation generally works brilliantly. The problem with it, as with everything the unconscious mind does, is that it cannot account for science and statistics. If you've smoked cigarettes every hour, every day, for years, without suffering any harm, the cigarette in your hand won't *feel* threatening.

Not even your doctor's warnings can change that, because it is your conscious mind that understands the substance of the warning, and your conscious mind does not control your feelings. The same process of habituation can also explain why someone can become convinced it isn't so risky to drive a car drunk, or to not wear a seat belt, or to ride a motorcycle without a helmet. And if you live quietly for years in a pleasant Spanish town, you're unlikely to give a second thought to the fact that your town is built on the slopes of the world's third-largest active volcano.[137]

We get used to the things that don't immediately hurt or kill us. And all that we categorize as "normal" and boring soon escapes our memory and attention. Thus, our brains have a tendency to focus more acutely on bad things than good. We thus overload and imbalance our minds with bad news at the expense of the good.

Real-world implications result from our emotions taking precedence over our reasoning faculties. These subjects of science, statistics, mathematics, and history require significant training and time devoted to understanding concepts that allow us to interpret counterintuitive phenomena. Some examples are trends in violence over time or a toxic chemical substance that is a hundred parts per million (ppm) that might be found in our drinking water. If we are not inclined to what probability and statistics are and the kinds of major historical events that transpired in the past to bring us to where we are today, then we are essentially intellectually handicapped in the modern world. That might come across as elitist, but it's an inconvenient truth nonetheless. Again, we need trustworthy experts to lean on unless we're willing to quit our day jobs and do all this deep studying and analysis ourselves.

What's more, we're easily deceived and taken advantage of by those who wish to capitalize on our fears and anxieties. For instance, the security industry is a prime example of how to market fears to those unaware of crime statistics in their area. Security system companies love a prosperous suburban community. That's where the money is, not necessarily the crime. These unsuspecting residents are targeted by companies with unsettling home invasion advertisements that convince them with horrible "what if" scenarios to install a security system in their homes, even though such communities are the least likely places for crime.[138] Many of these places are often already surrounded by fences and security systems! "Better safe than sorry" will win us over if we don't think too much about probability and utilize our local statistics. Essentially, every one of our brains comes with a reactive emotional operating system, but not everyone has invested or had the opportunity to invest in the synthesizing programs of the reasoning parts of the brain that are crucial to helping us mitigate our biases in the modern world.

Another psychological bug of ours is what is known as "negativity bias," where we give greater focus to and recall bad instances of our lives than the equally good or neutral parts of our lives. Negative thoughts, emotions, and cases involving harm and bad social engagements have been demonstrated to be more dominant in our minds and more contagious than positive and neutral instances.[139] We fear the bear attacks (less likely) more than succumbing to dehydration (more likely) in the wilderness because violent deaths scare the hell out of us. Professors of psychology, Paul Rozin and Edward Royzmann, developers of these principles, demonstrate that "in most situations, negative events are more salient, potent, dominant in combinations, and generally efficacious than positive events."[140] We stress out and feel humiliated over our bad presentations and speeches far more than we congratulate ourselves on when we nail them. Traumatic social events like terrorist attacks, school shootings, plane crashes, and cases of stolen babies carry far greater weight in our psychological states. Interestingly, one study found that there are nearly twice as many negative descriptors of our emotions in psychological literature as positive ones.[141] This also carries over into the broader English language, which has substantially more words for negative emotions than positive ones.[142] Then again, this makes good evolutionary sense that we'd be inclined to be more concerned with bad or potentially dangerous outcomes than good and neutral events. So, overall, it's a good thing that bad things are important to us. If we lived in a world where we were simply reacting to dangers in our environment this way, our behaviors would be more understandable, but due to the bombardment of bad news that won't likely affect us, it can have a dizzying effect. As we gravitate more toward negativity, we have to be more vigilant and not allow ourselves to become overly confused and make the mistake of thinking that the bad triumphs over the good, because real-world consequences can be severe and irreparable.

Let's consider a curious instance where statistics clash with our Stone Age psyches: plane versus car travel. It has been well-established among statisticians, psychologists, and engineers that plane travel is exceedingly safer than car travel. However, psychological factors at work, namely being aware that we are in a thin metal tube miles high in the sky and the feeling of being completely out of control of the situation, cause our brains to intuitively and inaccurately conclude that plane travel is more dangerous than car travel. If only we had a nickel for the number of Xanax and wine cocktails downed before boarding to calm the nerves. In *The Science of Fear*, Gardner opens his book with a poignant analysis of the terrible repercussions of trading reasoning for intuition during the post-9/11 aftermath when air travel plummeted and car travel swelled:

> [W]hat no politician mentioned is that air travel is safer than driving. Dramatically safer—so much so that the most dangerous part of a typical commercial flight is the drive to the airport. The safety gap is so large, in fact, that planes would still be safer than cars even if the threat of terrorism were unimaginably worse than it actually is: An American professor calculated that even if terrorists were hijacking and crashing one passenger jet a week in the United States, a person who took one flight a month for a year would have only a 1-in-135,000 chance of being killed in a hijacking—a trivial risk compared to the annual 1-in-6,000 odds of being killed in a car crash.[143]

He continues to elaborate further on this point by bringing our attention to the startling finding by psychologist Gerd Gigerenzer at the Max Planck Institute in Berlin, who analyzed travel and fatalities data five years before and five years after September 11, 2001. He discovered that in the year following the 2001 attacks, 1,595 people had lost their lives in traffic accidents *as a direct result* of the change in travel from planes to cars.[144] Inflated fears influence our behaviors and can have a very devastating impact when we succumb to OSD and let psychological biases trump us.

When it comes to such things as terrorists, serial killers, escaped convicts, crime waves, and child abductions, we allow ourselves to be overly captivated by their depraved and astonishing acts. The highly publicized and extraordinary cases are what grip our fears the most. Furedi effectively reveals this phenomenon by saying,

> It is unfortunate that high levels of anxiety about crime can only make the world more insecure...anxieties regarding the threat of crime against children often take on panic-like proportions. In the USA, where FBI statistics indicate that fewer than 100 children a year are kidnapped by strangers, the public concern with child abduction is pervasive. For example, a study of schoolchildren in Ohio reported that nearly half of them thought that they would be kidnapped. Such reactions are not surprising. Public information campaigns on milk cartons, posters, and videos have helped reinforce the impression that kidnapping is a widespread threat. The same inflated sense of danger prevails in the UK. Many parents simply do not believe that, over the years, the number of children murdered by strangers has remained fairly static. On average, it has been five per year. A few highly publicized child murders have helped shape the impression that such tragedies 'could happen to every child.'[145]

When we construct diabolical scenarios in our heads and continue to revisit them over and over due to how shocking and sickening they are, we wrongly convince ourselves and others that we or someone we love might just be the next victim of a similar scenario. While there are seemingly endless horrific and devastating events happening around the globe all the time—and I am not arguing for complacency or indifference—I remain convinced things "out there" across our immense planet are better than we're imagining them. What is morally imperative for us all to figure out is how we get more of us to broaden and balance our perspectives: *by becoming more directly engaged offline rather than passively engaged online.*

Now think of all this in the context of trying to encourage us to travel and explore more. We begin to see the challenge of being more adventurous. Consequently, we refrain from doing many adventurous things we might otherwise have done had we not let ourselves get so spooked. Most of the time, these things happen subconsciously rather than consciously. Try an experiment in which you invest time and attention watching a horror film late at night. Then try to go for a walk in the woods by yourself. You will find it incredibly difficult to be at ease, no matter how fantastically unrealistic you know your horror film was. Those film images are readily accessible to your mind and are putting you on edge for fight or flight. This is your intuitive limbic system overriding your reasoning neocortex. The same psychology can prove true after hearing about or watching life's depravities unfold on the news and other media outlets.

A third important psychological bias of ours (bear in mind the horror movie experiment) is called the "availability heuristic." Documented along with many other cognitive biases by renowned psychologists Amos Tversky and Daniel Kahneman, the availability heuristic shows that if we can recall something easily, such as a terrorist attack or an inner city homicide, we illogically conclude that it is common and likely to happen to us or someone close to us.[146] This is an unfortunate malaise that couples toxically with technological advancement and, more specifically, a consequence of our media-saturated culture and the extraordinary ease with which information is now delivered to us. When we are confronted with repulsive or frightening content repeatedly, we are far more likely to remember it. This, too, is a holdover from our evolutionary history. Scientifically, what is happening within the brain is that the amygdala is activated to release hormones that allow greater memory function, thus making it easier to recall in the future.[147] If you've ever reacted to a hose in the grass in the shape of a snake and nearly jumped out of your skin even before you realized what you were looking at, then you're familiar with how the brain targets and keeps available potential threats subconsciously.

"Confirmation bias" is also a glitch in our brains where we continually seek selected information that reaffirms our beliefs, and we neglect or downplay information that goes against or even discredits our beliefs. This is why conservatives predictively consume mostly conservative media and liberals consume mostly liberal media. This bias leads to much dishonesty in our discussions and prevents us from modestly admitting when we are wrong and accepting a nuanced perspective on things. Cross-pollinating our news sources might help alleviate the problem of everyone siloing themselves into divergent worldviews.

Closely related to "confirmation bias" is "group polarization," where individuals with similar beliefs commingle and their beliefs tend to become reinforced and more extreme. Again, conservatives reliably congregate with other conservatives, liberals reliably congregate with other liberals, and nazis, anarchists, and Marxists conveniently box themselves into groups where they each bolster and polarize their stances on current events and issues. We have a strong tendency to be "groupish" as notable social psychologist Jonathan Haidt has fabulously written about in *The Righteous Mind: Why Good People Are Divided By Politics and Religion:*

> Morality binds and blinds. This is not just something that happens to people on the other side. We all get sucked into tribal moral communities. We circle around sacred values and then share post hoc arguments about why we are so right and they are so wrong. We think the other side is blind to truth, reason, science, and common sense, but in fact everyone goes blind when talking about their sacred objects.[148]

Attending graduate school in an anthropology program recently, I can attest that I am intimately familiar with group polarization and groupthink now. Group polarization happens with virtually all other conceivable ways humans group themselves and is the foundation of the "us versus them" mentality, an unfortunate source of things like tribalism, nativism, and xenophobia. Even those amongst us who you'd suspect as being least likely to fall victim to these biases—the highly educated—are tragically just as susceptible. None of us is immune to this, no matter how brilliant you think you are.

Anthropologists and other social scientists have noted for a long time the universality of tribalism, where countless groups focus more heavily on how they are different from a neighboring group than on how they are similar. Again, looking at our biology and evolutionary history, it makes sense why certain groups might link up to defend and raid, or destroy other groups; therefore, placing a premium on traits and genes that select for aggression and patterns of behavior that separate people from one another.[149] Taken to an extreme, this makes it far easier to kill someone you perceive as "scum" or "an animal" than to see them as another human being. In an eye-opening text, *Humanity: A Moral History of the 20th Century*, author Jonathan Glover details this grotesque element within us, noting that "deep in our psychology, there are urges to humiliate, torment, wound and kill people."[150] Unfortunately, there are ugly, heinous parts of us that yearn to dominate, demoralize, and take pleasure in the cruelty and suffering of others.[151]

Glover details this dehumanizing process by illustrating the horrors of the Nazi concentration camps and the way Nazi mentality was conditioned to "seeing people as less than human" by creating "conditions which seem to confirm that view. In the Warsaw Ghetto, the Nazis' linking of Jews with disease led them to post notices that it was an area threatened by typhus. The imposed conditions of starvation, overcrowding, and filth soon created epidemics of typhus and other fevers…in the camps, the inmates were partly stripped of their human appearance."[152] Such tactics were carried out to deliberately make these people seem less than human, to make it easier to brutalize and kill them *as* vermin. We might believe we are high-minded enough and civilized today to not succumb to such extreme acts of barbarism, but our brains are little different than those that thrust spears into the backs and chests of our Neanderthal cousins some 45,000 years ago, and they are certainly nearly identical to the brains in the skulls of Nazis. Reconciling these truths is not for the faint of heart, but it is important to meditate on them nonetheless.

There are well over a hundred known and observed cognitive biases[153] that further distort the reality of our world in innumerable ways, and we should feel compelled to uncover more of them so that we can be better poised to understand our reality a little better. These five distortions, namely habituation, negativity bias, the availability heuristic, confirmation bias, and group polarization, are in some way related and contribute to why we obsess so much over safety, risk, and fear in modern American society. Together, they distort our reality and make it harder to see the good and beautiful aspects of our world. Habituation unsuspectingly dulls our response to things that don't seem to be threatening and has us focus more frequently on things that excite us and catch our attention. In a culture that places a premium on content that is sensational, alarmist, and attention-grabbing, these tend to be things like danger and violence. Negativity bias has us dwell on all the things clawing and tearing at the fabric of society, which skews our perception of the world to view it worse than it is. It makes us prone to remember serial killers and terrorists rather than Nobel Peace Prize winners. The availability heuristic makes us biased toward the most recent alarming events and has us conclude they are likely to happen. Confirmation bias and group polarization separate us into warring echo chambers, unwilling to concede that we all share more in common than we realize. Besides informing ourselves of these biases, there is something else we can more actively engage with to alleviate such distorted thinking. There is something we can *do*.

○

A sense of history eludes a great many of us if we do not find solace and optimism in the fact that we are the longest-lived, healthiest, safest, and wealthiest humans in history. One would think, because of this, that we would be some of the most *fearless* humans in history as well. Perhaps we share the same sense of dread and paranoia that infected the minds of countless emperors, kings, and czars of the past because, knowing we have it so good, we have the most to lose. Conjecture aside, let's reflect a little more on the consensus that civilization is decaying.

As Harvard psychologist and linguist Steven Pinker has observed, "By the standards of the mass atrocities of human history, the lethal injection of a murderer in Texas, or an occasional hate crime in which a member of an ethnic minority is intimidated by hooligans, is pretty mild stuff. But from a contemporary vantage point, we see them as signs of how low our behavior can sink, not of how high our standards have risen."[154] He encourages us to ask ourselves some less-examined inverted questions: "Instead of asking, 'Why is there war?' we might ask, 'Why is there peace?' We can obsess not just over what we have been doing wrong but also what we have been doing right."[155] The fact is, there is a plethora of human misfortune and depravity in our history that we can all be grateful is now in the past.[156] Things have unquestionably improved for humanity in a lot of significant ways, and we shouldn't be discouraged by cynics to at least *acknowledge* those improvements.[157] Nor does acknowledging the facts mean we are heartless and trivializing our current crises, because there are still many. We can have two things in our heads at once. Some of the more prominent works of late that highlight many of these positive trends are Steven Pinker's *The Better Angels of Our Nature* and *Enlightenment Now*, Hans Rosling's *Factfulness*, and Joshua Goldstein's *Winning the War on War*, which is just a subset of many of the other recent books in the recent canon of "progress literature."[158]

AN ANTHROPOLOGY OF WANDERING

A poll conducted for Reuters suggests that one in seven people worldwide and 22% of Americans believe the world will end *within their lifetime*.[159] That's a little over 70 million of our fellow citizens (some of whom probably vote) with an alarming, fatalistic belief to guide their actions. If all hope is lost, why be constructive? Think of the implications! When one in six of us, as a recent Gallup poll suggests, rank terrorism as the United States' number one problem, it's not at all a stretch of the imagination that terrorism and violence still weigh heavily on most American minds and the life decisions they've been making for at least the last two and a half decades.[160] Interestingly, the figure of 51% who said they were worried about being a victim of terrorism the week after 9/11 remained the same fourteen years later.[161] That's a long time for fear, unease, and frustration to be gestating in millions of minds. Many might find it troublesome and perhaps even foolish to travel and experience adventures during such seemingly dystopic times. But what if taking a daring adventure might relieve such suspicion and anxiety? How to bridge that gap? Maybe we all need to momentarily turn off the television and unglue our eyes from all our screens for a while and visit the world and experience what's happening "out there." Go touch grass! Is there not a place we all want to find ourselves in? Is it better to always lead with the heuristic "better safe than sorry"? What about "nothing ventured, nothing gained?"

Another plausible reason why so many of us might struggle to see the good in life could be explained by the fact that we are simply not encouraged enough, either by our society, community, parents, or peers, to explore in any meaningful depth with our world through more traditional means of wandering on our own two feet. Why are we not coaxed more to become driven, self-reliant, cosmopolitan citizens and engage more with adversity and diversity, to venture outside our comfort zones and see what's going on in the world around us? We haven't found a lot of easy ways to structure adventure in our society. Instead, we're more often taught to be cautious, to beware of strangers, and to have constant surveillance on all of us at all times. Many of us find it preferable to unquestioningly heed every warning that comes our way, staying complacently put in our little corner of the world where it is safe and comfortable and forever wait to be told by officials when the smoke has cleared and we can take our next sigh of relief. The late Hans Rosling wittingly sums up what's wrong with viewing the world from our lone vantage point:

> They worry about all kinds of dangers 'out there.' Natural disasters kill so many people, diseases spread, and airplanes crash. They all happen all the time out there, beyond the horizon. It's a bit strange, isn't it? Such terrifying things rarely happen 'here,' in this safe place where we live. But out there, they seem to happen every day. Remember though, 'out there' is the sum of millions of places, while you live in just one place. Of course, more bad things happen out there: out there is much bigger than here. So even if all the places out there were just as safe as your place, hundreds of terrible events would still happen there. If you could keep track of each separate place though, you would be surprised how peaceful most of them were. Each of them shows up on your screen only on that single day when something terrible happens. All the other days, you don't hear about them.[162]

If ever there needed to be a single meme quote remembered by everyone, that is it. But for some reason, there are a lot of us who reactively scoff, dismiss, and ridicule optimists like this. I'm still not fully sure why.

Being naturally drawn to the negative aspects of life, with such a slanted vision of the world mixing with the repetitive and terrifying news headlines, a potential positive feedback loop could be going on: as many of our firsthand experiences of the world decrease and we ingest ever more frightening news headlines and gossip we become more fearful, less adventurous, less informed, and less understanding of context, we could end up being convinced to travel less and remain less involved with real-world affairs. We could then continue living a type of complacent experience that relies heavily on a growing police and surveillance state with a media-dominated culture, which only increases a more narrow and insulated view. With the current events of mass unrest and fervent tribal aspects of nativism, nationalism, and xenophobia on the rise, it's not hard to see how all our fears and anxieties compound. We're becoming the complete opposite of a fearless people: truculent, insular, and self-absorbed. This is a view that seems to clash with the perspectives of those active in the real world "out there": those wandering the globe and engaging with the diversity of minds and cultures of our world. If there's one person who should already be a household name, it's Paul Salopek, the journalist who is spending a decade walking 24,000 miles across the *entire world* to retrace humanity's ancient journey. Talk about adventure!

Many of those who wander do not seem to share such a burden of fearfulness, cynicism, dread, and obsession with safety. This is partly due to having the experience of one's perceived fears extinguished as one encounters real obstacles like crossing a flooded river, dealing with menacing storms, or getting lost. These are the more probable things one is likely to face when placed at the mercy of the world, not the deranged monsters we conjure up in our mind's eye. However, confronting real fears and danger doesn't necessarily make someone immune to fear either. Likewise, this is not to say we won't face rare tragedies. It does, however, embolden a person to cope and manage their fear, anxiety, and apprehension more appropriately. More adventure might just mean coming to understand reality better.

○

The ultimate tragedy for me is if civilization were to eventually panic and fall into chaos and anarchy as a result of misperceived threats and confusion, swayed by an endless slew of disinformation and misinformation—out-of-context memes, AI-generated "deep fakes", and plain old lies and half-truths—while, objectively, everything was quite mild by historical comparisons. That our ancient brains are not equipped to parse fact from fiction is a disquieting thought. Thus, the madness of crowds should never be underestimated. Believing the world to be doomed is a grave mistake and could lead us to a self-fulfilling prophecy if the majority of us who hold such beliefs decide to act on them in irreparably dangerous ways: becoming more passive, enabling further legislation to pass that is more draconian, keeping children under greater surveillance, ceding power and authority to those who promise to keep us safe, cutting ourselves off from otherwise remarkable experiences because we are too afraid to venture out anymore. And, as Rosling further reminds us, "When people wrongly believe that nothing is improving, they may conclude that nothing we have tried so far is working and lose confidence in measures that actually work…in fact, the methods we are already using to improve our world are working just fine."[163] If we look hard enough, we'll discover that most things are not a crisis and that many people in the past and today have figured out some really important things about how to solve major problems and improve our world *for all*.

Instead of venturing out into the world to see what is really happening "out there", we're reverting to being armchair social critics railing against people on social media. We're confident that we're getting all the data we need from our televisions and internet sources. We're unwittingly cutting ourselves off from raw data out in the world of experience, and it is being replaced by insufficient data that is highly susceptible to corruption and manipulation. Consequently, we become more prone to such things as habituation, negativity bias, the availability heuristic, confirmation bias, group polarization, and plenty of other biases, the more we sequester in our isolated corners of the world. However, when out on an adventure, we're typically not surrounded by our usual group, we don't have access to our usual information, and we're not habituated and complacent to things we normally would be. Overall, we're more open and willing to engage with a lot more people and ideas in unfamiliar territory. That's not to imply that we become perfectly fearless and nothing ever goes wrong.

Many international travelers face real challenges and are right to feel justified in feeling vulnerable abroad for many reasons, including fear of con artists, pickpockets, or being held for ransom, which does occasionally happen. Tourists often stand out and can easily become targets. That said, the longer we spend globetrotting, the more biases we are likely to expel or mitigate in our minds. I suspect it's impossible to behave the way we do online and in our closed groupthink circles because we immediately come to depend on others for guidance and wisdom "out there." Ironically, then, adventuring into the realm of what we fear (other places and other people) might very well be the antidote that we are unwittingly preventing ourselves from reaching. We can transcend being a mere tourist and instead become a traveler. First, we need to discover how to unplug our ancient brains from the machine and more sensibly evaluate a primary source of our paranoia and confusion: our media and the age of information.

CHAPTER 6
Media and the Modern Paradox:
Paranoia and Confusion in the Age of Information

"The United States may be the best entertained nation on Earth, but a steep price is being paid."
—Carl Sagan, *The Demon-Haunted World*

"Today change is so swift and relentless in the techno-societies that yesterday's truths suddenly become today's fictions, and the most highly skilled and intelligent members of society admit difficulty in keeping up with the deluge of new knowledge—even in extremely narrow fields."
—Alvin Toffler, *Future Shock*

A gloomy, misty day dawned sometime in the early fall and somewhere in the New Jersey hills covered with an expansive palette of autumnal leaves. The sun was hesitant to reveal itself for most of the day, and rain continued to drip and drizzle. Fallen and splintered white birch trees lay like sun-bleached disarticulated skeletons strewn about.

Despite the grimness of the day's aura, we were enamored with the fall scents and colors the dampness drew from the soil and leaves. Plus, we were thoroughly rejuvenated by the nearly thirteen hours of deep, hibernated sleep the previous evening.

Being nearly two and a half months in, Hilary and I were well accustomed to the trail by now, or so we thought. Everything was going well until around five-thirty in the early evening when Hilary vanished.

We were together not five minutes before. Once I made it to the bottom of a steep hill, I stopped to wait for her. After a couple of minutes, I found myself puzzled as to why she hadn't appeared. I called out to her twice with no response. Something didn't seem right. I knew that she was just behind me and reasoned that surely, she'd still be able to hear my voice. How long had we been separated? I bolted back up the hill and returned to where I last saw her, or where I thought I saw her. She was gone!

Just moments ago, we had come to an intersecting trail, the other marked confusingly with a white blaze and red dot in the middle. Priding myself on always being calm and calculating, I should have taken the hint right here, but a twitch of panic was starting to override more level-headed thinking. She couldn't have walked far if she had gone astray, but which way? Again, I yelled out for her, "Hilary!" Her name felt strange on my tongue as we'd grown accustomed to calling each other by our trail names; Vulture was my adopted namesake, hers, Cactus. There was still no reply.

I ran down one way of the intersecting trail, cupped my hands around my mouth to accentuate another yell, listened, then ran in the opposite direction and did the same. Still nothing. I'd forgotten all about the weight of my pack, and it didn't even occur to me to remove it as the adrenaline started to surge through my veins. I was already armed with my heavy walking stick, and some months of training in Hapkido and Brazilian Jiu-Jitsu in college had me gearing up mentally for a fight. I tried to keep calm and rational, but my heart began to thump and my eyes widened with worry.

Twenty minutes or more passed, and my speech was becoming hoarse as my voice beamed relentlessly through the hushed forest. I thought surely she would have noticed she'd taken a wrong turn by now if that were the case. I continued yelling for her and felt like a trapped mouse in a maze, unsure of which direction to investigate. Dreadful thoughts started to invade my mind chaotically discerning, "People had been kidnapped out here after all…the woods are a perfect place for murders…there are crazy hunters out here…had we been stalked and followed by someone out of that short story we read in high school?…what was that?… *The Most Dangerous Game*…why did I let my guard down…why didn't we just stay home?" I couldn't recall ever feeling so helpless before.

My panicked emotional mind had me rush back up the hill again to where I last saw her and start searching for any sign that might indicate a struggle. Maybe she dropped something as a hint, like in every clichéd television crime drama. The fact that there was nothing to indicate such a thing should have reassured me, but I was sincerely panicked at this point. I'd already tried twice to call her on her phone since I realized I had service, but her phone was still off. Darkness was setting in, and I was close to calling the police, but I attempted a call one more time. This time, she picked up. My fear was quickly exchanged with anger and frustration, but I managed not to lash out. I was just relieved that she was okay.

AN ANTHROPOLOGY OF WANDERING

When the pack with legs came waddling up over the hill, she was oblivious to my near breakdown. I immediately teared up and hugged her. I noticed the earbuds dangling from her shirt, and I felt embarrassed. The easiest explanation had eluded me while I gave in to conjuring up the most ridiculous and frightful scenarios of what could have happened to her: listening to music and taking a wrong turn was all that happened. By now, we have a good idea of *why* my mind rushed to the implausible, but *where* did these rare, implausible scenarios come from in the first place?

○

Gloomy days and panic, paranoia, and confusion seem to be the broken record we spitefully label as "the media" keep playing over and over, and yet we still listen and gawk at the worst things happening around the world. Modern media culture has a fantastic ability to alarm and arrest us. It is not an uncommon news broadcast to follow like this: A young boy wading knee-deep in a Florida freshwater marsh was suddenly snatched and dragged into the waters by an alligator early yesterday morning while his parents watched from the shore helplessly; a serial killer and rapist from the 1970s has appeared but is thought to be still at large somewhere in California; Russian spies appear to have repeatedly hacked Democratic National Convention files to obtain opposition files; updates soon to follow on the Orlando shooting which claimed the lives of 49 people and wounded 52 others, America's worst mass shooting in modern history to date.

As we vigorously bounced over red, ironized ruts and gray-blue sagebrush through the dry windswept outback of south-central Wyoming on our way to our archaeological site, this depressing string of announcements was the first thing heard on the radio on an early morning commute. A co-worker cynically shook his head and mumbled, "What is wrong with the world today?" I've heard this same order of words time and again from countless others across the country over the years. A mere swapping of nouns and numbers will serve as a template for tomorrow morning's broadcast, and the frustrated and concerned voices of many of your co-workers, friends, and family members will likely echo those of mine.

We are constantly assaulted by symbols and left unprotected from "a hurricane of often fragmented, kaleidoscopic images,"[164] in Alvin Toffler's words. Not only does this modern media culture seem to be one massively attractive and irresistible oracle of complexity and contradiction we are perpetually enamored with, but it also seems profoundly skewed toward stories and events of human misery, aggressiveness, depravity, death, and destruction. This is the inherent selection bias of news media. Even when the data we receive from the media is accurate, it may not be representative of larger trends or may be lacking context. As we discovered in the previous chapter, there are several deep psychological and evolutionary reasons why our minds instinctively gravitate toward negativity, and our smart, albeit ancient, brains can be easily misled.

What's often trending on Twitter/X and repetitively circulating over mass media headlines are essentially obituaries. Those of us constantly gawking over doomsday tales are like those who work in sanitation services and find themselves standing in stagnant filth every day; the whole world tends to look and smell like shit. If we're staring at obituaries day in and day out, then it is of little surprise that it's going to always look like everyone and everything is dying. One doesn't even need to make the conscious decision to open the page to the obituaries anymore; it automatically comes to us on our newsfeeds. Unfortunately, this is what we give the bulk of our energy to with alarming ease in contemporary society. Because of this and how it mingles so well with our ancient brains, far too many of us tend to have an overwhelming sense that the very fabric of society is severely tattered and decaying.

Recall from the previous chapter that when it comes to such things as pedophiles and crime waves, our minds naturally exaggerate their numbers in the same way they do with terrorists, due largely to how often we hear about them and how easily such stories get primed into our brains. If a person is not privy to critical engagement with things like history and statistics, then it makes absolute sense to interpret the news as it is presented. This is why we need trustworthy institutions and experts we can rely on who actively study this psychology and sociology. Should we blindly follow scientists and other experts? Of course not. But we desperately still need the services of experts because our culture is currently highly deficient in trust. Ignoring the advice of what experts are offering and understanding how they think about the world is like watching a football game without an understanding of the general rules of the game, and ignorantly becoming suspicious of the referees whenever they try to flag penalties and enforce those rules.

Dizzied, disoriented, and disillusioned. We're incredibly frustrated and worried by everything we lay our eyes and ears upon. And it's difficult to watch or read a few segments of the news without feeling anxious and as though the world just might end tomorrow. And if it did? Well, some of us seem to be okay with that, too. We're exhausting ourselves into constant states of apathy at the same time. So what exactly is going on? Why the paranoia and confusion? Why so much divisiveness? Why the incessant gloom and doom? Always looking for a scapegoat, many of us idly point the finger at our media for all the disorder and bitterness we're feeling. That is *partly* justified. This is what is known as the "media-effects theory," where the dissemination of a disproportionate amount of frightening content for the sake of ratings or other ulterior political motives creates fear and anxiety in society.[165] Sociologist Barry Glassner highlights this point in *The Culture of Fear: Why Americans Are Afraid of the Wrong Things*:

> Television news programs survive on scares. On local newscasts, where producers live by the dictum 'if it bleeds, it leads,' drug, crime, and disaster stories make up most of the news portion of the broadcasts. Evening newscasts on the major networks are somewhat less bloody, but between 1990 and 1998, when the nation's murder rate declined by 20 percent, the number of murder stories on network newscasts increased 600 percent (*not* counting stories about O.J. Simpson).[166]

However, it goes even deeper than this. The media inherently *must* select for the troubling cases. That is why they are in the news business, to begin with. It is their job to cue us to potential threats, to let us know when a dangerous convict has escaped or when a fire is out of control. By design, they are required to cover the story of the lone plane that crashed, not the tens of thousands that fly every day without error. Regardless of whether the selection bias of the media is intentional or not, this phenomenon still, unfortunately, collides with our ancient brains, which causes us to feel unsettled and conclude the world is spiraling out of control. How do we address it? Can we? Is there any hope of ever getting a more balanced view of our world? And what does any of this have to do with travel and adventure?

It's probably not reasonable to expect the news media to change its imbalanced focus on the human condition because that is what they are designed and entitled to do, and it has a special duty to report on injustice, violence, and other critical information whenever it arises. This surveillance of bad behaviors is only escalating as everyone jockeys to become self-anointed investigative reporters armed with their iPhones, all from the comfort of their computer chairs on Twitter/X and other social media. But we need to be able to better define the issue and have a more sophisticated dialogue over the coming years concerning the disproportion in the ratio of bad things to good. The media's selection bias—whether deliberately political and disingenuous or wholly accurate and just depressing—is one of the dominant forces likely contributing to our culture of fear. How do we ensure we don't succumb to all these overinflated fears?

○

We live in an ever-increasing list of "ages." Our current era has been referred to as the Age of Information, the Digital Age, the Networked Age, the Age of Misinformation, the Age of Terror, and the Age of Empathy, to name just a few of the ages we appear to simultaneously inhabit. Based on these popular and contradicting titles, perhaps we can throw a couple more in the loop: the Age of Confusion and the Age of Paranoia.

One of the great ironies of our time, living within this "Age of Information," is that it is extremely difficult to get our stories straight despite the great ease of access we have to that information. Why is that? We tote around mini-supercomputers that fit loosely in our pockets. So much knowledge rests in our palms. However, *caveat emptor*!

Mass data collection is a very recent phenomenon. It has been estimated that more than 90% of *all* the data in the world has been created and gathered within the last couple of decades and is being stored and synthesized by computers. Former CIA analyst Martin Gurri, in his insightful work, *The Revolt of the Public and the Crisis of Authority in the New Millennium,* notes the stupendous "tsunami" of information that has battered us since the turn of the 21st century:

> More information was generated in 2001 than in all the previous existence of our species on Earth. In fact, 2001 *doubled* the previous total. And 2002 doubled the amount present in 2001, adding around 23 "exabytes" of new information—roughly the equivalent of 140,000 Library of Congress collections. Growth in information had been historically slow and additive. It was now exponential.[167]

This is astounding to think that we have acquired more bits of data in the last handful of years than has *ever* been recorded since the Sumerians started wedging and chiseling out clay tablets to keep track of taxes and pesky farm animals to trade in the 4th millennium B.C.E. [168] This is only growing exponentially with every passing year as society invests heavily in artificial intelligence and data centers. Take a moment to reflect on what this might mean if even a small percentage of data is corrupted, untrustworthy, and misinterpreted, and how this could affect how millions of us think and act in the world, especially if we continue to gradually outsource our time, attention, and critical thinking to machines, all based on faulty data. Consider all those internet memes and AI-generated videos designed to sway public opinion one way or the other. The floodgates of propaganda have only just been unleashed. Despite enormous benefits in communication and commerce, the ease of media dissemination on the internet remains a major source of confusion and misinformation.[169] We only need to peruse the comment threads of social media and news forums to see the intensity of misunderstandings happening in real-time. The implications of all this will be weighed out in time.

The magnitude of information ceaselessly pouring in and circulating in our culture is enough to nauseate and overwhelm us. The transient nature of knowledge is also highly problematic and might help explain the rising power of "fake news" and the philosophical claims we hear that objective truth and scientific fact do not matter. There's a sense of impermanence to our knowledge, and truth is increasingly seen as an illusion, opening up a disconcerting lurch toward moral relativism. New facts quickly replace old. This is another premonition that futurist Alvin Toffler accurately forecasted in his work.[170] From *Future Shock,* published nearly half a century ago, he observed,

> In education, in politics, in economic theory, in medicine, in international affairs, wave after wave of new images penetrate our defenses, shake up our mental models of reality. The result of this image bombardment is the accelerated decay of old

images, a faster intellectual through-put, and a new, profound sense of the impermanence of knowledge, itself.[171]

We are led to wrongly think that since some of yesterday's facts have become today's fiction, this means that today's facts will all too soon likely become tomorrow's fiction before too long. The truth seems more irrelevant and up for grabs. If we don't like someone's facts, well, we can just create our own "alternative facts." It doesn't take a philosopher to know this is a big problem. Do we truly want to live in a world where sophistry and emotionally charged rhetoric are preferable to truth and well-calculated objectivity? Even if objectivity cannot suffice for all truth claims and phenomena, it is nevertheless a sound goal to promote and aim for.

○

It might be helpful at this point to narrow our focus somewhat and specify what we mean by the term "media." The term carries a lot of baggage today, which needs to be unpacked. For many of us, "the media" has become an easy scapegoat, but what are all the mediums that structure it? In the broadest sense, anything we view on television or the internet in the form of advertisements, broadcasting, and popular culture; the content we read in the newspaper, magazines, tabloids, or a book; any kind of lecture, speech, or podcast; any kind of music, video game, painting, or sculpture; any photograph or movie; every image and video captured and shared on your phone is technically media.

All of this content directly influences and quite dramatically shapes our ideas about what the world is like and how we should respond to it. Thus, the totality of media carries significant moral and political weight in our culture. Ultimately, these are all imagined symbols and expressions of human ideas. From flags, statues, language, text, and iconography to ideology and religion, all these things are what cultural anthropologists study with the attempt to interpret their meaning and influence on human thinking, behavior, culture, and society. The renowned cultural anthropologist Clifford Geertz famously wrote about symbolic anthropology and that "man is an animal suspended in webs of significance he himself has spun, I take culture to be those webs, and the analysis of it to be therefore not an experimental science in search of laws but an interpretive one in seach of meaning."[172] Most aspects of our media and culture today are so intertwined that they can be thought of as virtually the same. So, if we're condemning and blaming the "media" we're essentially blaming our entire culture and, thus, as consumers of such media and participants in this exchange, ourselves as well (more to follow on this in the next chapter).

Perhaps the "mainstream media" is the source of much of our frustration and what we typically mean when we castigate "the media." This is the form of media that communicates to large audiences regularly through major news networks on cable TV and any other large-scale programs or individuals on social media with a significant following. The "mainstream media" is fluid, and soon enough, major podcasts and online magazines will be considered under this umbrella term, too, if they haven't already. For instance, is Joe Rogan's podcast now technically mainstream? These unmistakably hold a great deal of influence and control over the content and knowledge to which we are exposed. On his final episode of *The Daily Show* years ago, before his recent comeback, comedian Jon Stewart, perhaps reminiscent of Eisenhower's departure warning of a military-industrial complex, gave his final concise words of witticism on the topic of how obscure and distorted information can become at the hands of those who manufacture and disseminate it:

> Bullshit...is everywhere...There is very little that you will encounter in life that has not been, in some ways, infused with bullshit. Not all of it bad. The general everyday free-range bullshit is often necessary or at the very least innocuous. 'Oh, what a beautiful baby. I'm sure it will grow into that hat!' That kind of bullshit in many ways provides important social contract fertilizer and keeps people from making each other cry all day.
>
> But then there's the more pernicious bullshit; your pre-meditated institutional bullshit designed to obscure and distract; designed by whom, the bullshitocracy. It comes in three basic flavors. One: making bad things sound like good things, organic all natural cupcakes, because factory-made sugar oatmeal balls doesn't sell. 'Patriot Act' because 'Are You Scared Enough to Let Me Look at All Your Phone Records Act' doesn't sell. So whenever something's been titled "Freedom," "Family," "Fairness," "Health," "America," take a good long sniff. Chances are it's been manufactured in a facility that may contain traces of bullshit...Now the good news is this; bullshitters have gotten pretty lazy and their work is easily detected. Looking for it is kind of a pleasant way to pass the time. Like an eye-spy of bullshit. So I say to you tonight friends, the best defense against bullshit is vigilance. So if you smell something, say something.[173]

For those of us concerned about the inevitable issues that stem from all the bullshit we encounter, how do we begin sifting through this mountain of bullshit so we can gain a better sense of our world? After all, hardly anyone has the time (or willpower) to sort through what is true or false every time we sense bullshit is afoot. We can't fact-check everything on our own.

What kind of mandates and clever implementations can be designed to wean out the bullshit that we know is endemic and has become complicit in this media-industrial complex? This term "media-industrial complex" invokes, in a similar manner, Eisenhower's concerns of a "military-industrial complex" where profit-seeking companies would not only profit off of war but gain significant power and influence due to their vested interests and thus play an unchecked role in public policy. There is something quite analogous here to this "media-industrial complex" today that profits off of our fears and also has vested interests and unchecked power in shaping public policy and perceptions in negative ways. Whatever the solutions may turn out to be, the goal remains the same: we must develop a better way to ensure trust and truth in our information because getting to the truth can be existential.

Trying to make sense of the world today almost feels futile with the insurmountable amount of information beaming at us, but the answer is not to completely ignore it all. There are many more creative efforts being put forth to combat misinformation. But the most important first step to solving any problem is acknowledging that there is a problem. Some public figures are owning up to the dramatic impact the media can have on shaping the views and sentiments people have about the state of the world. Writing in the *New York Times* in the aftermath of the 2016 election, David Bornstein and Tina Rosenberg refreshingly opined,

Disillusionment and cynicism have become natural byproducts of everyday journalism…We're talking about a problem at the very core of journalism: the unstated theory of change that might be summed up as: 'Society will get better when we show where it is going wrong.' We are presenting what's wrong with the world as if that's all there is. As a result, what audiences see beyond their direct experience is a world of unchecked pathology, and it makes it all too easy to fear and demonize others. It shapes people's behaviors and choice of leaders…Journalism has a language with which to describe threats and failures, but it is tongue-tied when it comes to letting society know when there's a win. Part of this is simple sensationalism. But perhaps more important is that journalists have become afraid to cover remedies, lest we seem gullible (which, for a journalist, is the greatest sin). We are comfortable, however, covering failure, and adding to the narrative of decline.'[174]

By supporting those who are digging deeper into the truth of important issues and holding ourselves just as accountable for sharing and distributing content, we can help trim away some of the frenzied nonsense distorting reality. But is this media frenzy and concern about propaganda a new phenomenon?

O

When we revisit the embattling years of the American Revolution, we discover something about the nature and origins of our modern media-industrial complex. Arguably, America's first and bestselling propaganda pieces, *Common Sense* and *The Crisis* were written by Thomas Paine during the intervening years of the war. These two pamphlets alone arguably moved countless emerging Americans to support and maintain their morale throughout the Revolution and subsequent war by using hyperbolic and sensational writing to coax enough people and sway them to sustain the war effort. Due to the enormity and speed of the distribution of these publications, he virtually beat all his contenders to the punch. In hindsight, many of us revere and applaud Paine for his wit of communication, his patriotism for the American cause, the enlightenment virtues he extolled, and his insistence on separating from Great Britain. However, we also should recognize that, despite the brilliance of his writing and its effectiveness, some of what he argued was not entirely factual, but was purposely inflammatory, exaggerated, and sensational. It was designed to elicit an emotional response. Sound familiar? Even at the time, critics such as John Adams complained that *Common Sense* "will do more Mischief…He is a keen writer but very ignorant of the Science of Government."[175] Perhaps hyperbole and sensationalism are prerequisites and necessary evils to politics.

Here lies the duality and double-edged sword of having a free press (especially now in the age of the Internet): anyone can write, publish, criticize, and distribute what they please, barring a few restrictions like libel, incitement to violence, fraud, and defamation. There are always bound to be self-interested agendas and ulterior motives mixed into things like journalism, politics, history, and culture. An unfortunate consequence of free speech and our modern media-industrial complex is that so much information is wrought with sophistry and confusing rhetoric. This becomes quite the tonic for a headache because simply reading information on paper or screen does not ensure we will be informed of anything at all. There is much to be read between the lines. Even worse, time just isn't on our side. No one has the time to read and critically analyze all the details of everything that is out there and give everything a fair trial, especially for those of us with a demanding workweek. We are forced to make assumptions and give faith to those we hope won't deceive us. We can easily be deceived and misled into thinking thoughts that are disingenuous or completely erroneous. This can consequently become a key source of our vicious divisiveness that bleeds not just into our politics but into personal relationships. And popular culture only helps to fuel the fire.

How we spend our money, time, and attention is a crucial indicator of what we value, or perhaps what we are addicted to. Popular culture is saturated with incessant cynicism, misanthropy, and self-destructive sentiments and is, therefore, just as guilty as news programs that draw our attention to such negative content. Though it is now highly contested by many scholars whether violence in media *causes* violent human behavior, it surely plays a role in shaping our perceptions of human behavior. The abundance of post-apocalyptic drama shows and films is a testament to our current perceptions and phobias of an unraveling and declining world that may serve as a useful metric to measure our attraction to destruction. These are just some of the more recent popular blockbusters to keep the dreadful collapse of civilization alive in our minds: *The Walking Dead; Mad Max: Fury Road; The Road; Planet of the Apes; The Matrix; I Am Legend; The Book of Eli; Oblivion; The Quiet Earth; 28 Days Later; Land of the Dead; This Is the End; The Terminator; Resident Evil: Extinction; The Hunger Games; Children of Men; Armageddon.* And for every film, there are surely thousands of popular books and songs to complement the soundtrack to the tragic fall of humanity soon to be. We eat these films up, and with good reason; they're extremely addictive and entertaining. As Carl Sagan observed, "The United States may be the best entertained nation on Earth, but a steep price is being paid." How much of a price are we paying for the amount we invest in being entertained all the time? Endless streaming services, 24-hour news cycles, and sports events are the modern bread and circuses.

Consider also the institutional changes that have occurred within news organizations in the 20th and early 21st centuries. Back when CBS, NBC, and ABC formed a powerful triumvirate of media dominance from the late 1940s until the early 1980s, the charges against mass media holding the greatest influence on public perception were appropriate. However, today, as Alvin Toffler poignantly opined, our news apparatus has been systematically "de-massified" over the last few decades, toward the breakup of mass audiences into segments and subgroups, each receiving a different configuration of programs and messages."[176] With the advent of the internet, media became more democratized, thus giving birth to seemingly endless outlets and a wide spectrum for news dissemination and discussion. Mass media still exists, but there is now a bountiful supply of many other sources on the spectrum, confusingly stirred together with high-quality journalism mixed with the most god-awful tabloid sensations fit only for a dumpster fire. Democracy is cumbersome and messy. It will take time for all of us to develop better ways to synthesize our information. And we ought to consider being better stewards of how we respond and behave with this information because it all siphons into our culture of fear.

The content of our televisions and the internet is heavily curated to select the most engaging material, much like the archaeologist sifting his piles of dirt through the screen in search of rare artifacts. What's mostly going through an archaeologist's screen are endless grains of soil, dried-out seeds, insect parts, and boring, untouched pebbles of rock. On a very rare occasion, they'll find something of interest, and it might make it to the museum for a display in an exhibit. An innocent bystander who visits that museum might get the impression from looking at all the rare artifacts in the exhibit that an archaeological dig would be an extraordinary experience full of enchanting relics of ages past. *It is not!* Archaeological excavations are as monotonous as watching paint dry, and it is as though you're slowly cooking in an oven under a burning sun all day. If only there were a museum exhibit full of giant mounds of sand and dried-out vegetation with one display in the center of the room containing a few chert flakes and part of a broken spear point, then that would more accurately give a visitor the sense of proportion of mundane dirt to enticing trinkets. Likewise, journalists and reporters now anxiously wait on Twitter/X to diligently sift through the mundane mounds of existence, all for that rare, exciting piece of human misery, depravity, and scandal to curate and display on our newsfeeds. And then once they find that story, they all simultaneously talk about it at once.

From his analysis of the culture of fear, sociologist Frank Furedi notes something key about the source of our media content:

> The media play an important role in the shaping of perceptions of risks. Since most people gain their information through the media rather than through direct experience, their perception is moulded by the way information is communicated...However, it is important to remember that the media amplify or

attenuate but *do not cause* society's sense of risk. There exists a disposition towards the expectation of adverse outcomes, which is then engaged by the mass media. The result of this engagement is media which are continually warning of some danger. But the media's preoccupation with risk is a symptom of the problem and not its cause.[177]

Even more to the point, Hans Rosling comes to the defense of journalists and documentarians by pointing out that they are not:

> ...deliberately misleading us—when they produce dramatic reports of a divided world, or of 'nature striking back,' or of a population crisis, discussed in serious tones with wistful piano music in the background...and blaming them is pointless because most of the journalists and filmmakers who inform us about the world are themselves misled...they have the same mega misconceptions as everyone else.[178]

○

Our modern world, so bloated with information, has given birth to mediums like Twitter/X and Instagram that optimistically attempt to make our information quickly accessible and digestible in a few hundred characters or with images without words. Even if pictures are worth a thousand words, that's still not adequate to be properly informed. These models of communication were brilliant in theory, given how much data we have to synthesize, but they are simply failing us. There remains much information in our world that simply cannot be synthesized in such a way and requires time and discipline to be properly informed. Hefty books still need to be read and carefully considered, no matter how archaic it feels. Long conversations must still be endured, especially between those who stridently disagree with one another. Evidence still needs to be followed. Lots of time and energy still need to be expended. But this proves to be a paradox when the rate of society and the turnover of new information continues to quicken its pace. As Alvin Toffler remarked,

> [T]o function in a fast-changing society, to cope with swift and complex change, the individual must turn over his stock of images at a rate that in some way correlates with the pace of change. His model must be updated. To the degree that it lags, his responses to change become inappropriate; he becomes increasingly thwarted, ineffective. Thus, there is intense pressure on the individual to keep up with the generalized pace.[179]

We're fighting an uphill battle with information, but not fighting at all would be far more consequential.

Can we say in this present moment and with any amount of confidence that we are an informed citizenry, especially in the midst of a supposed information age? Being properly informed was one of the prime civic duties held to a high standard in the early formation of the United States (which is why several had doubts about citizens taking it upon themselves to become learned enough and thought democracy more of a risk than having a republic where elites called the shots). What does it mean to be an informed citizen in today's rapidly changing world with such an insurmountable amount of information (and bullshit) pouring and mixing like quick-drying concrete into our skulls? What do we have to rely on to obtain the most reliable information?

The problem of convoluted information and misinformation is so interwoven into the fabric of our culture that it has become a firmly set Gordian knot, and we are a new kind of Sisyphus[180] tragically condemned to a new sort of punishment to sever the knot only to watch it reform again and again with each swipe of the blade. This analogy captures our misfortunes with the current climate of ceaseless misinformation and suggests that the problem is likely not going away for some time. There will always be a significant collection of distorted information in circulation, and we will, therefore, need ways to adapt to that fact.

○

Now, what does any of this have to do with travel and adventure? One of the best insurance policies against ignorance is to confront issues and arguments directly. Though this will sound old-fashioned, the two best ways to do this are through travel and reading as extensively as we can. Engaging with ideas directly can be uncomfortable but rewarding. This is a far better, albeit more time-consuming, way to know and understand a place and people because all our senses are present and engaged while traveling. What type of reading? Anything that causes a person to critically judge reality: a book that intimately grips us into seeing the world from the mind of another; considering the viewpoints of someone you abhor in an attempt to see their perspective; following a blog that challenges our preconceived notions of life in another area of the world; examining a journal or article that completely tunes us into something so bizarre and abstract that never before entered our mind.

If we let ourselves get outraged with every hot-button political and social issue and ruminate on these issues all the time, then we're stealing our time away from activities that might prove more productive and fulfilling to our health and well-being. The line has to be drawn somewhere. Also, we lose sight of the bigger picture of fixing the problems we've always faced as humans. Is the world changing rapidly? Yes. But not everything in the world is freshly complex. We still have old blueprints to fix persistent problems.

Part of our social currency depends on being up to date on current events. But how much do we need to be aware of current events, especially those that will likely have no significant impact on our lives? At what point does this information become psychologically damaging and more costly than beneficial? With a finite amount of time on this earth, we owe it to ourselves and the time we have to be a bit more serious with how we choose to spend it. We can ask ourselves, "Is what I'm doing *right now* truly fulfilling? Is this issue I've been ruminating on all day worth my time? Is this contributing to human flourishing and an example of the values I want to see more of in our world? Am I going to *do* anything with this information to improve my life or those of others whom I care about?"

○

One of the most striking things found in hiking for four months on the Appalachian Trail was the incredible sense of ease and reduction of my anxiety and worry about the ongoing social, political, and economic problems tirelessly circulating the airwaves above us in silence. Life was put on mute for a moment. It made me think of just how much our technological connectivity has become both a blessing and a curse. On the one hand, by being "connected," we gain our social currency and can deem ourselves "informed." On the other hand, we are strangely disconnecting ourselves at the same time from our immediate surroundings. It seems increasingly difficult to divvy out what actual events and issues are pertinent or impact our lives.

I was astonished one day when I phoned my best friend from Hanover, New Hampshire, and he clued me in on all the recent news headlines, nearly all of it devastating and terrifying: the uprising protests in Ferguson, Missouri, another beheading of an American journalist somewhere in the Middle East, airstrikes on ISIS killing civilians, migrants fleeing from several countries in the Middle East and northern Africa. His tone was sympathetic though nonchalant. This was just another day in his world. However, this flood of awful stories hit me in an unusual way for some reason. I suspect that I would have been just as nonchalant and far less impacted emotionally had I not been on the trail and still wrapped up in the mire of my normal life, one that now struck me as desensitized. After being on the trail and experiencing repeated cases of overwhelming kindness and respect, this utterly shocked me like diving headfirst into a lake that had recently thawed. I wondered if the world I was facing was more the reality or if I had just become naively blind to the world at large as a result of this semi-solitary experience. Perhaps, in a sense, I was doubly insulated, once by the protection of U.S. security and another by the trail community. Was this a fair and normal sample of people, or did the trail just attract an unusually high amount of friendly, privileged, adventurous folks?

The people who do something like travel solo to a foreign country or backpack a long-distance trail are likely already inclined to set aside personal prejudices and open to meeting new people. Being in unfamiliar territory, it is advantageous and rational to be friendly, as we are often more dependent on others than they are on us. Would we sincerely pick a fight with someone over a minor political disagreement if we were desperate for a bath and they were offering their home to us for the evening? Would it be worth it to make our point? However, in our experience, it wasn't just the people on the trail acting so kindly, but virtually everyone else living their lives throughout the towns and communities bordering the trail: the numerous folks who offered us a ride to and from town, those who left piles of food and beverages alongside the trail as "trail magic" for people they would never meet, those who welcomed us into their homes for hearty meals and warm showers. Small acts of altruism manifested outside, beyond the trail into the "larger society" after all.

As part of our blog, we featured a "People of the Trail" segment, inspired by *Humans of New York* posts on social media. But we were keen to not just document the voices of those hiking the trail, but also those who were connected to the trail in other ways: the park rangers and faculty of the National Park Service, the volunteers who maintained sections of the trail, the "trail angels" who offered rides and food. Julia, short in stature with graying hair drooping over her broad shoulders and donning rounded Benjamin Franklin-looking spectacles, was one of these "trail angels" we met on our way up Mt. Greylock, Massachusetts' highest point. She purchased our burgers at Bascom Lodge when we arrived at the top and elaborated on her prideful connection with the trail, "I've been a trail angel to many. I've hiked a number of sections of the AT, and I used to work at Bascom Lodge. I love being a part of it. I moved to North Adams, Massachusetts, and made sure that I bought a house so I could see Mt. Greylock. It's one of my favorites to climb." Immediately after our lunch with Julia, a group of New Jerseyites, unaware of what the AT even was as they hiked on it, took so much fascination in what we were doing that they pushed three twenty-dollar bills into my pocket and refused to take them back. Humbling stories like this grew after each day. None of these people had the incentive to aid us, and we wouldn't have thought less of them if they hadn't. They simply went out of their way to help us. They restored some of our faith in humanity and taught me why it is so important for all of us to wander and have adventures in a seemingly fearful world.

Tramping along the trail and encountering real instances of distress also made it much easier to put many of our perceived fears and worries to rest or in a greater context. We were forced to deal with the present moment and dispel all our excess, abstract fears. The longer we hiked, the more apparent it became that the majority of our fears about the trail we originally started with were not brought to us in any direct sense. They had been delivered indirectly by the toxic brew of media, popular culture, and hysterical gossip, and had been firmly nestled in our ancient brains from the many symbols brewing in our culture. The trail allowed us time to relearn something about human reality and reframe many of life's fears and anxieties.

MEDIA AND THE MODERN PARADOX

○

The day was damp and cold again. All the aftermath of another storm, and, of course, we were unfortunately caught in this one as well. I lost count of how many times we were caught on top of mountains in a torrential downpour with lightning scaring the shit out of us. Soaked, cold, angry, and smelly, every time we asked ourselves the same predictable question, "Why the fuck are we doing this!?"

Once dry under the comfort of the tent and feeling the warmth of a partner beside you, the mood pendulum typically swings back to calm, content, and grateful for doing something so extraordinary. It's amazing how much a person comes to appreciate the smallest and simplest things. Being entitled to nothing in the woods, we found ourselves at the mercy of the weather, terrain, and other people. No law requires any of these factors to be kind. Surprisingly, we found people to be remarkably caring in virtually every case. The same could not be said for the terrain and weather. Nonetheless, every warm meal, every item of dry clothing, every shower, and every chance to be and feel comfortable is sacred and is never taken for granted while on an excursion like this.

The day was a depressing, sluggish one, but we still managed to tackle Mahoosuc Notch. Many consider it the hardest, yet the most thrilling mile of the trail. I took my first hard fall halfway through, but luckily, no serious injuries resulted. To add to the difficulty, Hilary's pack frame gave out again; it was formerly MacGyvered with super glue and duct tape. This put her in a frustrated mood because her pack kept wrenching her backward. Everything was wet and slick, which was perfect because Mahoosuc Notch is an entire valley of massive boulders! Even amid the warm summer, there remains ice beneath them, and you can feel the coolness exhaling below the granite rock as warm sun-heated beads of water drop down into the abyss of these chasms to strike the frozen patches. It took us nearly two hours to find our way through this maze. The trail was poorly marked, and we lost our way for fifteen minutes at one point. There were times when we needed to take off our packs and push them through the narrow crevices.

Utterly exhausted, we'd managed to make it through and discovered another shelter. Only 5.1 miles to tally up for the day, but it was a bitch, so we had no qualms about stopping for the evening. We'd met several "trail families" along the way by now, but never an actual family. All-In and Momma Bear were a young, healthy-looking couple, maybe in their mid-thirties, with their two children, a young girl, Cartwheel, her nine-year-old brother Robin Hood, and their big, shaggy dog Orion. It seemed unusual to happen upon parents with such young children going the full distance of the Appalachian Trail. We've even read about parents who carried their one-year-old the entire length. Remarkable! Being anthropologists, we know humans are capable of such feats, but seeing it in person is still surprising and uplifting. We've been wandering like this as a species for most of our existence, yet seeing such a sight today seems antithetical to our lifeways now. Our technology and culture cradle us in a protective womb of comfort and luxury. In the abstract, we often think about how impossible things are until we set out to do them. We then realize that things weren't even close to being impossible and that we just didn't give ourselves enough credit.

One of my long-running personal fears was bringing a child into the world. It's not so much that I didn't think I'd be able to care for and raise them properly, but more about what I'd be sacrificing as a result. Would there be as many adventures? Witnessing parents doing the things I love with their children relieved me of that fear to know that with the right amount of determination and forethought, I wouldn't need to sacrifice nearly as much as I once thought. Only new adventures will abound with the right perspective and attitude. Personal fears and worries only seemed to fall away the further we wandered.

○

Much of what we hear and see is indirect, warped out of context, and bundled together in a two-minute sound bite that doesn't mesh very well with our ancient brains. As a result, the world seems foreboding of destruction and misery. Things seem bad because of how disproportionate the ratio of negative to positive information is delivered to us. Often, what adventurers say about human nature and diversity contradicts what is being told by our media-industrial complex. It's not that media sources are purposely inaccurate or blatantly lying all the time, but that they have an innate selection bias for stories that amplify the negative or extreme aspects of the human condition. Consequently, we've become more familiar and fascinated with the demons of our nature while neglecting our better angels. Maybe the doomsayers are right and, indeed, we're merely riding on a wave that is heading to an ominous and firmly set concrete wall. Climate change, nuclear war, or totalitarianism will destroy us all. We can't predict the future, but it should come as some reassurance to us that neither can the doomsayers. Before we get ourselves too panicked, we ought to consider more of the evidence that disputes such cynicism. Things might not be as bad as we think they are after all.

The good news is that we have more than sufficient knowledge of our world, our technologies, and all the capabilities necessary to solve a lot of our current problems if only we can learn to take the temperature down on our politics and culture wars. The current American crisis is not an external "tyranny" like in Paine's time, but a very deep-seated internal crisis in the format in which our media is delivered to us and how it shapes our thinking, our understanding, and our behaviors. More than anything, we have a personal responsibility to not be so lax about our culture and the content it produces. We do have control over our movements. We have agency and, therefore, possess the power to venture out into the world and challenge what we hear in the media. Is the world a scary and uncertain place? Of course, it can be. Should that deter us from exploring it and gaining new experiences? Absolutely not! If we appeal to the former and cower to fear, we will only beget more fear. We only need the courage to see things for ourselves and desire the much more fulfilling perspective that adventures have to offer.

Dreadful stories will continue to proliferate, and music and film artists will adopt the overall musings of the news and convert them into hauntingly catchy cinematic and musical entertainment. Billions of us are misled by information every day. Many, if not all of us, have probably been misled and deceived many times, so we all have that in common. The pervasiveness of lies and deception will continue throughout our lives and will still flourish long after we are gone. Misinformation and propaganda will always abound. Therefore, bad information and bad ideas leading to bad actions seem inevitable. The only choices we have are how we respond to it, how we adapt to it, and how we alleviate it in ourselves and others. Like the Hubble telescope, fixated on its long exposure to the deepest realms of our universe, we too must mirror our long exposure to a diversity of ideas found exclusively in the interactions we have with cultures, landscapes, and literature. One of the few ways to overcome our world's most sinister vices of prejudice, hatred, and ignorance may be achieved through direct travel and adventure. I, along with countless others interested in understanding the world through these mediums, feel anxieties and fears diminish, a sense of peace overcomes me, and an appreciation of the human condition with each step in the direction of another adventure. Next, we will meditate on the final factor that influences our culture of fear: the choices we make.

CHAPTER 7
Agents of Fear:
Responsibility, Trust, and The Choices We Make

"It is by acting in the face of danger and by habituating ourselves to fear or courage that we become either cowardly or courageous."
—Aristotle, *Nicomachean Ethics*

Thirty days of living life on the trail came to pass. It wasn't entirely normal, but there was a comfortable regularity to it by this point. We still experienced our "off" days, but we felt much more adaptable. By "off," I mean excruciatingly sore, utterly exhausted, and 99% sure we made a huge mistake in choosing to do such a ridiculous thing as attempting to backpack the entire Appalachian Trail. These are the damning physical and psychological struggles the thru-hiker continuously faces. The body is never absent from aches. The mind is never fully absolved of decisions. Wandering isn't just a carefree stroll after all, but requires a level of grit and foresight far more demanding than we typically encounter in "normal" life.

The first part of our trip was incredibly tough and anxiety-ridden due to many factors, including our overall inexperience with the trail, the time needed for our bodies and minds to physically and mentally adapt, and, of course, the added loss of my grandfather. All of these factors made for a stressful and confusing time for me. That said, we had yet to encounter any of the perceived fears and apprehensions only Hollywood screenwriters and worried-to-death grandparents could fathom: No lunatics looking to rob or murder us at gunpoint; no bears or mountain lions lurching for our throats; no life-threatening diseases or flesh-eating plagues; no getting severely lost and forced to eat each other. We were, however, being confronted regularly with some real risks and challenges: crossing rivers that could have drowned or severely injured us; losing our way numerous times; and climbing mountains in lightning storms. We often relied on strangers to guide us and take us into towns. We suffered minor scrapes and bruises from falls and endured days walking with painful headaches from dehydration or throbbing plantar fasciitis, in Hilary's case. We were swarmed by black flies and mosquitoes (Hilary once counted nearly 250 swollen bumps all over her body; I somehow only had about a dozen, yet my complaints were somehow louder and more anguished). We made it through with our wits intact, but we had months to go. Maybe the real monsters were further south, and we were still just naïve. The future "what ifs" are always going to be plausible in our minds because that's how our brains function, as we saw in previous chapters. Nevertheless, we had gained some remarkable insights into what we were capable of.

We were empowered by overcoming so many obstacles. Our endurance had greatly improved. We had most of our daily routines down to a science and were generally confident in our abilities to "survive." The rain and storms still managed to piss me off a lot, and there were always going to be mishaps and common mistakes, but we accepted these inevitabilities and prided ourselves on making it through Maine and into New Hampshire so far in good health and good spirits.

The time the trail allowed us to let ourselves simply think and talk was something unexpected and extraordinary. We discussed every topic that came to our minds: whether there were species on other planets that reproduced using more than two sexes; the nature of consciousness prompted by a podcast Hilary listened to by philosopher David Chalmers; Carl Sagan's novel *Contact,* which we read out loud to one another in the passing evenings under our headlamps. We had discussions on trees, wildlife, our future home, other adventures and aspirations, our favorite past high school teachers, our family and friends, and the cherished memories we shared with them. Hours upon hours, we got lost and wandered in our heads as our feet unconsciously carried us forward. I've always thought walking was the best form of meditation. I'm curious how often people can do something like this, to fully allow themselves to focus their time and energy on these well-deserved things in our lives uninterrupted, and how important it is for our imagination to explore these deep, meaningful questions. What's life really about? Why do we fail to prioritize the things that matter most to us? I can't help but return to the thought that we've devised a society that has far too many distractions in it to properly think these things over to a satisfactory degree. The trail provided us with rare opportunities for time, self-reflection, and mindfulness.

A part of me felt like we had escaped from a lot of society's distractions. Something I've always had a difficult time dealing with is the idea that "there aren't enough hours in a day" complex. On the trail, thoughts feel remarkably clear, the recurring anxiety I typically feel vanishes, and nothing feels more normal and right. Time opens itself up and expands, as does space. The world comes to feel boundless and something you want to keep exploring. Walking for so long welcomes you to the true size of our world, and it feels as though you've been let in on a guarded secret. So many others on the trail have the same aura about them. Nearly everyone we crossed paths with often met us with a smile and had an exciting anecdote or word of advice they were willing to share. This camaraderie exists simply because there's so much more time for it; there's no rush, no hustle, and bustle, no market-scheming interactions to try and sell or be sold a product or service, no endless tasks to keep one running on the hamster wheel. We were relieved from all the social constraints to exercise our agency, prioritize what mattered, and carefully choose our path. *That* is what allowed us to feel most alive.

○

Agency. No, not your insurance company or the CIA. Another type of agency. The term, used by many stuffy academics in various fields of the social sciences and humanities, is defined simply as the capacity of a person to act in a given situation or environment. It has to do with how much control we feel we have in our lives. By taking some time to dwell on who we are and our power to act and make decisions, we gain an informed sense of our and others' responsibilities and beliefs, and how we make things happen out in the world. This has to do with the choices we make (or fail to make) and the effects that result (or don't result) from those choices.

The famous Trolley Car dilemma, introduced in every Ethics 101 course, illustrates the case in point: A train is careening down a set of tracks. You are standing beside the tracks when you notice five individuals strapped to the track that the train will imminently collide with. You cannot reach them in time to cut the rope that binds them, but a lever is beside you that will derail it. The rub is that a single individual is strapped to the other track, in which, if you were to pull the lever, they would surely be killed. How do you act? Do you intervene to trade one person's life for five? And remember, doing nothing *is* still a conscious act and a moral decision too![181]

Besides biased brains and the fearful rhetoric generated in our culture by news, entertainment, and hysterical gossip, a lapse of individual agency represents a third and final force contributing to our culture of fear. Fearing the unknown is something all too human. However, by not exercising our agency, we prevent ourselves from becoming more adventurous. By consciously choosing not to invest in opportunities that would otherwise introduce us to instances of nuance, perspective, and context, we do a disservice to ourselves. For instance, when we fail to engage with our neighbors and communities, we are choosing to close our minds off from vital social information about the interests of our neighbors and the functioning of our communities. This can lead to a variety of bad thinking and habits, perhaps attributing evil and malice to others who may not deserve it. Our minds have a funny way of filling in the gaps in our knowledge when we have little to go on, and often, we ascribe the worst attributes to one another. This chapter is ultimately about introspection and how we, as individuals, can better exercise our agency to piece the world together in a more charitable way.

As we saw in previous chapters, the values and lessons of adventure elude many of us because adventure means danger and risk, and our American culture has become allergic to danger and risk. We've cultivated an unhealthy obsession with safety that feeds into our culture of fear. While we do not have full control over all the things trying to scare us, and of course, there is plenty in the world we should genuinely fear and pay attention to, we do have more control over fears than we give ourselves credit for. In this chapter, we'll explore the choices we make as they relate to our fears that can cripple our sense of agency. In many ways, *we* are the cornerstones and puppet masters orchestrating our society and culture, whether we realize it or not. We all bear some responsibility for stoking our culture of fear. Together, we share a complicit role in the spread of unreasoned fear and anxieties in our culture. Together, we share a duty to think better and be better actors in the world. Together, we possess the creative power and capacity to improve things and to venture out of our comfort zones both with our bodies and in our minds.

○

Few of us desire or actively seek challenges in our lives. Like water, we opt for a path of least resistance. Again, "better safe than sorry," we reassure ourselves. Many of us even go to great lengths to avoid challenges. This is understandable behavior because challenges often force us to confront the many things about ourselves that we are scared or ashamed of to some degree: few of us want to feel weak, powerless, lost, ignorant, or misguided, much less admit it. What's more is that this lack of courage and foresight to face up to the challenges and fears of life helps explain why so many of us fall in line and often conform to the crowd or like-minded tribe, trying not to be noticed, and inactively mimicking our neighbors because we also fear the scrutiny and ostracism of the group.

However, overcoming passivity and conformity, by breaking away from the crowd from time to time, venturing down our paths, and thinking things out for ourselves, is an experience we should consider. This critique isn't meant to degrade. On the contrary. Feeling weak can enable us to become strong. Being lost can guide us to discovery. Placing our ignorance on trial can lead to having our eyes widely opened. As journalist Paul Salopek has poetically mused about wandering while making his 24,000-mile *Out of Eden* journey from Ethiopia to Tierra del Fuego:

> Being lost can be stressful, of course. But it also wakes you up. You stand a little straighter. Your eyes and pores open. You become more alert. You study the world carefully, scanning the horizon for landmarks, signs, clues—for a way forward. (Sometimes, you backtrack.) But ultimately, you become alive to possibility: a new compass bearing, a new story, a trail untaken. Being a little lost can be a good thing. Being found all the time is overrated.[182]

Invaluable lessons await us when we challenge ourselves and face what we fear.

There is no doubt that immense propaganda and dedicated groups and organizations full of conniving and disingenuous people exist to sway public opinion one way or another to obtain votes, prestige, power, or money. As detailed in the previous chapter, this media-industrial complex is responsible for the exacerbation of many fears in society, but that is only part of the story. Expecting "the media" to change incentives and practices is probably not very realistic, at least in the near term. Therefore, the responsibility rests with *us*, the consumers, to learn better ways of curating and engaging with all this information. And that's far more empowering than it may seem. Becoming aware of how our minds are disposed toward negativity and bias grants us agency and moral responsibility. Thus, we can no longer just idly condemn the media when we become conscious of the fact that we, too, are part of the equation of fear.

"The media" is not just some abstract or independent thing apart from us. The media comprises thousands, if not millions, of our fellow citizens. We, too, are the very consumers and producers of that media. We, too, are complicit in giving power to fear. We are the subscribers and supporters. We are the ones who reliably tune in. We are the ones who comment, complain, gossip, share, react, and spread these ideas about the world to an incessant degree. We *are* the media, or at the very least their middlemen and messengers. We are the most active ingredient or causal factor in the perpetuation of society's greatest woes. We are ironically the producers and victims of the culture of fear, though we fail to see the connecting dots of where and how exactly we contribute. Like a game of dominoes, we are constantly, and often unwittingly, tapping these chains of events into motion. We are the real agents of fear. There is no one in the world left to blame but us.

○

Each of us is responsible for spreading unreasoned fear and inaccurate information about the world. Many of us do this *daily*. It might be a subtle act of gossip about an unsettling story we accept unquestioningly as true and then casually share with our peers. It could be an act of restraining our children from playing outside and keeping them barricaded at home under constant surveillance out of an overly cautious feeling that "someone out there" will take them and hurt them. This does fully protect them but inadvertently exposes them to other dangers from inactivity that could lead to serious mental, physical, and social problems. It could also simply be the decision to abandon an otherwise noteworthy trip in our lives out of fear and being convinced that it just sounds too risky "out there." Rather than living up to the challenge of an adventure and taking control, we often cater to erroneous suspicions.

These anxieties might seem unrelated and even trivial at first. However, it's been argued that "our paranoia regarding the safety of children is driven by cultural forces that are very similar to the ones that make us apprehensive about climate change, ecocide, or the food we eat."[183] In a culture of fear, virtually anything can be interpreted as potentially deadly, despite how innocuous something is. Though we can never know how much harm some casual gossip or sharing disinformation on social media is, we should not underestimate the subtlety of our actions and how they can add up over time, especially when we consider that millions of others are doing the same thing at any given time. A lot can compound over time from something small. Like littering, one person throwing some trash in the ocean won't upset an ecosystem, but millions of people throwing trash in the ocean can contribute to creating the Great Pacific Garbage Patch.[184]

History beckons to open us to a wider context. We are not unique or the first culture to find ourselves bothered by fears:

> Every culture has something distinct to say about fear. In ancient societies, people were instructed to fear their gods or ancestors. In medieval times, communities were incited to fear witches and other malevolent supernatural forces. Some cultures fear death, others are concerned about unemployment. Until recent times, Western cultures were preoccupied with the threat of nuclear war. Today we are simply encouraged to regard fear as our default response to life itself. As Christopher Lambert observed in his study of French society, *The Fearful Society*, his compatriots are haunted by 'fear of the future, fear of losing, fear of others, fear of taking a risk, fear of solitude, fear of growing old'.[185]

Every culture throughout time has likely experienced a whole swath of fears because risks are an inherent feature of life. We fret over our particular moment in history and imbue significance in recent events like 9/11, COVID-19, threats from domestic and foreign terrorism, and climate change. We presume these are the leading causes of our culture of fear. Yet previous generations also lived in a culture of fear with their world wars and fears of nuclear annihilation during the Cold War. If we could travel back to the Ice Age, we'd see parents concerned about a whole host of risks, from getting too close to mammoths, sabertoothed cats, and other wild game to fears from neighboring tribes and not knowing how to combat mysterious diseases. The case can be made that human societies *always* live in varying cultures of fear because there are always legitimate threats and fears to worry about. In that sense, our times are not all that unique after all, and perhaps may be quaint and mild, historically speaking.

What may be a distinctive feature about our present type of fear, however, is how much imagined and unreasoned fear people possess today as a result of *indirect* experiences. We like to think that we are not as susceptible to irrational fears as pre-scientific or pre-literate societies, but current trends in conspiracy thinking and the discovery of all our underlying cognitive biases suggest otherwise. We keep the door locked on the many things we deem unknown and uncertain about, and this is a problem. We haphazardly focus on wildly different fears from week to week, too. As Frank Furedi further observes, "Fear has an unpredictable and free-floating character. One day we fear gun-crime, a week later our attention is drawn to car-jacking…in contemporary times, fear migrates freely from one problem to the next without there being a necessity for causal or logical connection."[186] This habit many of us possess ought to give us pause: the fact that what we were concerned with last week, last month, or last year has, in all likelihood, faded from memory demonstrates the ethereal and non-threatening nature of that fear coming to fruition. In other words, we ought to find some relief in the fact that the many things we fear fail to happen to us.

No matter the obstacles each of us faces, we are all gradually being granted greater access to knowledge and opportunities to improve and better inform our lives. Individually and collectively, we're obliged to own up to the perpetuation of fear and ignorance in our society. After all, aren't we all a little tired of seeing our grandma spooked by all the garbage she's being fed on television or the internet? Though we have many legitimate challenges to confront in our society, all things considered, we still live in a country of abundant resources, abounding security, and opportunities for change.

○

There is a curious phenomenon we've likely observed between our behaviors on social media and our behavior in real life. We act monstrously toward one another while on social media. Common decency and civility seem in short supply on the internet. As a result, we don't appear all that sympathetic or have the capacity for perspective-taking. Like the insufferable Mr. Hyde that creeps out of us in moments of road rage, we feel unashamed and secure when entering the realm of anonymity and distance on the web. Thus, this perception of people being brutally honest and completely fearless behind their computer screens can translate to a lot of minds the idea that people deep down are overwhelmingly petty, arrogant, extremely judgmental, and even hostile. This likely contributes to much of the hysteria, anger, and frustration in our culture. Another consequence of living more of our lives in cyberspace is that we tend to create echo chambers or small communities of like-minded individuals. We wean out those we dislike or disagree with and eventually form groups with distorted views of the world because we only communicate with those who share our ideals. Here is where confirmation bias and group polarization reign supreme. Tribalism manifests itself in cyberspace just as much as it does in the real world, maybe more so.

Although our temperaments seem more in control when not hidden behind a computer screen, the twitch of unease masking some of our pessimistic sentiments still manages to reveal itself in a face-to-face conversation. As linguists and anthropologists are well aware, how we talk and what we talk about are subtle clues to our worldview. We may notice that many we encounter share a very cynical, dystopic, and downright misanthropic view of other people and where the world is headed. This is one of the few areas where most of us ironically find common ground: we can all at least agree that the world is falling apart. One survey asked 'Generally speaking, would you say that most people can be trusted or that you need to be very careful in dealing with people?' Fewer than 40% of people responded that 'Most people can be trusted.'[187] Confidence in the government's ability to protect U.S. citizens against terrorism has been gradually diminishing for more than 14 years now, with a new low at 55% being confident they can defend against it, with about half saying they worry about becoming a victim.[188] At the same time, our investment in security steadily increased. As Barry Glassner puts it,

> [W]e compound our worries beyond all reason. Life expectancy in the United States has doubled during the twentieth century. We are better able to cure and control diseases than any other civilization in history. Yet we hear that phenomenal numbers of us are dreadfully ill.[189]

Psychologist Robin Rosenberg famously opined in a 2013 article how the latest version of the *Diagnostic and Statistical Manual of Mental Disorders* (DSM) could effectively diagnose 50% of the American populace with a mental disorder at some point in their lives.[190] For more than 40 years, there has been a steady decline in the trust we have in others.[191] The least trusting of which is that of the youngest Americans.[192] We are "significantly less trusting of each other and less confident in large institutions, such as the news media, business, religious organizations, the medical establishment, Congress, and the presidency."[193] This is an alarming observation and unfortunate, given the overwhelming benefits trust has to offer society. As applied sociologist Josh Morgan points out:

> Trust is the glue that binds people together. It is a rare concept in the social and behavioral sciences in that the evidence for its benefits is overwhelming. Trust is correlated with increased civic participation, decreased corruption, increased resilience to disasters, decreased economic inequality, and decreases in illegal activities. It is also correlated with increased health, happiness, and intelligence. Practically all researchers studying trust have concluded that it improves the human experience.[194]

Next time we're engaged in a heated debate online, we ought to ask ourselves, "Would I honestly say this to someone if they were right in front of me?" If it's a nasty, thoughtless comment, the answer is most likely 'no' because a true social interaction has immediate consequences that cause most of us to pause with self-restraint and measure our responses before spouting off like we do at our keyboards. There are many social cues, intonations, and behavioral consequences lacking in online conversation, so it ends up corrupting our ideas of others and being, at best, a quasi-social connection that often leads to unrealistic and misinterpreted human behavior.

Branding social media as "social" and online communities as genuine "community" may go down as some of the greatest shams in history. If anything, we are witnessing *antisocial* media dominate our lives. Relationships are becoming more tendentious, frayed, and severed in the real world, all the while people obsess over their likes and comments on social media. People are retreating within and finding false consolation online. A major societal transformation may be underway where we are self-isolating from one another, staying locked in the machine, and constructing a far more dangerous world in our minds than the actual reality. The American biologist Edward O. Wilson famously observed, "The real problem of humanity is the following: We have Paleolithic emotions, medieval institutions, and godlike technology. And it is terrifically dangerous, and it is now approaching a point of crisis overall."

The takeaway of all this is that these jaded sentiments carry over into the real world, where far too many of us end up holding a very unhealthy outlook about others; always suspicious and always projecting bad intent on others. If our ideas about the world are this gloomy, disdainful, and untrusting, how will this affect our actions in the real world and the interactions we have with others? Similar to the classic example of the bystander effect, where we assume someone else will save the screaming person in the street, will we eventually be standing beside the tracks as we watch the train run down five people or one person, as something to not even be morally startled by? Is apathy our destiny? What happens to a world when all sense of trust, responsibility, and agency collapse?

○

In the last handful of years, I've come to love science fiction. This fantastic medium of literature allows us to think deeply about the future we're creating in the present. English author E.M. Forster is perhaps most famous for writing *A Passage to India*. Few are aware that he wrote a powerful prediction of our present moment in the form of a startling dystopia. In 1909, his science fiction short story *The Machine Stops* was published. His imagined world depicts an ominous scene of a planet raked clean of its resources, where some ambiguous, yet suspected man-made catastrophe has coerced humans to live below Earth's surface and live isolated and confined to their tiny self-contained rooms or cells within an enormous subterranean machine. They communicate with others only via the machine through instant messaging, email, and something akin to today's Zoom, yet it suspiciously "does not transmit nuances of expression." The passengers' minds and bodies have nearly atrophied, their figures becoming a "swaddled lump of flesh…with a face as white as a fungus" and "without teeth or hair." The machine even has the power to make crucial decisions on human life, like carrying out infanticide of those "who promised undue strength" since it was a "demerit to be muscular." The machine provides all they could ever want or need at the touch of a button and no longer requires people to interact face-to-face, despite the ironic fact that "human intercourse had advanced enormously" through telecommunication.

Over time, it becomes common knowledge that the surface of the earth remains uninhabitable, merely "dust and mud," and people are encouraged to fear traveling to the surface and to fear anyone who wishes to do so. It becomes illegal to travel to the surface and punishable by "homelessness," a euphemism translating to death, as mandated by the machine. The protagonist is Kuno, a young man, rebellious, precocious, and eager to venture to the surface. He attempts to encourage his mother, Vashti, to travel to the surface with him, but she replies that she has no time or interest in such an unnecessary and silly thing.

Kuno's mother lives contentedly in her room on the other side of the planet with no ambition other than participating in her "lectures," essentially gossiping on widely unrelated and unoriginal topics. She remains apathetic and reluctant to visit her son and perceives going to the surface as foolish and dangerous. When she first attempts to make the journey to see her son, all of which is completely automated by the machine with little to no physical exertion required, she becomes "seized with the terrors of direct experience." The only means of travel is through the machine on its airships. As passengers on the airships speed high above the seemingly desolate and appalling earth, they are unnerved and deeply distressed by the direct sensations of natural phenomena. Seeing such things as the stars, sun, islands, and mountains "give me no ideas," Vashti complains when viewing the Greek islands and the Himalayan and Caucasus Mountains aboard an airship, finally en route to see her son.

Aside from making the rather extraordinary anticipations of the Internet, instant messaging, visual communication, and artificial intelligence, Forster's dystopia reveals other striking and rather uncanny parallels with our contemporary world and the potential consequences of technological overdependence. Despite being virtually liberated from physical work or demanding schedules, people still feel as though they have no time and certainly no time to waste on traveling and adventure. In their online communication networks, it is far more popular to discuss second-hand ideas rather than the original content. People no longer value the source of their ideas, but rather the opinions of those who originated the ideas. They feel completely comfortable and confident interacting and sharing ideas via the machine, yet feel utterly alienated, uncomfortable, and repulsed by face-to-face interactions. Indeed, it has become a high-brow culture and a sign of being an "advanced thinker" *not* to engage firsthand with a person or any other direct experiences. Over time, the knowledge and ideas they possess become so far removed and diluted from the truth that understanding devolves into disjointed hearsay; some may deem it "fake news." When they need a word to express themselves, they summon the machine to do it for them. Indeed, the machine, Kuno suspects, "penetrates our blood and may even guide our thoughts." The substance of their "lectures" is about places on Earth and the history of those places, but none of the passengers has been inclined to physically visit the sites, for fear of venturing to the supposed barren surface of Earth. What's more, they feel sufficiently informed by other people's opinions and arrogantly talk about them as though they have been there and know all about them.

Discontented and curious, Kuno journeys to the surface and discovers the earth to be green with life in recovery, and finds a few other rebellious people who have managed to forge a life free of the machine. He uses some information he received in a lecture to pinpoint his location based on the stars, but then has the epiphany that "this is the first bit of useful information I have ever got from a lecture, and I expect it will be the last." This is shocking proof to him of how far true knowledge has disintegrated over time and how grand the illusions that so many possess are. Kuno now feels emboldened by these revelations and becomes enlightened about how absurd life has become. He comes to pity everyone who is living according to the misplaced fears and ignorant opinions of others.

The climax of this tragic world unfolds when the machine begins to break down. Everyone is in denial as they try to convince themselves it is merely the "whim" of the machine, which by now has been mystically interpreted as a god, and they have forgotten it was once built by humans. As the complaints and panic grow and their conditions worsen, it leaves them idle without the skills, knowledge, self-reliance, or will to repair it and save themselves. This horror show is the extreme vision of a world devoid of human trust, responsibility, and agency.

Stories like this provide a lot of food for thought. Though the predictions of future gadgets by science fiction authors are fun and surprising, the impacts on society and culture as a result of technology are far more interesting and relevant for us to consider. We might reflect on the role technology plays in our sense of adventure. How much is our technology restricting us as well as liberating us? How close are we to enabling technology to override our sense of exploration and mold our experiences for us? Is this something we want, living out our experiences through machines? Is this just inevitable? Do we have any agency left in the matter? What impact is this having on our relationships with one another, and especially, our children and upcoming generations? Are we truly connected like never before, or are more of us becoming more isolated in our rooms within "neighborhoods without neighbors?" Are we as comfortable with ourselves and others in real life as we appear to be on comment threads? Though dystopias naturally dramatize the extremes, are we so confident that in a hundred years hence we won't be as distant from nature and the lives of others as Forster detailed?

Whatever the technology of the future brings, Kuno's spirit is what most resonates with me. Defying conventional wisdom is not always easy and rewarding. Nor is it necessarily wise. It leads to a lot of self-doubt, anxiety, and dead ends. In my own life, I've seen the value of not always going along with the crowd and learning how to chart my own heterodox path, which can be gratifying. But it does come with costs. Doing uncommon things like pursuing an archaeological career or backpacking the Appalachian Trail sounds adventurous on the surface, and it can be. However, they are also fraught with insecurities, and you're always wondering if you've made the right decision. At the end of the day, I do think it is worth it to challenge our conventional wisdom and defy what others say is impossible or unwise, which is the essence of being adventurous.

○

What traveling and research into the sociology and psychology of fear suggest to me is that much of our current societal unrest, distrust in others, and unreasoned fears are related to a lack of adventure in our lives. The neglect of travel and exploration of our world and other cultures is related to the decrease in the quality of personal connection with one another. Thus, a general lack of personal firsthand experience with wide and diverse geographies, landscapes, people, and ideas escapes many of us, even despite the incredible gifts of telecommunications. *Technology is a supplement, not a surrogate for life's experiences.*

The explosion of modern technology has undoubtedly done wonders for humanity, but it will never supersede the physical relationships we seem to effortlessly build when in direct contact with another human being. Close relationships are often devoid of mistrust and fear. If we are so well connected, why do we then see such heightened levels of fear and anxiety in public perceptions?

Technology is supposed to alleviate that which is tedious and give us more control over our lives. After more than a century of substantially accumulating material assets that promote comfort and leisure, why are we still so restless, alienated, and fearful of one another? If we are connected, maybe it's only in a very superficial way. The assumption that technology and such things as the internet and other forms of telecommunications have connected us "like never before" may be somewhat premature, misleading, and perhaps illusory. How connected are we? And to what or whom specifically? There is a greater resolution and quality of human experience that becomes strikingly apparent the more we explore our world offline.

We must learn to exercise our agency and come face-to-face with problems more directly, not from behind a television or computer screen, where people are unrealistically fearless and loose-lipped about their opinions. Although our sense of agency can vary, we ought to recognize that we have more control over our lives and how we respond than we may realize. By not seeking wide and fresh experiences in the world, by severing ties with our communities and disengaging with ideas and cultures unlike ours, and by succumbing to unreasonable fears, we risk becoming *more* scared and indifferent to new ways of thinking and seeing the world. If we find ourselves more often amid a daring adventure, chances are we would respond to situations and people in a much more reserved, patient, unassuming, and contemplative manner.

There is an overwhelming sense that a lot of us do not understand how adaptable we truly are, that we possess agency, an innate ability to take control and change our circumstances for the better. "Adaptability" is one of the most astounding traits of humanity and something one must see to believe. As an anthropology student, one quickly becomes indoctrinated with the term, and it becomes common sense that, of course, people are adaptable. But nothing made us confront this truism more than our experiences on the Appalachian Trail, where every day was a test of adaptability and resilience.

○

In our contemporary culture and society, we unfortunately do not place much value on the acquisition of new knowledge and new experiences. Consequently, we may be trading too much of our time away in favor of isolation instead of interaction. Examining the statistics on how we spend our free time: on a given week, the average American over the age of 15 spends nearly 17.5 hours watching television, while the *combined* amount of time dedicated to exercise/sports/recreation, reading, relaxing, and thinking amounts to just a little over 6 hours.[195] And the older we get, the amount of television consumed nearly doubles to 31.5 hours per week.[196] This is nearly a whole workweek of staring at the TV! Recent data suggests children spend a meager 15-25 minutes a day in outdoor play and sports.[197] On average, children and adolescents between the ages of 8-18 spend nearly 7.5 hours a day using one or more types of media (video games, television, cell phones).[198] At the 2017 TED conference, NYU psychologist Adam Alter warned how, in the ten previous years since the advent of the iPhone, our attention to screens had increased quite profoundly, showing that the few hours we do have on a given workday, we give to a screen.[199] These are all choices we are making for ourselves.

We should not view these as light matters but as extremely consequential to our society. A recent nationwide survey of 20,000 Americans, in close alignment with previous surveys, found over 50% responding that they felt a variety of emotions, ranging from feeling isolated or unwanted and having a sense that they lacked companionship, or that their relationships were not meaningful, thus indicating a rise in loneliness, especially among younger generations.[200] Some lean heavily on anti-depressants and other medications to overcome this, while others turn to alcohol or illicit drugs. What a person could very well need to suppress such anxieties is embarking on their long-envisioned adventures. That might sound overly optimistic, perhaps naïve, and by no means is this meant to suggest a complete substitution for seeking professional help for serious mental and emotional issues. We'll cover some of the major benefits of wandering in the next chapter.

What all this is meant to illustrate is the trade-offs we make in our everyday lives and have us reflect on the decisions we make and the power we possess to reorient our lives. When we devote 17.5 hours each week passively absorbing insipid information, it not only has a debilitating effect on our physical, psychological, and intellectual health, but in addition, 17.5 hours have been squandered where much creativity and intellectual growth might have thrived. For drama's sake: this 17.5 hours per week of television plays out to 70 hours per month, and

840 hours per year. And if the axiom about us sleeping a third of our life away is accurate and we tack on the hours we spend working, eating, and bathing, this paints a very depressing picture of the average American life: work, watch, eat, sleep, rinse, repeat. It should come as no surprise, then, that so many of us are enraged, confused, depressed, and disillusioned with everything. What's more ironic, given how scornful we seem to be toward "the media" nowadays, is how much time we devote to it.

We don't have to be this way. We have a great deal of choice or agency in how to invest our time and the incremental changes we make to our lives. We could take those same 840 hours of television consumption and spend them cultivating a new skill or art we've always desired to learn, a new language, an instrument, the next big novel, mastery of martial arts, expanding our culinary repertoire, or taking micro-adventures right out our door. Based on the 10,000-hour rule, we could master a new skill every 12 years with this added time. We have it in our power not to let television and the internet dictate our lives with so many distractions and shape how we should feel. But due to our overall indifference, lack of inspiration, and lapses in agency, we are to blame for some of the costs and flaws in our society. We must own this. Doing nothing is still doing something.

Our overall character flaws may just be unfortunate consequences of biology and social upbringing: "bad" genes, poor parents, and shady friends. But that same biology and social upbringing have also given us mental faculties and tools to cope and even overcome our psychological, moral, and intellectual deficiencies. This is the essence of having agency. These flaws require defining if we hope to re-engineer better ideas and behaviors. Today, we seem to favor cynicism more than optimism and realism. We cater to our emotions and opt for prejudice, tribalism, divisiveness, and shamelessness in our ignorance more than we value appealing to careful reason, trust, and patience with others. Many of us do not think it is worth our time to learn new things, update what we thought we knew, and adapt to an ever-changing world. We are at a disadvantage when we fail to exercise our agency.

○

The average American today is fearful, confused, anxious, depressed, and outraged with current politics and culture wars. But this is understandable given the context and structure of our society. As we age and work hard to procure the things that make our lives easier and safer, for ourselves and our families, it becomes natural to "settle down," as we say. However, "settling down" has its consequences too. It seems like the safest bet to take. But we can easily fall victim to our success and accrued safety. We can become idle, reluctant to change our minds on long-held beliefs, unwilling to go out of our way to make positive changes in ourselves, and less likely to take a chance on adventure and travel. We can lose or keep dormant our sense of adventure in the process, and with it, challenges become seen more as dreadful rather than inspiring. An instinctual thing we all do under uncertain times is to err on the side of caution when we fail to fully understand something.

However, we don't need to leave our fears in the dark. As technology and opportunities for social mobility continue to enhance our society, fewer of us have a good excuse to be uneducated and unadventurous about the wider world. Today, it is all too easy to keep feeding the fear machine. What is not so easy is detecting how much of it is true. What is also easy is finger-pointing and scapegoating. What's harder is determining how much we, too, have contributed to the frenzy. To a large extent, this kind of unreasoned fear and insecurity is a choice we're all deciding to make together. *We* choose to be involved or uninvolved in our communities. *We* choose to work or not work to cultivate bonds with others. *We* choose to educate ourselves or remain ignorant of the realities and falsehoods of fear. *We* choose to live by the dictums of either "Better safe than sorry" or "Nothing ventured, nothing gained."

These ideas on fears and anxieties in our society, our passive neglect for new knowledge and understanding, and our inattentiveness toward new experiences of adventure are more closely connected and influence each other more than we may realize. As citizens and human agents, how can we hope to navigate reality, become properly informed, and develop sound policies both domestically and abroad if an overwhelming majority of us remain ignorant of so many aspects of the world's landscapes, cultures, and minds? If our media is inadequate and flawed, then we must find alternative ways to gain access to the truth. If we wish to be leaders and role models in an increasingly globalized, pluralistic world, we must learn to immerse ourselves deeper in the adventures and experiences of different cultures, landscapes, and ideas.

Far too many of us experience other people's lives through a few-minute video clip, or condensed article, or a mere headline. Even the best writers can fail to capture the depth of a person this way. It is very easy to caricature and stigmatize another human being in these contexts. Many of us are under the illusion of being connected because the cameras are always rolling and our closest kith and kin are a phone call away. Social media never sleeps, but our shortened attention spans, coupled with the amount of information surrounding us, prevent us from focusing on the gravity of what we're seeing and hearing.

The explosion of information beaming toward us every day fills us with the impossible task of soaking it all up. As much as we'd like to absorb it all in one fell swoop, a lot of time and patience are required to understand our world. Our minds are not sponges, but leaky pails. Important information requires long-term exposure. Adventurous experiences are the same. There is simply far too much emotion and stimuli wrapped up in the visitation of a place that cannot be translated through cameras, pictures, or the machine. One must be present, with all their senses, to feel and grasp the weight of these experiences. And yet, as many of us painfully know, it can also be extremely difficult to simply tell people anything contrary to their well-established beliefs and ideas, even when it is in their best interest. Often, the only effective way for a person to understand something is for them to discover it on their own, hence the saying "seeing is believing." Finding creative ways to encourage people to experience travel and adventure for themselves becomes our challenge.

We can at least begin to actively condition ourselves to view our world through a more adventurous lens. As Thoreau states, "It's not what you look at that matters, it's what you *see*." Adventure is dependent on *our* creativity and willpower. Some things do come down to willpower and agency. Take boredom, for instance. Boredom is something we do have a great deal of control over. It is not just a random mood we all unwittingly and uncontrollably become victims of at various intervals throughout our lives. Boredom, too, is a perspective. It's a dull state of complacency we allow ourselves to fall into. What's important to recognize is that we can consciously avoid such a state with concentrated meditation. As the anthropologist E. Paul Durrenberger remarked, "Boredom, of course, is self-generated. It isn't what we see but in how we respond to it." The origin of boredom is the same origin of adventure. They are things of the mind. It only takes some practice to reroute our thinking. If we're adventurous people, we'll likely never have a chance or good reason to be bored. By being more introspective and by exercising our agency, we can begin to quell our culture of fear and take steps to cultivate a more resilient, charitable, trustworthy, and responsible culture and society. Now that we have unpacked the major forces behind our culture of fear, we can finally explore the benefits and challenges of wandering in the 21st century and beyond.

CHAPTER 8
The Trade-offs of Adventure, Part I: *The Benefits of Wandering*

"Travel can educate tourists about other places and peoples; it can also help them better understand their own culture and society. In an age where we are overwhelmed with images, symbols, information, and misinformation, travel can be an important way for us to communicate directly with one another. No computer, travel brochure, or television ad can ever replace that."
—Deborah McLaren, *Rethinking Tourism and Ecotravel*

"[I]f a person does take the time out to reflect…it becomes clearer that money, power, status, and possessions do not, by themselves, necessarily add one iota to the quality of life."
—Mihaly Csikszentmihalyi, *Flow: The Psychology of Optimal Experience*

For months, the days continued to meld into a persistent rhythm. Our routine had become that of methodical Spartans: seven o'clock peel off the sweaty, fart-infested exoskeletons of our sleeping bags; turn on some cheerful folksy tunes; boil up water for oatmeal and mix in hot cocoa; break down camp and hit the trail; walk. Ten o'clock break for a Clif Bar; walk. Noon, peanut butter and jelly wraps for lunch, walk. Three o'clock, scout for water sources and force down another Clif Bar, walk. Six o'clock set-up camp, debate which dry meal to eat for the 30th time, break out the chocolate and peanut butter again, mix up some lemonade, and crank up the tunes once more to watch the sun go down and then crawl back into those ghastly sleeping bags for twelve more hours of hibernation, repeat. Our bodies had relinquished all excess fat and trimmed us down into pure-muscled hiking machines.

Towns came and went. Some made quite the impression and stoked feelings of homesickness in us. We savored our time in the welcoming town of Hanover, New Hampshire, where a passerby appeared out of nowhere to nonchalantly plop down a cold bottled IPA pint at our picnic table and just as quickly bid us good luck in one swift motion. It was as if we were celebrities in some of these towns: so many good-natured people went out of their way to help us, raising our spirits to keep moving. We engaged with a Dartmouth undergraduate and casually debated Beatnik literature and our favorite authors. We decided to indulge in a swanky hotel room and a gluttonous amount of wholesome local town food. We would have loved to spend several more days there, but that would have meant the death of our budget, and Hilary, ever the numbers-crunching stickler, wasn't letting up on that.

I woke up early the following morning and slipped away to Lou's, one of Hanover's famous diners. Walking around the Dartmouth campus, I admired the architecture of limestone-brick buildings, and the campus brought me back to our recent years in Bloomington at

THE TRADE-OFFS OF ADVENTURE, PART I

Indiana University. In all the lounging around, I started to think about the importance of taking meaningful risks in life and what that could mean for a person down the road. Our society tends to put a lot of unnecessary pressure and fear into us; so much that we're constantly obsessing over risks and all so determined to avoid them without understanding what we might be gaining or missing out on. I thought about Robert Frost's poem "The Road Not Taken," which hung cheaply framed on the wall in a dimly lit basement of a church we had recently bunked at for the night, and how often we all stand at divergent paths anxiously contemplating where each one could lead us to wildly different outcomes. I began to wonder more about these courses we chart out for ourselves and what we might be doing had we taken a different path. Consciousness then guided me to reflect more about some of the fears we had overcome and how, in hindsight, they were not the spooky, heinous types of fears our minds imagine and assume when we start picturing the journey to come. Again, I wondered how often we all forfeit our dream adventures because we're misled by fears when, in all probability, what we more often face are the physical and logistical challenges that are difficult and anxiety-ridden, but manageable and worth doing. The right amount of stress propels us into becoming better versions of ourselves.

Many previous *perceived fears* had been finely tuned by our experiences. In the passing months, we found we no longer felt uneasy about throwing our thumbs in the air for a lift into town. Indeed, this is how we would eventually choose to travel home. We have more time to engage with the strangers we pass on the trail and discover that the term "strangers" might just be a poorly chosen descriptor for others we simply haven't met and bonded with. Most "strangers" aren't strange at all but are often comical, perceptive, and overwhelmingly friendly and helpful. A part of me became more compassionate and attentive to the stories of others along this journey. One man, in particular, made a lasting impression as one of the funniest people we met on the trail. Detour, as he went by, was a stocky barrel-bodied man with the face of Andre the Giant and the voice and humor of George Carlin. He told us of many of his adventures across the country and where he witnessed his most beautiful view. "I was out hiking Pike's Peak, and I was on my way home. Hadn't slept in four days; I don't sleep much, life's too short, ya know? So I stop in Kansas to get a few hours of sleep before I keep driving. So I'm sleepin' and I get woken up to this loud noise; it was a train whistle. I'm immediately pissed, ya know? I just slept for two hours. I need to wake up in two more hours, and this train is waking *me* up! Sure, I was by a train track, I knew that. But it was in the middle of nowhere! Why would he blow the damn whistle out here? So I see this conductor leaning out the side, pointing. He wants me to see something, but I'm like, whatever, I'm tired. But he keeps pointing. He even crawled around the side to make sure I had seen him. The train finally passes, and there it is—have you ever seen twelve rainbows in the sky all at once? Well, I have! The most beautiful view I've ever seen. And it was in Kansas, Dorothy!" We had only meant to stop at the shelter for water and a quick break, but he had us rolling with laughter and endless stories for more than an hour.

Then there was Forester Gump, a lean man with deep dark eyes and legs like old hickory trees. He was a veteran who had witnessed the brutality of war and been marred by several personal tragedies, yet remained surprisingly energetic and Zen-like in his outlook. "Do you *really* want to know how I first learned about the Appalachian

Trail? When I was a ten-year-old sexually-repressed boy living in the Midwest, I was flipping through the only source I could find 'boobies,' *National Geographic*. And I came across an article on the Appalachian Trail, and it really inspired me. There were two things my brother and I said we were going to do together: one being to hike the Appalachian Trail, and two, to ride motorcycles to Alaska. He died of a massive heart attack last year, and I, too, likely have those genes, so I thought, 'Uh oh, time's ticking.' So I put my knee replacement surgery on hold and left for the trail."

I've always been a quiet, reserved person; Hilary is typically more the extrovert and approachable. But it's something I have always wanted to change about myself because I am enthralled by the remarkable stories so many have to tell. These experiences gave me a wonderful opportunity to "come out of my shell," as they say, and further enabled me to gain incredible value from being a part of such a dynamic community of wanderers. What's more, being on the move gave me immense pride and self-esteem in knowing I could accomplish goals I wouldn't have thought possible a year ago: all this in a matter of a few months. What would life look like if it could always be lived in more adventurous ways? What kind of people are we capable of becoming?

○

In every instance of our lives, we are losing out on something as well as gaining. Life is all a grand orchestra of trade-offs. We owe our very existence to those, in the face of the unknown, who dared to wonder and wander. Instead of complacency and security, our ancestors chose the path of unknown perils. There is no doubt our forebears of the distant past were conscious of the inherent risks of acting boldly to explore our world, but so too were they conscious of the potential rewards of doing so. Some of them reaped those benefits by discovering wondrous new lands with plentiful game and resources to exploit, and thus consequently charted a better world for themselves. We are indebted to them for their courage and wanderlust. Had our ancestors stayed in place and been located in a small ecological niche, we might very well have gone extinct by now, in the way of all our previous hominin cousins: the Neanderthals, the Denisovans, and the Australopithecines. By painfully pushing into the unknown and spreading around the globe, we unwittingly ensured a greater probability of existence for our future kin because it forced our ancestors to divide, cope, and adapt to a wide range of earthly climes, thus safeguarding a greater chance of survival during unstable times. And yet, our species is still young, being approximately 300,000 years old. What does it mean for an already globalized species to maintain wandering in a seemingly claustrophobic and overpopulated world?

It's not only in our interest to know a wide array of our physical and intellectual world, but it is deeply critical to our collective interests as well. And if we care anything for our future kin, we must keep moving, learning, and wandering even if it appears as if we've already explored the entire globe. We instinctively understand this and know that we must continue to venture. We yearn to explore, and it's neither guaranteed that progress will continue trending upward nor that "civilization" will last forever. In an interview with Charlie Rose about humans traveling in space Carl Sagan once urged, "It is important for us, humans, to be out there...we are an exploratory species, the last ten

THE TRADE-OFFS OF ADVENTURE, PART I

thousand years we've been sitting around in civilization, before that, for the last 100,000 years we were wanderers, explorers, nomads, and that is in our blood." One of the reasons we have been so successful at becoming the dominant species on earth and outlasting our hominin kin is due to this inherent feature of humanity, along with standing upright, having opposable thumbs to craft tools, and the use of language.

Why should we continue to explore in a world that already seems fully explored, known, and filled? What's the value of adventure in our contemporary world? What is it that we come to gain or lose for the sake of adventure? What are some of the social, economic, cultural, and ecological consequences of travel and adventure? Is it all worth it? We've haphazardly encountered some of the answers to these questions throughout the previous chapters. This chapter and the next intend to bring together the reasons why we need to be adventuring more and the trade-offs we make for doing so. The reasons for adventure are vast, as are the responsibilities of the 21st-century traveler. What follows in this chapter and the next are some of the more significant pros and cons of succumbing to wanderlust.

○

Perhaps the most fundamental thing we gain from an adventure is *increased physical and psychological well-being*. Though the physical aspect is pretty obvious and common knowledge by now, there are some interesting scientific findings on the benefits to our psychological health. It has been found that hiking in natural environments for even a short period (90 minutes) reduces rumination, more commonly known as brooding, or repetitively dwelling on negative thoughts that can lead to depression, anxiety disorders, and other forms of mental illness due to the increased activity in a part of the brain known as the subgenual prefrontal cortex.[201] In a world with an expected population of 70% living in urban areas by 2050, it will be crucial for us to maintain access to and be engaging with natural areas, and especially incorporate more green spaces into our ever-populating cities, where urban areas have been known to have negative cognitive effects on people.[202] A growing consensus urges urban planners to reflect on the ecological and psychological benefits urban design can have in alleviating the stressors of cities by promoting such things as greenways for walking and biking, more street trees and parks to reduce extreme heat, and community gardens.[203]

Natural settings also boost creativity. In a tech-free hiking experiment where participants were immersed in nature for four days, performances on problem-solving tasks increased by 50%.[204] Another study has found that engaging children in green outdoor settings can reduce symptoms of ADHD, the most common neurobehavioral disorder in children, which is estimated to affect approximately 2 million school-aged children in the United States.[205] What the current research suggests is that exploration of the natural world is vitally important to both our physical and our psychological well-being. For the regular outdoor enthusiast, this is not news. I'm often amazed at how a short hike in the woods radically boosts my mood on the days when I'm feeling down. In addition, I also noticed a significant decrease in anxiety while venturing on the trail, and I suffered from few, if any, headaches during the entire time on the Appalachian Trail; something

I was prone to before our experience. For the majority of us who have become or will eventually become absorbed by the organized chaos of modern city or suburban living, we should bear in mind this innate dependency our minds seem to have on nature.

The four months spent trekking along the Appalachian Trail tested the physical limits of what our bodies could endure. Within a couple of months, our bodies had reformed into pure hiking machines: fat traded for muscles that gripped strongly to our frames, lungs beat more efficiently to a new rhythm, and overall body weight reduced and shifted to counterbalance the external weight of our packs. What's more, the greatest enhancements may have been in our psychology. We became more engaged with the present instead of dwelling on the past or trying to anticipate how we would manage our future. Anxiety and fear seemed to diminish as we conquered challenging obstacles. Confidence and self-esteem were renewed, and it felt as though we could walk the circumference of the earth if we needed to. We felt more trusting of strangers, and friendships came with much greater ease. Overall, we became empowered physically and cognitively, gained a greater affinity for others, and were now eager for more adventures and challenges.

Another positive attribute to be gained in venturing, already briefly mentioned in the second chapter, is that *adventures can be therapeutic in coping with the suffering and strife of life.* One of the most astounding things discovered on the Appalachian Trail was the unusual number of people who were suffering from some significant physical or emotional tragedy: the woman overcoming her divorce, the man who had been blown up in war, the nurse who had gone blind at the same time her husband's body was fatally deteriorating. Indeed, many people in moments of transition find themselves on the Appalachian Trail or similar adventure. Instead of allowing grief and misfortune to define their identities, these people had the tenacity to seek therapy in nature. Left Turn was a woman with short, graying hair hiking alone and brandishing a very becoming smile. She had "hit a brick wall" in her life when she was confronted bluntly with a divorce. "I went to a talk and the speaker said, 'When you hit a brick wall, turn left.' I really liked that, but I was in my 50s, so I didn't know what my left turn would be." Reading a book about the Appalachian Trail at the time, she called up her daughter asking, "Would you think I'm crazy if I hike the Appalachian Trail?" Her daughter quickly responded, "I think you would be crazy if you didn't!"

Doing something like hiking a long-distance trail helps remarkably well with coping with many stressors of life because, we suspected, the crucial components of what a person needs the most are present here, namely other people, a community, a purpose, and an opportunity to fashion a new identity. In addition, plenty of *time*, *distance*, and *place* grant an individual an environment to share their grief amidst a common struggle with the physical and mental obstacles of the trail. Being with others, along with having the chance to be alone to process and evaluate these misfortunes, can be a tremendous life-improving event. In a society that incessantly pleads for our time and attention, requiring us to keep in lockstep at an ever-increasing speed, we unsuspectingly trade away these personal connections and intimate moments that are seemingly antithetical to our contemporary system of living. I, too, would come to unsuspectingly benefit from the therapy the trail provided.

THE TRADE-OFFS OF ADVENTURE, PART I

O

Our journey for the trail was supposed to begin in early June, but was unexpectedly postponed by two weeks when I received a call from my mother informing us that my grandfather (Papa) had been diagnosed with brain and lung cancer. Radiation treatment would begin immediately on the lesions in his brain, and chemotherapy would follow after two weeks. I fought back my gasps and tears as best I could while on the phone with her. Through my mother's quivering voice, I mentally noted her courage and hope.

After I hung up the phone, I went through a spiral of emotions: emptiness to helplessness to anger, to deep sadness. This hit me very hard because I'd never lost anyone so close to me before. These next two weeks might be the last moments we have to see him alive and well. This added another challenge to what we were already planning to face because we originally planned to tackle the entire trail in one fell swoop, and this could mean not accomplishing the purist thru-hike we were hell-bent on doing. But family came before all else. We spent two weeks with my family. Most, if not all of us, remained optimistic, yet when I looked into their eyes, I was saddened by the harsh truth of it all. It was all unspoken, but what we all knew, or at least strongly sensed, was that these were his final days. The attitude he expressed to all of us was remarkable: he was fearless and accepting, embracing whatever may come. What bothered me most, though, was the thought of what he was thinking and facing when he was alone at night, and how my grandmother was coping. I couldn't imagine the torment they were both going through, knowing death was so rigidly near. We always hope there will be more time...

I owed much to my Papa. He had impressed upon me an endless supply of values, wisdom, and inspiration. The bounty of colorful postcards my Nana and Papa sent me from their own journeys across the United States while I was growing up may be what prompted my wanderlust: stunning images of the California redwoods and sequoias, a rustic locomotive balanced on tracks somewhere in the Colorado mountains between Durango and Silverton, Death Valley, and Monument Valley. And I know the reason I yearned to go to college was in large part because of his insistence. He was the most generous, honest, modest man I knew. Humbly, he implored us not to hold up our trip because of this. What I can be grateful for is that we were able to be there when he was expected to be of sound mind, and yet as our car tugged us away and we waved goodbye, my heart was torn.

We had hoped that the doctor's six-month prognosis would be accurate, but we were back just under a month later. Once out of the Hundred Mile Wilderness, we received unwanted news. Papa's condition had taken a rapid turn for the worse, and my mother urged us to fly home as soon as we could. Stunned and in denial, I tried convincing myself that she was exaggerating, but I knew her to be sensible and wouldn't have asked us if this was not serious. We were saddened to be leaving the trail and friends we'd already met so soon, but even more distraught to be returning to Indiana under such sorrowful circumstances.

We were fortunate to have my grandma Paula only two hours away in Belfast, Maine. She picked us up the following day in Monson, and we celebrated Hilary's birthday that night at her cottage, where we were treated to lobster, clams, corn, potatoes, wine, and homemade sugar cream pie. We owed her dearly for her hospitality and for easing the stress.

THE TRADE-OFFS OF ADVENTURE, PART I

After a week of being home, Papa passed just before six in the early morning of July 16th. Only 40 days had passed since his initial prognosis; appropriately biblical for such a devout man. None of us could believe how quickly death came for him. The experience of watching the life of someone so instrumental in your own life rapidly fade away and cease is tormenting. The pain is deeply felt, but he will forever remain one of my greatest sources of inspiration.

The support from the local community, friends, and family was remarkable and touching. It goes to show he meant so much to so many. His character was a rare one, and he will be greatly missed. I hated to leave my family so soon after the funeral, but I'm certainly glad we were able to make it back to the trail. It was an emotional ride those sixteen days off the trail, but so is the way of life, I suppose. Papa himself would always proclaim that "Life goes on." Simple, yet true.

○

Hearing the personal stories of those who had felt loss in their lives greatly helped alleviate the pain I felt for the loss of my grandfather. We all cope and grieve in varying ways, but what became quickly apparent, walking in the open piney air along the trail with so many others who came here specifically to "walk the war out of their system" or stop allowing their divorce to define their lives, was that this provided a unique experience for people to actively meditate and walk through their struggle. *The trail provided a process of healing.* Being a part of this community and witnessing others overcome their obstacles uplifts a person to see that we are not alone in this world after all. Despite being in a society surrounded by many others coping with their struggles, we all appear so indifferent to each other's pain a lot of the time. The trail openly brought many people together and provides a powerful form of therapy in the midst of wandering.

Another critical lesson *is confronting and overcoming fear and anxiety*. Adventure puts fear in its place. As it is often the fear of others that preoccupies our minds, one of the most central things a person becomes aware of with consistent new contact with other people and places is a diminishing sense of fear and apprehension about the world. We become more familiar with human nature and thus gain a greater affinity for others. This allows us to see through the eyes of those who may, on the surface and from a distance, appear wildly different from us and our cultural ways. Eventually, we gain an insight into just how complex being human is, and that though there be differences, the similarities bind us more than we realize. In the end, our adventures have us look back in hindsight at our previous fears to see how ill-informed we once were—we are enabled to see more clearly the difference between *perceived fears* and *actual risks*.

Since our time on the Appalachian Trail, it has been a goal of mine to pay close attention to all the dangerous or violent instances I might encounter whenever traveling somewhere new or just experiencing daily town life. Rarely are such instances encountered. And if they are, they're never at the level imagined. This is important for each of us to be more cognizant of because we are so bombarded with worrying information all the time that we rarely notice how little of it happens to us. Unreasoned or perceived fears have a great tendency to lead us astray. A benefit of wandering, thus, brings our risks and greatest worries into sharper focus.

THE TRADE-OFFS OF ADVENTURE, PART I

A growing sense of self-reliance and confidence in our ability to adapt is another major practical and psychologically uplifting lesson from the adventure. Adventures make us more confident and thrifty. When we come to experience life on a long-distance trail or abroad, immersed in a foreign culture where our accessibility to familiar technology and things we previously depended on are limited or nowhere to be found, we can quickly become unsettled. We're forced to confront our ignorance and inadequacies. But in striving to overcome such obstacles, we meet the creative side of ourselves that once lay dormant within us, and we gradually come to adapt to unforeseen circumstances. As we persevere, we come to find a renewed appreciation and confidence in our adaptability. We often "wow" ourselves with our brilliance for improvisation, and those epiphanies can inspire us to take further steps toward adventures that give us similar experiences. Problem-solving and being innovative are essential and innate components of our identity and a hallmark of human nature. It is very much a part of everyone, whether we recognize it or not. Trust that it is there within you. And when we ignite that spark of self-reliance and self-discovery for the first time, we find ourselves full of life because we are reminded that this is what links us to our species' sustaining ingenuity and resilience. Ultimately, what we have to re-learn is our capacity to adapt. Our greatest collective obstacle may just be enabling more people to see that they inherently possess the capability to alter their behavior, to be self-aware of their agency, and to channel it more fruitfully. Adventures then provide one of the best ways to see these things for ourselves by dropping us into uncomfortable situations that allow us to tap into our creativity and adaptability.

Many people have responded to us since our days on the Trail,

"There is no way I could do something like hike the Appalachian Trail!" This isn't so. What folks are saying here is that they don't have faith in themselves to adapt and overcome their initial fears. Most people actually could hike the Appalachian Trail, travel abroad, or do whatever their dream adventure is if they truly wanted to, because they already possess this innate adaptive ability as a human being. We've seen children as young as nine, ranging up to people in their seventies, able to hike the trail. Every one of us has a dream adventure, but far too many of us fail to make it a reality because of our inability to see this self-reliant, creative, and adaptive side of ourselves. That is the paradox I've been discussing throughout this book. We encounter apprehensive people with this heavy self-doubt all the time. Know and trust that you are far more capable than you may realize.

During her time at Indiana University, Hilary spent a few days getting allergy shots every week, gearing up for her trip to South America, and became familiar with some of the nurses at the medical center. There was a small section of the building designated for the Travel Immunization Department. The walls were covered in postcards and foreign currency, along with smiling photos with "Thank you!" written on them. Both nurses were extremely kind, but one was particularly loquacious. One day, Hilary asked her if she had visited any of the places that she's sent eager college students off to. "No," she hadn't, "but I have always dreamed of going to South Africa." That was her dream trip. "What's holding you back?" Hilary prodded candidly. She described her lifelong desire to do a two-week safari in Africa, but the financial and logistical burden of doing something like this felt beyond her. Nevertheless, she had been saving for the trip for some time. "But really, the biggest thing is, I don't want to go alone. My sister won't go with me, and I haven't found anyone else."

These things are always rooted in some underlying fear. Here was someone with a persistent dream that may never be realized because of her trepidations. Her life's work was to prepare young people to jet-set on countless adventures to far-off corners of the world. Every day she came to her office, walls lined with photos of every thinkable destination and currency to match, only to go home knowing that she was not working *mentally* toward South Africa. Hopefully, something has since changed in the nurse and prompted her to indulge in her adventure. Maybe she convinced a friend to join her. Nonetheless, the wish remains to see that more people realize the power of travel and adventure and just how much one can discover on their own if one would only take a chance and go for it. Solo traveling might turn out to be the very thing someone needs.[206]

Closely related to adaptability is seeing *how much we can do without*. Adventures teach us the value of frugality. One of the critical things one comes to learn in wandering is how much we can do without while still living a high-quality life. Indeed, self-inflicted deprivation is the *sine qua non* of backpacking the AT. As Bill Bryson humorously put it in *A Walk in the Woods*:

> [T]he central feature of life on the Appalachian Trail is deprivation, that the whole point of the experience is to remove yourself so thoroughly from the conveniences of everyday life that the most ordinary things—processed cheese, a can of pop gorgeously beaded with condensation –fill you with wonder and gratitude. It is an intoxicating experience to taste Coca-Cola as if for the first time and to be conveyed to the brink

of orgasm by white bread. Makes all the discomfort worthwhile if you ask me.[207]

When we're forced to carry only what's on our backs, we think very carefully about the things we truly need and want. With a burgeoning population, unsteady markets, increasing pressure on the environment and its finite resources, climate change, and culture still encouraging conspicuous consumption, it could be a wise societal move for more of us to fine-tune our needs and wants. We are at a time where senselessly owning and casually discarding things is no longer an ethical or sustainable option. Amusingly, people have even been purchasing items in their sleep.[208] In 2017, Americans spent $240 billion, twice as much as in 2002, on non-essential goods from jewelry and watches to clothing and phones.[209] We spent *on average* $972 on clothing and seven pairs of shoes.[210] Houses continue to bulk ever upward to accommodate such excess. The average size of a single-family house increased by 23% last year from two decades ago to 2,426 square feet.[211] With so much time, money, and energy expended in accumulating all these things, where do we all find the time for our adventures? Chapter 1's critique of our society and culture reminds us that most of us don't. The motto from *Fight Club* seems to be evergreen: "The things you own end up owning you."

When we return home after months of travel with just the things on our backs, look at our apartment or three-story house or gluttonous garages with no room for our cars overflowing with things in disarray, we might well ask ourselves, "Why the hell do we need so much stuff?" These experiences in an adventure just might inspire us to refine and simplify our lives. This is a good thing for reducing our carbon footprint. If more of us experienced such an epiphany, we could potentially have a larger impact on alleviating some of the pressure placed on the earth's resources and our landfills. Perhaps most of all, we may realize that living a more minimalistic lifestyle might turn out to be more liberating than limiting. By living out of a backpack for an extended period, one comes to realize how little they need to live a quite sufficient and fulfilling life. This might then encourage us to seek alternative ways of living. After all, the consensus is that our modern cluttered lifestyles need to be altered and reduced in one form or another if we desire to soften the blow of any future environmental, population, or economic crises—it is highly questionable that an economic system premised on constant growth can go on forever without serious trade-offs. In addition to changes in technology that force our behavior to change more sensibly, another effective way of meeting that goal could be getting people mobile again in an adventurous, less cumbersome way. But traveling more also comes with environmental costs to consider, as we'll see in the next and final chapter.

Adventures can also lead to *moments that instill humility, gratitude, and mindfulness.* Adventures can make us more thoughtful and sympathetic. Having these emotions and experiences is not exclusive only to people who get lost in the depths of the wilderness or venture out into some far-flung foreign culture, but there can be much more heightened or impactful experiences of such feelings when we are in a place without the usual comforts and conveniences of our society. When we find ourselves putting up a tent in the darkness on a cold, rainy night, we might tend to reflect a little bit more about the parents who took the long, difficult steps to provide us with the warm, well-lit bedroom of our childhood. When we pass through a small, economically deprived town and see neglected, malnourished children wading in a stagnant, manure-filled canal, we might feel a tinge of guilt for never giving a second thought or thanks to the community and neighborhood that never allowed such conditions to be a problem for us. What's more, witnessing such abhorrent conditions may even inspire us to take action to help fix such issues. In facing any radically different environment and experience, we are bound to contrast many of the things we once took for granted, and better yet, become more actively involved in changing the world for the better. After all, things left out of sight are left out of mind. What's more, many of the prejudices and biases we may hold could very well be uprooted and tossed aside through wandering. We can begin to see that some of the formerly taken-for-granted aspects of our lives can take on a new hue and a renewed sense of appreciation as we gain insight from our adventures.

A sense of ecology and a value for and connection with nature is a complex subject. Nevertheless, adventures unite us with the landscape. For some, nature is little more than a vast resource for humans to exploit. We have dutifully done this for centuries and profoundly engineered the earth to suit our needs—hence our moment in time being labeled the Anthropocene. Many of us have long feared the consequences of actions that completely alter the natural world to the point that it is utterly unrecognizable. We've sensed that without it, there would be a great deal of moral, emotional, spiritual, and physical loss. Even the most hardened individuals deep down can understand this. Without natural settings, would we be able to experience the solitude and peace we find unique in its depths? Would we still be able to appreciate and understand the dynamics of change and the intricate web of biodiversity teeming throughout the planet? Would we still be able to find a place that makes us feel so small and vulnerable, yet simultaneously empowered and connected to life? Would we still be able to capture that ultimate feeling of timelessness when immersed in it? Without it, the natural environment would slowly be severed and lost from our collective memory, fading into the past like a mystical Ark of the Covenant. The natural world would eventually come to be a legend, rumored to contain within it great lessons and values for humanity, but nothing more than a myth and a never-ending pang of remorse for those in the future left only to their imaginations of what used to be. For most of us, we need to physically and emotionally see and feel this, having all senses present, and step into the forests and canyons to truly appreciate its attraction. Without a healthy majority of us in favor of conservation, this hyperbole can become a reality.

An eighth and final lesson is the experience of *connecting with other people and sharing a sense of community within a common experience*. Adventures restore our faith in humanity. In anthropology, this sharing of a common experience within a community has been characterized by the term *communitas*.[212] Establishing relationships is something we inherently do. Again, this isn't an exclusive thing among adventurers. However, entering unknown territory in the heart of travel can be daunting. We often find ourselves relying much more heavily on the goodwill of strangers and become overtly committed to building a rapport with others. Upon arriving in Hanover, we found ourselves dripping wet from more torrential rains. We were utterly exhausted and our moods were souring. The supermarket was crowded, but we needed to gather supplies before figuring out where to stay that night. A young woman exiting the supermarket spotted us with an openhearted smile. Former thru-hikers can instantly spot other thru-hikers, no matter the size of the crowd, like an archaeologist can spot a piece of worked stone amidst a scatter of natural pebbles. Then again, the days-old sweaty stench emanating from their weathered clothes and grungy gear doesn't make it all that difficult for the layperson either. Without thinking twice, she invited us to stay the night and clean up at her apartment. She hiked the trail two years before and could easily relate to our situation. And when she offered her apartment to us, she was quite literal: she was leaving for the weekend and left us with plenty of food, her Netflix account, a shower, and a bed without wanting anything in return.

These shared experiences of community struck me as profound and unexpected, despite being recently steeped in the study of anthropology. Another critical lesson dawned on me: learning something from afar, say in the classroom or reading a book at home, doesn't mean we fully grasp something; many lessons of life require the full physical immersion of all our senses. These cases seemed to occur so regularly that it has made me wonder if all we need to do to gain a better sense of human altruism and unadulterated kindness is to simply wander a bit more throughout the world and inspect humanity a little more face-to-face. Throwing ourselves out into the world forces us to make contact and establish a rapport. When we are nestled in a familiar place, we become habituated. We know how to move around with ease and acquire the things we need and want almost without thinking about it—we don't necessarily need to interact and engage with anyone on any meaningful level. We can easily click purchase online, and the closest we get to human contact is merely hearing a knock at the door when our package arrives. Technology can also distance us just as much as it can connect us. When we find ourselves in the grips of an adventure and a new place, we're almost forced to interact with others more authentically. On an adventure, we tend to connect with others more intimately, establishing camaraderie or companionship with those sharing our experience.

One major positive to wandering in the world is that we not only expand our vision of our planet, but also our circle of sympathy casts a wider net. In his study, *The Expanding Circle: Ethics, Evolution, and Moral Progress*, moral philosopher Peter Singer observed in 1981 a historical trend of how the "circle of altruism has broadened from the family and tribe to the nation and race, and we are beginning to recognize that our obligations extend to all human beings."[213] The fact that we feel the pain and suffering of those affected by a natural or man-made disaster halfway around the world, and may even send relief money to those with whom we'll never meet or have our kindness reciprocated, says something quite extraordinary about our moral progress. Stepping out into the world in more direct ways will allow us to see this less media-driven side of our humanity.

The renowned primatologist and author Frans de Waal echoed this sentiment of expanding empathy in his 2009 book *The Age of Empathy: Nature's Lessons for a Kinder Society*, stating that,

> [I]f I could change one thing, it would be to expand the range of fellow feeling. The greatest problem today, with so many different groups rubbing shoulders on a crowded planet, is excessive loyalty to one's own nation, group, or religion. Humans are capable of deep disdain for anyone who looks different or thinks another way, even between neighboring

groups with almost identical DNA, such as the Israelis and Palestinians...Empathy of "other people" is the one commodity the world is lacking more than oil. It would be great if we could create at least a modicum of it...If I were God, I'd work on the reach of empathy.[214]

As an anthropologist and traveler, I can't think of a more important reason for people to be traveling and having adventures than for us to come face to face with more of our shared humanity so that we can eventually shed the sheer silliness of tribalistic thinking and "othering" one another that has plagued our species for far too long.

Due to those willing to wander about the globe and engage with others in trade, in storytelling, in sharing ideas, in creating networks and links with people and cultures different from themselves, our sympathies for others slowly enhanced over the ages to overcome painful and deep-seated prejudices. And yes, there was plenty of senseless bloodshed too along the way, but the trends have been rapidly declining in our modern age, all the while population continues to go up. Recognizing this progress should give us pause and encourage us to stay in contact with others and share our ideas so that we may further improve our global society. But we must lastly reckon with the many challenges our world is still inundated with, and what the responsibilities of the modern wanderer are.

CHAPTER 9
The Trade-offs of Adventure, Part II: *The Challenges of Wandering*

*"That's the problem in making travel television.
When we succeed, we inspire others to travel to the places
we care about and, in a sense, help kill what we love."*
—Anthony Bourdain

*(1) "Everyone has the right to freedom of movement
and residence within the borders of each state.
(2) Everyone has the right to leave any country,
including his own, and to return to his country."*
—Article XIII of the Universal Declaration of Human Rights

We entered the mystical and aptly named White Mountains of New Hampshire, and the days were effortlessly colliding and in sync like pleasant musical measures. Having over a month's experience hiking through Maine gave us confidence, too much confidence perhaps. If we could have had the ability to skip a day, this would have been the one. But on second thought, truly good stories come from hair-raising misadventures, not quiet hand-holding excursions on the beach. What kind of story would we have without the misadventures and challenges of today? In hindsight, I titled today's journal entry "Momentary Negligence: The Day All Went Wrong."

The day began with smiles, good fortune, and a breakfast buffet. Like a giddy hobbit, breakfast fills me with an irrational sense of joy, but after finding a $20 bill on the ground on our way to the Pinkham Notch Visitor Center, I had an unusual pep to my step. Luck wouldn't run out on us today, I thought.

After the excusable slow start, Hilary and I headed out for what we thought would be another tough, but doable climb up Mt. Madison, the first on our end of the Presidential Range in the White Mountains. The weather was gorgeous, and the forecast was only predicting a slight chance of rain, but what about up there, closer to the sky? Had my mind not been running on a lackadaisical pancake high, I might have been more diligent in checking the weather and maps that were abundantly emblazoned along the walls and counters of the visitor center. Full of carbs, we set off feeling well-energized and chatty. Only seven miles existed between us and the next hiker hut (Madison Spring Hut), and we anticipated being there easily by six that evening.

Hiking through the White Mountains presents a challenge because it feels like a spider's web network of other trails that intersect the Appalachian Trail, which makes the method of simply following the white blaze trail markers especially difficult. Also, numerous wooden signs, neglected for some years, were down or pointed in obscure directions so that we were unsure where they were meant to point. The white blazes that we were so accustomed to, and that were so ubiquitous through Maine, were few and far between. Indeed, ever since we'd arrived in

THE TRADE-OFFS OF ADVENTURE, PART II

New Hampshire, I had asked myself time and again, "Where the fuck are the blazes!?" I guess they were trying to save on paint. Though frustrated with the confusion, we were forewarned to get a map, which we neglected to do, so I suppose we'll have to take the blame for that.

We thought we were following the correct trail, but after a while, things didn't seem right, and I started to get concerned because the elevation profile in our data book showed that we should have been ascending Mt. Madison at a rapid incline. Instead, we were gradually climbing along a modest stream. I kept shaking my head and thinking, "This can't be right." Then all went steadily wrong.

The trail completely vanished before our eyes, and we were facing a steep climb of boulders, loose rock, thick, spongy, heavy moss, and a fairly benign waterfall. We were climbing on all fours, and the higher we climbed, the greater the wind picked up and the steeper the incline grew. The clouds looming above us felt ominous. They were darkening, and the anger and rage I was feeling for being so damn careless and stupid quickly changed to worry and fear. I was slowly losing my nerve; Hilary was not. She remained stoic, yet became increasingly impatient with my temper and outbursts. I thought maybe we should just turn around, but she was hell-bent on going forward, so we continued the relentless push upward into the sky.

The clock on my nearly dead phone now read 6:30 p.m., and we were definitely lost. All we could do was keep climbing, scout for rock shelters for some meager cover in the event of serious weather, hope the storm didn't break, and hope some more that we'd find the trail at the top. It was exhausting work lugging our full packs and bodies up this seemingly vertical angle.

We eventually made it to a sign, and when the clouds lifted for a moment, I thought I could spot our trail. "Do mirages happen in the mountains, too?" I wondered. We should have been on a longer, more circuitous route ascending Mt. Madison to the north, but had inadvertently made a beeline east, straight up the wrong mountain! To our dismay, the sign read, "Mt. Washington Summit - 0.5 Mi." We almost couldn't believe it. We had accidentally climbed the highest mountain in the entire northeast, one of the windiest places on the planet, at 6,288 feet on a side that wasn't even intended to be a trail. Even after hiking over three hundred miles through Maine, we were still morons.

Earlier that day, I'd been reading a plaque at the visitor center about all those who had lost their lives on this very mountain range due to falls or exposure. The words on one of the plaques had been sounding an alarm in my mind the more I climbed. They read,

> There have been joys too great to be described in words, and there have been griefs upon which I have dared not to dwell, and with these in mind, I must say, climb if you will, but remember that courage and strength are naught without prudence and that momentary negligence may destroy the happiness of a lifetime. Do nothing in haste, look well to each step, and from the beginning think what may be the end.
>
> —Edward Whymper, who made the first ascent of the Matterhorn with six others in 1865. On the way down, four of his companions fell to their deaths.

Now, Mt. Washington isn't even half the struggle of climbing the Matterhorn. I understand this. Indeed, climbing gear isn't even required here, excluding the winter season perhaps. Nevertheless, these words that emphasized momentary negligence painted a chilling, sobering scene in my mind, and not because of the wind, though it too bit and pushed us to walk and balance ourselves all the while leaning at what felt like a 45-degree angle against the wind.

We'd made it to the top. An eerie scene with fog, thick and stagnant, confronted us. All the lonesome buildings, scarred by years of elemental exposure, were locked. No other souls haunted this landscape. I wondered if perhaps we shouldn't have been out in this misty haze. We were walking through a dense, rupturing cloud, and visibility was extremely poor; the sight of my fingertips outstretched looked phantom-like as they breached the wall of whiteness. Dampness mixed with the wind made my skin shake with spastic tremors. We scampered around the summit trying to find the sign that would point us in the direction of the closest hut, which was, unbeknownst to us, only another 1.2 miles away. Our adrenaline had kicked in and had us motoring over the trip-hazard stones. I'm not sure how either of us kept from falling. The wind was unlike anything we'd experienced, and each step required careful placement. We later learned that wind speeds were 63 mph.

En route to the hut, I had joked to Hilary that Ridge Rat's (a humorous old trail volunteer we previously met in Maine) prayers either had not come to fruition or he had forgotten altogether. Ridge Rat had been through here numerous times on his wanderlust excursions, and now we knew what he was talking about. He compulsively smirked when we informed him of the upcoming White Mountains and our thrill for the view, saying, "Oh man, Mt. Washington, I tell you what, I'll pray for you up there and for one reason, to have good weather. I've hiked up that mountain in every way possible, and I've never had a view. NEVER! Sometimes you could reach out your arm and just barely see your hand, but that's about all. Everyone talks about 'Oh, Mt. Washington, yeah, the view is beautiful.' Well, how the HELL would I know!?" Now we could fully relate.

The clock read 8:00 p.m. and darkness arrived when we happened upon a sign that read "Lakes of the Clouds Hut 0.1 Mile." We were filled with relief, and the wave of adrenaline circulating through our bodies quickly phased out. We'd made it, but not without realizing our fortunate circumstances. Another sign reminded us of just how serious things could have been had we failed to reach the trail and remained lost in the misty darkness. It read, "STOP. The area ahead has the worst weather in America. Many have died there from exposure. Even in the summer. Turn back now if the weather is bad." It was the area from which we had just emerged. I shook my head, wondering how bad is "bad?"

We stood inside the entrance of the hut, our labored breathing and chilled bodies slowly returning to normal. The lounge was crowded with people carrying on with laughter, games, and conversation. Some were eating and sipping warm beverages. All were completely unaware and indifferent to our recent fright. I felt lucky we hadn't received the wrath of a truly heinous storm, and we had made it safely to the hut before dark. We would sit out the following day to allow the rest of the storm to pass.

So many have suffered far worse and been in much more extreme circumstances, so I'm not going to contend that our experience was anything more than a brief potentiality for danger; that wandering comes with genuine costs if one is not prudent. Nevertheless, it certainly has

THE TRADE-OFFS OF ADVENTURE, PART II

inspired me to "wise up" a bit more, to not get distracted by breakfast buffets, and to never slip into "momentary negligence" again.

○

What are the harms or unintended consequences of pursuing our travels and adventures? What are the arguments *against* travel? Is it wise to encourage more of us to wander? Does an ethical middle ground exist for travel and adventure to continue in the face of its negative consequences? Before setting foot on our wandering paths, we should lastly reflect not only on the personal risks we take by exploring our world more but also on the ugly sides of traveling and the impacts global tourism can have across the planet. The consequences of large populations of humans temporarily shifting around the globe for the sake of travel are multifaceted, but can have significant impacts socially, culturally, politically, ecologically, and economically for many of the world's geographic settings and the indigenous and/or local people found living there. The demanding role of the adventurer of traveling in the 21st century is a conscientious one and far more demanding than in years past. Today's travelers, if we care to be ethical and considerate, must be conscious of their actions and the consequences of their behavior if they wish to retain something of the place that originally attracted them there. We must be willing to educate ourselves about the complex and sometimes detrimental relationships the tourism industry has with local communities in "host countries." Thus, it requires 21st-century wanderers to become more mindful stewards of lands and cultures.

Being a mindful adventurer in today's world comes with some important, perhaps conflicting demands. We're asked to understand something about ecology and why things like biodiversity, preservation, and conservation are critical for sustainability and mitigating climate change. We're asked to reduce our rates of consumerism, development, and pollution that can inadvertently damage environments and undermine or displace local people's way of life. We're asked to understand local economies and their relationship with the tourist industry so that we will be better informed to prevent such inexcusable things as the exploitation of child labor, forced displacement, mass human migration, the spreading of disease, prostitution, alcoholism, drug addiction, human trafficking, and other human rights abuses. These are, unfortunately, things some travelers' money and presence unwittingly support. Like a long chain reaction, our decisions and actions have the power to put these consequences in motion. Because of all this, we are asked to learn something vital about culture and developing meaningful relationships in an ever-globalizing world. This list of demands can be overwhelming and burdensome for someone who merely wishes to venture out and "see the world." But as challenging as it may seem, becoming more conscious of these issues can unexpectedly make our adventures more wholesome and inspiring.

○

Let's revisit some brief history for a moment and consider the actions and consequences of previous generations of developers, industrialists, and other supporters of mass human movement on indigenous communities. Many anthropologists and ethnologists, beginning in the late nineteenth century and continuing through much of the early 20th century, forebodingly sensed the impact Western civilization and an emergent tourist economy would have on indigenous peoples across many areas of the world, as it often pressured conformity, acculturation, and assimilation within many cultures for their land and resources. By this time, numerous native groups had already been ruthlessly decimated by disease and genocide committed in the name of Western civilization and progress. They were pushed to the margins for the sake of energy and infrastructure development to fuel an ever-expanding and insatiable economy. Many of these cultural anthropologists who had intimately studied and lived with diverse cultures still surviving couldn't help but foresee the imminent threat to these peoples' lifeways and their landscapes from outside forces of industry, bureaucratization, and commercialization. Notable anthropologists were convinced that significant changes had completely altered most, if not all, indigenous cultures the world over. The English anthropologist W.H.R. Rivers noted in 1910:

> It is almost impossible at the present time to find a people whose culture, beliefs, and practices are not suffering from the effects of European influence, an influence which has been especially active during the last fifty years.[215]

Likewise, the famous Polish anthropologist Bronislaw Malinowski, writing in the foreword to his magnum opus *Argonauts of the Western Pacific*, published in 1922, confidently stated,

> For though at present, there is still a large number of native communities available for scientific study, within a generation or two, they or their cultures will have practically disappeared. The need for energetic work is urgent, and the time is short.[216]

Many of these emergent ideas for "progress" were antithetical to traditional ways of life for many native groups. Joseph Epes Brown, an American scholar who dedicated his life to studying Native American traditions and spirituality, wrote in the 1940s and 1950s about this historic clash of cultures, forced disruption of their societies, and the subsequent dilution of the Native way of life:

> Governing techniques based on the accumulated wisdom of the elders were replaced by an imposed bureaucratic system, which could never, even if it wished, understand the real problems of the people under its charge. In accord with the Euro-American concept of ownership, the random distribution of parcels of land on the basis of individual family units shattered the cohesive unity of the Indian's own larger consanguineous groupings, and the prohibition of plural marriages disrupted the immediate family units. School systems were imposed that had as their avowed goals the suppression and eventual elimination of traditional values in order to hasten forcefully the process of total assimilation. This policy, with all too few exceptions, is still basic to today's school system on the reservation. Ill-conceived government attempts at economic rehabilitation have ended again and again in total failure, largely due to the fact that agriculture, then identified by

white people with civilization, was a practice contradictory to all Indian values, which held the earth as sacred and inviolate and not to be torn up with a plow. Among the most difficult trials, however, were the hostile attitudes toward the Indian's religious practices. Sacrificial elements of the Sun Dance were prohibited, as were the rites held for the departing souls of the dead, and it is well known how participation in the much-misunderstood Ghost Dance ended in the infamous massacre of Wounded Knee in 1890.[217]

Some contemporary observers originally predicted that these long-running colonialist forces would inevitably erase these cultures from the face of the earth and, therefore, felt obliged to document everything they could before it was too late so that some semblance of a past culture could be preserved for posterity.[218] Others aligned themselves with indigenous social and political movements to use what leverage they had and fight back against this wave of morphing neo-colonialism growing through much of the mid to late twentieth century up to the present day to preserve, protect, and keep intact what they felt were unique and sacred expressions of the human condition.

The impacts of globalization continue to ripple and abound across many areas of the world. The tourist economy is the logical outgrowth of this system that relentlessly puts pressure on local communities the world over. In recent years, numerous anti-tourist protests have erupted in a backlash against "overtourism" across many European countries.[219] There are many underlying causes to explain this phenomenon. In her book *Rethinking Tourism and Ecotravel,* author Deborah McLaren details the economic, ecological, and ethical ramifications the tourism industry has on local people in "host countries" around the world, arguing that tourism often degrades a local community because of the vast resources required to develop the resorts that travelers demand. The outcomes are reduced natural resources, infertile lands and increased cost of living.[220]

This is a shared problem. As we saw in previous chapters, the responsibility of shaping our (mis)perceptions of our world rests not entirely with "the media." Likewise, we can't simply blame "the tourism industry." The responsibility also lies with us, the travelers, and the demands we unsuspectingly cause those with large capital to develop in a given area. We are the first domino to fall in this charade, and therefore, some of the onus rests on us, too:

> As tourists, we consider travel an inherent economic right. Yet we are supporting the loss of jobs, subsidizing corporations, and cooperating with governments known for human rights abuses. Tourists and locals must become active citizens and make clear the connection between the corporate path of globalization and the multitude of injustices taking place under the guise of a vacation.[221]

As one of the largest industries in the global economy, it's easy to see that tourism means big business. As a consequence, many assume that with all the money being generated, assuredly a fair amount of that money trickles down to help locals and their communities and is, therefore, a plus for everyone. However, in many cases, communities of the "third world" who were previously self-reliant and self-sustaining using fishing, farming, or hunting before globalization and privatization are now dependent upon "a global economy, leaking many economic profits outside of the community back to the companies and countries that control most of the travel infrastructure...Tourism decreases dependence on local resources, as technologies, food, and health services are imported. Local people may also be pushed out or sell out, and local prices for commodities and services rise, as do taxes."[222]

In many of these cases, people have been forced from their traditional lifeways, thus losing once valuable skill sets that ensured their local status in the community to assume low-wage unskilled service jobs such as hotel clerks, maids, porters, dishwashers, and cooks in an unstable economic tourist environment that is often highly fluctuating and seasonal. Additionally, we ought to bear in mind that such things as labor unions and robust laws that typically protect workers from unethical work conditions, and ensure benefits that we often take for granted, such as legal contracts, minimum wages, insurance, healthcare, sick leave, and paid time off, do not necessarily exist for many workers in some foreign countries. As if this weren't enough, foreigners from various other countries looking for work who hawk these destinations can often fill these positions far more cheaply, which further prevents locals from gaining any socioeconomic standing in their hometowns.[223]

We also should be aware of environmental and human rights issues. One tactic many corporations use is what is known as "greenwashing," or painting a thin veneer over their products and services to give the impression that they are being "eco-friendly." We've all seen the green-labeled shampoos and signs at hotels that encourage the reuse of towels to help "save the planet." In reality, many of these companies have a hand in the destruction of the local environment through the heavy development and consumption of natural resources, which should be considered far from ecologically friendly.[224] What little they do to project a concern for the environment can be inconsequential and fail to make up for the damage they've already incurred on the environment.

Furthermore, the tourism industry can sometimes establish itself in countries despite oppressive governments with deliberate human rights abuses such as child labor exploitation, forced displacement and migration, sex exploitation of women and children, and human trafficking, as has been a trend in places within countries like Kenya, Myanmar, Tibet, China, Sri Lanka, the Philippines, and Indonesia.[225] Unassuming tourists visiting these countries may not realize that some of the money they spend in these areas can potentially support such ignoble acts. As travelers, we're cautioned to be on the alert and inform ourselves beforehand of the ongoing social and political events and issues—to use our money and opportunities wisely and ethically—voting with both our feet and pocketbooks. Proper research into the country or region of our soon-to-be adventure should be a priority for any ethical modern traveler. A good starting point can be the State Department's travel map, which lends insight into the variety of developing problems around the globe at any given time.[226] Seek out trustworthy travel guides and experts, preferably ones who live in your sought-after destination.

Such economic, environmental, and cultural exploitation is not absent from the United States either. Many indigenous peoples have been fighting for a long time against the devastating impacts brought about by global tourism and encroachment on their tribal lands. One contributor to McLaren's book, Kaleo Patterson, a native Hawaiian, portrays the perspective of tourism from his vantage point and captures what many other natives around the world feel and live with when confronting tourism in their homeland:

> From our experiences and our history with tourism, to turn the other cheek, to ignore the tide of visitors, and to refuse to sell the crafts and the flower leis is not enough. Inevitably and very quickly, others will take our place in the venture of tourism; any other brown-skinned or well-tanned replacement will do. A time will come when our most sacred of words and traditions, cherished dreams and ideas, become common property to the world—all because tourism has no real purpose but to make money. This desire is so strong that the development of tourism in a place like Hawaii is like a tsunami, washing away all that is real and once was, and leaving behind something new and foreign. When all that sustained a people in the past is gone, we shall one day look and sadly see that nothing is left and that we have lost everything.[227]

Many indigenous and local peoples, the world over, take these impacts on their homelands very seriously, and so too should anyone else considering traveling within these regions.

The erosion of natural settings has also been the case with a number of our national parks within the United States. Several of our parks seem unbelievably crowded, which can incentivize the clear-cutting of important natural forests and the further development to make way for more hotels, roads, restaurants, toilets, and campsites. Some of these places seem destined to become mere amusement parks soon enough. By adding ourselves to the gluttonous crowd, we have the potential to completely undermine and destroy everything that was once pristine and everything that originally attracted us to a place. The same can happen when we go abroad into the homelands of others.

What can be done about this? One simple alternative would be to seek out places that are not already highly targeted destinations or overly touristed. For those of us in the United States who wish to travel domestically, we can consider spreading out and widening our vision of alternative destinations. We certainly favor national parks over national forests. For instance, national forests make up nearly 300,000 square miles[228] and saw an estimated 149 million annual visits in 2015,[229] while national parks comprise under half that, a little over 131,000 square miles[230], and saw more than double the people, an estimated 331 million visitors in 2016 (up 24 million since 2015).[231] National forests can be just as awe-inspiring as our national parks and often give us more of the quietude and raw experience we seek out in national parks. The same is true for the Bureau of Land Management (BLM) lands, which make up an additional 385,000 square miles.[232] This is just one example of how we can come up with less-traveled places to explore and relieve pressure on high-density national parks and other hotspot destinations.

Also, if we are committed to traveling to national parks and desire a higher quality experience, perhaps we can schedule our adventures in the off-season. One of the most memorable experiences traveling to our national parks and monuments was a solo trip I took to the southwest, visiting Mesa Verde National Park, Aztec Ruins National Monument, Chaco Canyon National Historic Park, and Canyon de Chelly National Monument. Certain areas within these destinations were still closed off for the season, unfortunately, and the weather was not optimal in the early parts of April, as my tent was blanketed with snow and rain on more than one occasion. However, I took enormous pleasure in the fact that I was one of the few visitors at the time. Walking through the canyonland of Chaco, an archaeological and spiritual mecca, alone to wander among the great houses felt as though I were the first one discovering them. Without the overbearing crowds, I was able to connect with these remarkable places in a much more intimate way. And I was even able to connect with a few people by sharing stories and sips of scotch well into the night around a soporific scene of a campfire illuminating the petroglyphs etched into the burnt red sandstone, something the noisy ambiance of a packed campground doesn't usually allow for. With generators running into the night, powering dozens of RVs, dogs barking, and babies crying, it's hard to appreciate a place originally designed for a raw elemental experience of quietude under the glow of the moon and stars. Traveling to these areas during the off-season will have some disadvantages. Some areas will not be open, certain conveniences will be absent, and hazardous weather can bring about some logistical challenges. However, not only will we not be adding ourselves to the crowds, but we may come in touch with a more heightened sense of adventure and learn things about ourselves and others we would have otherwise missed out on had we been consumed in the more cumbersome and raucous crowds of the peak seasons.

Understanding the pressures we unwittingly place on coveted tourist destinations is important because we have the potential to destroy or completely alter things for the worse for local cultures, economies, and the environment on which they ultimately depend. This is a challenge inherent in our own highly individualistic capitalist culture and something to be kept mindful of. If we must travel to such places already teeming with tourists, then we ought to be willing to tread lightly on the landscape, be supportive of authentic local growers, shopkeepers, guides, and other businesses, to educate ourselves on the local politics and issues affecting the community, and push for companies to change their practices if they are deemed exploitive and unjust. It all simply boils down to being respectful, conscientious, and humble.

Perhaps the best policy, however, is to listen and learn the desires of those living in a given place and not assume what people want or don't want for their culture and society. How do *they* feel about globalization and large swaths of tourists coming to town? Is it something they welcome and wish to be a part of? Many of these places rely heavily on tourism, and some welcome the crowd. Things are not so one-sided after all, and there's much more nuance to be found in these debates. In 1996, Jon Krakauer illustrated the commercialization and aesthetic degradation of the region surrounding Everest in *Into Thin Air*:

> [T]o handle the growing traffic from Western climbers and trekkers, new lodges and teahouses are springing up across the Kumbu region…longtime visitors…are saddened by the boom in tourism and the change it has wrought on what early Western climbers regarded as an earthly paradise, a real-life Shangri-La. Entire valleys have been denuded of trees to meet the increased demand for firewood. Teens hanging out in Namche *carrom* parlors are more likely to be wearing jeans and Chicago Bulls T-shirts than quaint traditional robes. Families are apt to spend their evenings huddled around video players viewing the latest Schwarzenegger opus.[233]

However, Krakauer further points out, "I didn't hear many Sherpas bemoaning changes." Due to the money brought in by climbers to economically uplift such things as schools and medical clinics, reduce infant mortality, and help boost critical infrastructure projects,

> [I]t seems more than a little patronizing for Westerners to lament the loss of the good old days when life in the Kumbu was so much simpler and more picturesque. Most of the people who live in this rugged country seem to have no desire to be severed from the modern world or the untidy flow of human progress. The last thing Sherpas want is to be preserved as specimens in an anthropological museum.[234]

For every argument against tourism, there happens to be one for it. A review of a seminal anthropological text, *Hosts and Guests: The Anthropology of Tourism,* adds much nuance to how multidimensional the effects of tourism are and how varied people's reactions can be toward it.

> [T]he research...indicates overall that tourism is *not* the major element of culture change in most societies. Given the pervasive indigenous demands for modernization, for the materialism and gadgetry that make human lives physically more comfortable and easier, the labor-intensive tourist industry has progressively served as an economically viable and socially permissible vehicle to provide wage employment. Tourism is especially favoured where significant segments of the population have minimal education or technical skills, inasmuch as other industries may require extensive training.[235]

Thus, it seems a middle ground approach to all this then is to listen and learn from the local inhabitants of a given area as to what their aspirations are for their country, not assume we know what is best for them from afar. But to do this thoroughly, we have to make some of these treks ourselves, learn the languages and customs, and befriend others to know their true hopes and desires. Modern travelers can heed the advice and practice of anthropologists, and in a sense, the modern adventurer eventually becomes a kind of anthropologist themselves.

As suggested, an alternative and potentially more rewarding way to travel can be to seek out places that are not already swarming with tourists and heavy development. There is a mode of travel that has been taking off for awhile now, known commonly as ecotravel or ecotourism: a form of travel that is principled in limiting one's environmental impact, promoting sustainable practices, and being cognizant of local and indigenous peoples' culture. Through this means, people actively volunteer to aid things like farms, vineyards, artisan workshops, and many other variants of sustainable communities. In recent years, a growing trend in eco-agro tours known as the World Wide Opportunities on Organic Farms or Willing Workers on Organic Farms, known more commonly as WWOOF, and its adherents as "woofers" have enabled many travelers hoping to have a more authentic adventure experience and limit their impact on the environment by becoming a part of the global network of organic farmers. In exchange for food and a place to stay, volunteers work and learn ecologically sound methods of growing and sustaining local communities, all the while immersing themselves in a completely new country, culture, and community. Tasks range from sowing seeds, making compost, gardening, planting, cutting wood, weeding, harvesting, packing, milking, feeding, fencing, making mud bricks, wine making, cheese making, and bread baking.[236]

These travel alternatives have great potential to not only immerse a traveler in a more engaged experience but also offer one the opportunity to give back to a community and establish reciprocity with their "hosts." That said, it should also be mentioned that some problems can stem from this type of travel as well because, as McLaren points out, "neither tourists nor locals understand the global forces transforming their lives, and no mechanism seems to exist for educating either hosts or guests to evaluate their own roles in the circumstances that are bringing about disillusion on all sides."[237] For all its intents, ecotravel can be almost as problematic environmentally, economically, and culturally as regular tourism. For instance, eco-travelers still typically utilize the same transportation networks as regular tourists: planes, trains, and automobiles that consume large amounts of fossil fuels. Increasing population in previously balanced communities, consuming large amounts of natural resources, and generating waste and pollution are other noted problems that inevitably result, even if someone is consciously attempting to reduce their impact at their intended destinations.[238]

In doing something like hiking the Appalachian Trail, it is paramount to maintain outdoor ethics and practice "Leave No Trace" ethics. One of our indicators for the blog we maintained while on the trail, kept a running total of "scats buried" as a humorous way to show the waste generated by only two people. Our running total tallied between the two of us for the four months on the trail was around 230 piles of poo that we buried six to eight inches deep every single time. With the amount of increasing traffic along the trail, it's rather remarkable just how clean the scene is, so kudos to all the Leave No Trace practitioners and volunteers for doing your part to keep the trail clean. Nevertheless, we can see the inherent tradeoffs we make when we encourage others to travel to these amazing places. As Anthony Bourdain once observed, "That's the problem in making travel television. When we succeed, we inspire others to travel to the places we care about and, in a sense, help kill what we love." We are left wondering whether the benefits of more people wandering outweigh the risks or costs.

The only truly eco-friendly way to entirely prevent such impacts would probably be to just stay home, but this is an unrealistic expectation for wanderlust individuals. Taken to an extreme, McLaren comments that to have the least amount of impact, a tourist:

> ...would have to walk to the destination, use no natural resources, and bring the food that she grew and harvested. She would also have to carry along her low-impact accommodations (a tent) or stay in a place that is locally owned and uses alternative technologies and waste treatment. Of course, she would also leave the destination in no worse and perhaps in even better condition than she found it, and contribute funds to local environmental protection and community development. And most importantly, ecotourism would be the development choice of local people who would be fully in control.[239]

This is assuredly an extremely high standard and an unrealistic expectation. Most people are not going to commit themselves to that much effort, no matter how much they might care about the environment or climate change. Nevertheless, this is merely food for thought, and even if more of us opted to choose a few ways to change our traveling habits, then over time we could conceivably make a significant positive impact on local environments, economies, and cultures as we develop an improved traveling ethos. This stuff is still a work in progress, and we have a long way to go. However, I don't believe in being a rigid puritanical environmentalist, but I do think we can all do better to live more conscientiously on this planet in a way that is suitable to our wants and needs. Healthy middle grounds and compromise exist if we are patient and clever enough to aim for them.

While tourism can sometimes seem to be an insurmountable problem wreaking inevitable havoc on the planet, we can see that there are also ways to alleviate it. The upside is that we can educate ourselves on many of these issues, boycott companies that flagrantly dissolve local cultures and impoverish or exploit people, and be more involved in our communities in promoting positive change through conversation, organization, and sustainability. Much like becoming aware of our psychological pitfalls will make us more adept at combating them, becoming aware of all the ways our actions as travelers and adventurers can harm a local culture and economy will help prevent such destruction and help preserve what is true and valuable in these regions of the world.

○

Wandering and travel take on various meanings in various contexts. As the contemporary forced migrations and refugee crises become all too apparent, wandering comes to mean very different things to different people. Wandering, as discussed in this book, is about a specific kind of adventure, one typically of luxury and privilege. Many of us are only gifted these opportunities to freely explore our world with relative ease and comfort because of an incredibly complex and tumultuous history that is both dark and beautiful. That history, despite all the misgivings, has provided us with an unbelievable bounty of liberty and security. And it is a history we ultimately inherited, both the good and the bad. We owe it to ourselves and the generations past to always be learning more about it so that we can appreciate the fortune we've been gifted. Nevertheless, this type of adventure is still a distinct type of luxury at the end of the day. And while it may be a luxury, it is not a luxury like many other indulgences. Adventure and the art of wandering have the potential to bring incredible meaning and experience to our lives, to open our eyes wider, to fill us with humility, and to take greater control over our lives.

Wandering opens up a world that is more perplexing and bizarre than we could have ever imagined if we were merely "vegetating in one little corner of the earth all one's lifetime," as Mark Twain put it. It opens up the doors of perception and makes us realize just how much there is to learn about the only habitable world we can know at this moment in time. We still need to see firsthand how volatile and fragile our planet is, how vulnerable we are, how limited our resources are, and how immense the knowledge we still have yet to possess as a collective species. With our lifestyles currently undergoing radical changes as we transition ever more into a more media and technology-saturated culture, it would be wise to bear in mind the potential impacts on our physical, emotional, and cognitive well-being.

○

In closing, I wish to reiterate the benefits and challenges of wandering in the 21st century. What we tend to gain when we venture is an enhanced physical and psychological well-being that allows us to tune into the world in a more pleasing and tranquil way. It gives us a chance

THE TRADE-OFFS OF ADVENTURE, PART II

to heal and cope with life's most unwelcoming tragedies. We're granted opportunities to discover our adaptability, self-reliance, and ways of being in the world in a less constricted fashion. And we can uncover a renewed appreciation for life that reveals a deeper connection with the natural world and with others found wandering in its midst. But we're also presented with a paradox of wandering. We travel to far-off places with high hopes of experiencing something new and foreign, but many of us have high expectations that we carry with us and don't always desire things to be "too foreign" or "too exotic." We still demand many of the conveniences of home, and the travel industry is more than happy to provide such products and services. Before too long, a once-balanced environment and culture can become uprooted and sabotaged right before a local community's eyes. Overtourism is a significant problem and can breed conflict, resistance, and unnecessary violence, something none of us want. All the while, we remain ignorant of the social, cultural, economic, and environmental depredations our demands brought about. The elimination of natural and cultural landscapes is an unfortunate and serious side effect of more people being encouraged to travel more. By undermining and transforming unique places and only preserving and spreading elements of our own homogeneous culture, we're left with nothing to compare it to, nothing to hold a mirror up and question if the values and customs we hold dear are truly right and fair. What do the people who live there think of others visiting their homeland? Do they welcome the change or abhor it? Shouldn't we know what they desire first and foremost? What right do we have to have an adventure in these places, to begin with?

Most of the world's countries subscribe, at least on paper, to fighting for and upholding human rights. Of the 195 countries of the world,

192 subscribe to the United Nations' Universal Declaration of Human Rights, of which Article XIII grants freedom of movement to and from one's country of birth or residence. Although this is often invoked to argue for the human rights of refugees, internally displaced persons (IDPs), political dissidents, and asylum seekers, does this also grant *everyone* the right to openly explore any country as they please? Strictly speaking, yes, it does. In other words, we all have the right to travel, but it can be legally restricted based on things like public health, national security, and other safety justifications. That said, common sense and deferring to ethical considerations are also paramount when deciding where to travel.

A final ethical consideration is that adventure is not open to all. There are lingering and entrenched socioeconomic and racial barriers that prevent some of us from enjoying the extensive outdoor adventures that many of us take for granted. Even on the Appalachian Trail, a space praised for being open, free, and democratic, it is still largely accessible to a predominantly white middle class. As author and ecologist Susan Power Bratton comments in her sociological analysis of the ethics and spirituality on the Appalachian Trail,

> The trail itself is also free—there are no admission fees, and the emphasis is on public ownership and use. The trail and related events have an "everyone belongs" atmosphere, which is in itself an ethical statement. Because of relatively low ethnic and socioeconomic diversity on the trail, however, this democracy and openness to others operates within a largely white middle-and professional-class framework. Intended as a respite for urban residents and industrial laborers, today's

THE TRADE-OFFS OF ADVENTURE, PART II

trail is, if anything, less accessible by public transportation than it was immediately following World War II, when most medium-sized Appalachian towns still had daily bus and rail service. Although many AT thru-hikers consider themselves to be of limited means, and some borrow money to make the trip, the majority are financially buffered by generous parents, a retirement account, savings from a well-paying job, or college-age exemption from fiscal obligations.[240]

Thus, if we wish to be critical and honest, there are still many societal, economic, and racial obstacles that can prevent large numbers of us from experiencing these empowering forms of adventure and travel. And we can always be doing more to open the channels of travel and adventure to everyone.

We must take note of the many ethical consequences of wandering and not take the opportunities to wander for granted. We must also understand that the more time we spend traversing the world, the less time we may spend with friends, family, and our communities at home. Adventures sometimes require greater risks and potential dangers. It's not a sure thing that we won't face serious injuries, long-lasting ailments, or even death as a result of living adventurously. And we may lose ourselves in the clouds while we climb the wrong mountain. That said, I strongly believe the benefits outweigh the risks and challenges of wandering. If longer life requires us to be complacent, fearful, and merely imagining what life is like in other places, then all we're doing is standing in a long line of monotony waiting for our death. On the other hand, if a fulfilled and examined life is what we yearn for, then being daring with the time we're given is a logical step to take.

AN ANTHROPOLOGY OF WANDERING

The famed Russian author Leo Tolstoy once wrote, "If we admit that human life can be governed by reason, the possibility of life is annihilated." Thus, if we try to calculate every instance of our life with reason alone, we may well lead a life cloistered up, never venturing, never gaining, never dreaming, and never taking any life-fulfilling chances. Learning to wander our world has something to offer each one of us once we unburden our minds from our perceived fears and limitations.

EPILOGUE
To Wander

> "Nothing in life is to be feared; it is only to be understood.
> Now is the time to understand more, so that we may fear less."
> —Marie Curie

We had been home for over two weeks, having returned on October 31, 2014. The first snow blanketed the ground, and we were gratefully protected by the sturdy, insulated walls of our room, the same room we spent so much time planning out and envisioning our trip over a year ago. We made it happen!

Weather reports of similar frosty conditions from our departure point in Shenandoah National Park in northern Virginia and along the rest of the East Coast reassured us that our decision to return home early was not all ill-conceived. We did wonder where we would be and if we would one day return to finish the trek of our remaining 800 miles. What would we be facing had we chosen to stay? Probably a lot of snow and many more shivering nights were in store for us.

I'm astounded to think that our experience of the trail is over for now. It seems to have passed as quickly as the snap of a finger, and all that remains of our trek are snippets of colorful photos, journal jottings, and vivid memories charging through our brains. The changing of what we conceive of as time is so curious and remarkable to me. When I think back to our walking of 1,300 miles over four months, it does feel far more distant in my memory and almost as if it could have just been something I dreamed up.

It is a strange and provoking feeling to have done something so remarkably contrasting to everything else I've done in life so far, to now be placed right back into the normalcy of life. I'm already restless again, eager for another adventure. But if I've learned anything from the trail, it is that I'm already on it and have been all this time. Maybe that sentiment sounds a little trite, but it is still true nonetheless.

We too often think of nature and adventures in glorified romantic ways, as something distant, afar, and something we designate to seek out at particular moments in our lives, as moments somehow separate from our lives. We think we need exotic experiences from far-reaching foreign lands to give us our greatest thrills and insights, yet we may notice that something interesting happens once we've arrived, settled, and been in these distinct places for a prolonged period: the mist of romantic allure that we imbued these places with and that originally ensnared us lifts and fades. We come to find that the mist was never there at all, that these places we instill with fairytale expectations eventually become just another commonplace experience, and a place we now understand a little more. They become familiar. It is interesting how we then shift our restless gaze back toward home or another far-off place and allow the same romanticizing phenomenon to begin to ensnare us once more, urging us to keep moving, to keep wondering and wandering: this is the wandering ethos that compels us to keep exploring. This is what it means to have wanderlust, a craving to put

EPILOGUE

the world together in our minds, coalescing like a constantly evolving puzzle. We will never be able to put it all together because life is too dynamic and vast, but we are nonetheless humbled by the depth of this world in reaching for the unattainable.

It then dawns on me that these yearnings and curiosity for adventure must be both inspired by our culture *and* deeply embedded in our biology. I can't help but return to wondering when it was that the first hominins, standing upright, looked beyond the horizon and felt the sparking sensations bolting through their brains and lifting the hair upon their skin, sincerely compelled to journey into the unknown just to see and feel what was there. Every day, regardless of where we are in the world, can be deemed an adventure so long as one's focus and imagination remain captivated by the unknown and unexplored. We have to fight to never lose this sense of wanderlust and keep handing it off to our children and each subsequent generation.

○

I owe a great deal of my identity and chosen career in archaeology and anthropology to two things: books and an insatiable appetite for travel and adventure. Though I can't claim to be as intrepid as Anthony Bourdain or Jacques Cousteau, and will never make it into The Explorers Club, I have spent an unusual amount of time researching and thinking heavily about the significance of travel and adventure for humanity. I have had my fair share of adventures throughout many regions of the United States, along with a handful of countries abroad at this point. By profession, I am an anthropologist and archaeologist.

AN ANTHROPOLOGY OF WANDERING

I am interested in the intricate way in which our behaviors, society, culture, and ideas are formed and influenced. The central anthropological question that intrigues me most and what I've wanted to explore with my readers in this book is why humans yearn for travel and adventure, how societies and cultures restrict or encourage their members to travel and explore, and how we might begin to restructure travel and adventure into our lives. What I wanted to learn about over ten years ago were the underlying anthropological and psychological reasons for going on an adventure like the Appalachian Trail. What was the meaning of this? Why did people feel compelled to do this? What did they have to say about their experiences while doing it? Underlying these questions on adventure in society brings us to one of the perennial questions of anthropology, namely, what is the relationship between the individual and society?

I am most intrigued by human groups that have taken many forms of social organization and gone by many classifications by academics—bands or tribes of hunters, gatherers, fishers, foragers—but are known most frequently in the popular consciousness as hunter-gatherers. In general, these are people who lived in small groups, acquired all their food from hunting, fishing, and foraging, and traveled consistently, albeit variably, throughout the year. This was our way of life up until yesterday, when we settled down and became more or less stationary, boxed in by many layers of borders, property boundaries, fences, and walls. Although there have been centuries of debate in philosophy and anthropology about what the "human condition" is—whether we are violent or peaceful at our core or whether nature (genetics) or nurture (society and culture) shape our behavior more—what I've come to learn and appreciate is that the reality is humans are highly variable and, most importantly, adaptable and resilient creatures dependent on a whole cacophony of internal and external variables.

Ultimately, it is yet to be seen whether our newly adopted forms of social, economic, and technological organization, i.e., urbanization, industrialization, and capitalism, will play out as the most conducive environment and system to our health and well-being. While these new systems have undoubtedly brought about tremendous benefits and opportunities for humankind's flourishing, I also believe we have lost something vitally important to who we've been in all our years of transitioning to our modern system, and we are severely impoverished because of it. Reframing how we think of ourselves and others has profound social and political implications. Restructuring how we participate and engage with that world in all its natural and cultural diversity is the vital first step we must take. This "anthropology of wandering," I hope, will help to reorient some of us toward more fruitful habits, values, and goals well into the future.

O

Years before our time on the Appalachian Trail, a romantic and restless dream had spawned in my undeveloped high school brain. I wanted to experience the life of a modern nomad, drunk on wanderlust, exploring our country and any other place on the globe that fate might whisk me away to. I had a resonant surge of inspiration when I first read Jon Krakauer's book *Into the Wild* and saw Sean Penn's 2007 film adaptation detailing the life of Christopher Johnson McCandless, a restive and idealistic young man (also coincidentally studying anthropology and history) in the early 1990s. In a Buddhist-like fashion, McCandless had forfeited his privilege, life savings of $25,000, relationships, social network, and predictable existence in favor of living a nomadic lifestyle on the road. This was an attempt to exempt himself from societal conformities, namely, consumerism, materialism, and the many inherent self-destructive and unjust elements of our society, as many an angst-ridden young man perceives it anyway.

Krakaeur's narrative captivated me immensely and aligned with my adolescent worldview as no other story had. I connected deeply to this ethos of *escaping* modernity, shunning our unjust society, and transcending a world I found insufferable and deeply flawed. Like McCandless, I, too, had been engrossed in the works of Thoreau, Emerson, and Tolstoy, along with much of the philosophy of anarcho-primitivism (think Ted Kaczynski minus the bombs). And like many restless teenagers, angry with so much of the world and the seemingly ludicrous system previous generations of adults had created, I yearned for an escape and to be free from the mindless societal games everyone else seemed to be unhappily playing—leading "lives of quiet desperation" as Thoreau would say. Breaking away from society was the closest thing to self-reliance and unadulterated liberty I could imagine at the time. I wasn't going to be a wage slave, beholden to the rat race like all the rest of these suckers in society, I told myself. *I* was going to transcend it all, commune with nature, and live in Zen-like bliss in the wilderness. *I* was going to be the one to crack the code of living life unencumbered by debt, mindless work, materialism, and unwanted responsibilities. Egotistical know-it-all? No question about it! But surely we all can sympathize with the fantasies and ideals of our youth. Such passion is important to cultivate, after all.

EPILOGUE

I thought I'd have the courage to go on a McCandless-esque voyage of my own after high school. I didn't. I entered community college and reluctantly began accumulating debt like everyone else by taking out too many student loans to learn an eclectic mix of psychology, history, philosophy, religion, literature, archaeology, anthropology, and architecture. In other words, I had no idea what I wanted to do. I was interested in just about everything and thought I was just biding my time before the great escape. I had plans to first make my way to one of my best friends' properties in eastern Kentucky in the foothills of the Appalachians. There, they had a remote cabin deep in the woods where I could begin training to live independently before making my way out to the western states. In the meantime, I was exercising and conditioning my body and mind in various ludicrous ways to endure what I anticipated would eventually be a harsh but rewarding lifestyle, living a wayfaring existence. As embarrassing as it is to admit now, I would do things like run barefoot on gravel and meditate in cold water (please don't ever ask me what the hell all this was about), and I learned to hunt and build traps (not very well, mind you) and identify wild plants for food. I told myself I'd break away from it all after this second stage of schooling. That didn't happen either.

Next, I ironically did the last thing someone hell-bent on self-reliance should do: I joined the military, the Air National Guard, that is. This didn't last long, though. I stuck around for a year, doing all the necessary pull-ups, sprints, rank-structure memorization, and bathroom mopping until I wised up, became my own self-appointed lawyer, read through the contract I had blindly signed, and got out on a technicality. I should have listened to my grandfather, a veteran of the Korean War, for he knew I had severe problems with authority and could not stand being told what to do. I joined for all the wrong reasons, and I'd concluded this path was certainly not for me. However, I was now more confident about what I wanted to do with my life, which was to study anthropology and archaeology, but fear and anxiety from somewhere had convinced me it wouldn't be wise or financially savvy (that last part is most certainly true by the way, you will never grow wealthy as an archaeologist no matter how much you dig in the dirt). Nevertheless, I committed to the study of these disciplines anyway and haven't entirely regretted it yet.

Although I was never daring enough to burn my money and catapult myself onto the road like McCandless, I came to inculcate a model of adventure into my life in my unique way. It turns out that following the model of someone else's life isn't all that bold or interesting anyway. In choreographing my life, I discovered a whole new set of adventures I never would have experienced had I followed a path of narrow reckless abandonment, as I now perceive some of McCandless's decision-making. Although I undoubtedly would have experienced a whole realm of adventures living the vagabond lifestyle I spent years planning for, looking back from the vantage point of where my life is now, I can't help but feel confident it would have likely been far more impoverished than the life I am leading.

Since meeting Hilary over a decade ago at our archaeological field school, we have found a sustainable way to incorporate adventure into our lives. We thru-hiked 1,300 miles of the Appalachian Trail in the summer of 2014 from Mt. Katahdin in Maine to northern Virginia, ending up in Shenandoah National Park. We spent three winters living in Steamboat Springs, Colorado, learning to ski and snowboard. I also spent those summers out west as an archaeologist, surveying and excavating all across parts of Montana and Wyoming, and spent a summer working with the Forest Service in Steamboat Springs, where I was paid to backpack throughout the Medicine Bow-Routt National Forest, conducting archaeological reconnaissance surveys. We embarked on many trips exploring the Colorado Rockies and the Utah desert during that time. We've been able to venture abroad on occasion to explore Italy, France, Belize, Guatemala, and Mexico together. Hilary and I moved in 2017 to Knoxville, Tennessee, where I continued cultivating my archaeological career, working throughout many southeastern states. In 2022, I earned my M.A. degree in anthropology at the University of Tennessee. Our son, Walden, was born in 2019, and we've since learned how to sustain our wanderlust as parents as we attempt to instill in him a love of travel and adventure, doing our best to keep him off the screens and out in the woods.

As any bibliophile knows, many books conspire together to shape who we are and how we think about the world. But *Into the Wild* wasn't just a book that inspired me; it was a book that propelled me into action and compelled me to live a life of adventure as best I could. If I'm being honest, on my more jaded days, I still feel like escaping from modernity. There's a lot in this world that still rankles me to the point where I no longer want to be a part of the messiness that is humanity. However, there's a funny thing about aging: When I first read about Christopher, I felt nothing but envy and admiration for the lifestyle he enacted. I remember thinking that he had probably witnessed far more beauty and adventure in his short sojourn than most of us do in a lifetime, and yet, as time has passed, I now feel a sense of pity for his early death and the impact that must have had on his family and friends. As contentious as some of his relationships appear to have been, I can't help but wonder if the risks he took were truly worth it in the end. There was so much more of life he had yet to cultivate, experience, and contribute to.

What I once imagined as the takeaway from this book was a young man living the adventurous life everyone else was scared to live and giving the middle finger to a broken, unjust society. As with many great stories, I now see this story very differently in my mid-thirties with a burgeoning family. There is a timeless tragedy, a deep sorrow wrapped up in Krakauer's story—McCandless is a symbol of passionate and intelligent, yet angry, self-righteous, damaged, and vulnerable youth. In the process of becoming adults, we easily forget what adolescence was like. Although there is a lot of variability in how each of us undergoes adolescence, there are overall shared qualities to the experience. It is a time of painful uncertainty and deep, directionless emotions as we search and grapple for our purpose and meaning. We mustn't forget that even the most privileged of youth suffer these maladies and can have fraught relationships, which adds to the depth and poignancy of Krakeur's tale of a very personal narrative. As young adults, we face a paradox in self-doubt as we are simultaneously conscious of our ignorance and inexperience, yet eager to prove our worth and value at a young age. What we dream for ourselves often conflicts with what parents and others in society may envision for us, and many of us have to fight like hell to gain some semblance of respect for carving our paths. Being young is never easy, and the world is often seen as ruthless, unjust, and unforgiving to us and others through the lens of our adolescent eyes, so much so that we act out in radical ways and desperately attempt to escape in whatever way will get us there, be it drugs, suicide, or physically running away. We need to remember that

EPILOGUE

underneath the veneer of all that adolescent angst and anger is a child simply trying to make sense of this world.

As adults, we have to be better at conveying to younger generations that if they can hold on long enough, there will be untold joys and adventures they cannot yet fathom. But how do we do so without being too patronizing? We must all learn to better channel the passions of our youth in ways that guide them toward living a life in balance within a world we all know is less-than-ideal. I could have easily been one of the many youths who threw it all away and been none the wiser. The challenge that remains for us all is how we can reach a better mental state of equanimity with the modern world in all its chaos and ugliness, rather than veering toward the longing to escape it. Despite my changing views on McCandless, I still share the sentiment that I believe is at the core of *Into the Wild*: that adventure has a much larger role to play in our personal lives and society than we may realize—one that is more wholesome, sustainable, and conducive to our well-being.

O

What I hope to have provided readers with is a yearning and zest to explore our world more intimately and to envision every day with a more adventurous lens. After all, so much of whether we will travel and have our adventures depends on more of us learning to value travel and adventure. I believe by peering through that lens, we will begin to alleviate our culture of fear. We are and have always been adventurers deep down, and we are resilient creatures at our core, though the comforts of a sedentary lifestyle have made us lethargic and amnesiac, causing many of us to forget these truisms of our species. Adventures require us to make more conscious efforts to engage with the world so that we may gain from the many perspectives humanity has to offer. Ultimately, wandering is a means toward greater social solidarity because we are forced to interact and engage with cultures, languages, lifestyles, and beliefs distinct from our own, and this forces us to reflect more heavily on our thinking and preconceptions of the world. Will adopting a wandering spirit lead to world peace? Probably not, but the more we engage with the world firsthand—in ways no longer purely mediated through the highly curated lens of social media and television—we may begin to feel a little less restless and a little less fearful of others, restoring some faith in our humanity.

One of the greatest epiphanies from our experience on the Appalachian Trail was looking back in hindsight at how wrong our past apprehensions were of such a grand experience of life. This is an insight analogous to so many other inexperienced moments in life that fill us with dread, urging us to avoid the risks and isolate from one another. Life has always been fraught with risk, and life will always be a dangerous business. But we shouldn't need a warning label for life. What we do need is perspective and nuance in our lives. We need to lean into risks sometimes, for there are also risks of not taking risks. As those who wander teach us, there are many unique things adventure has to offer a fearful culture. We must only be willing to see beyond our initial apprehensions and test the hypothesis of whether or not adventure can heighten or lessen our sense of fear. With more of us becoming engaged in living through our adventures, I believe we will eventually dissolve many of our apprehensions. And if we share the desire to build a truly sustainable cosmopolitan world where we are all citizens free to fearlessly wander and explore the only planet we've ever known, then we must take a more committed step by witnessing life in more adventurous ways. As counterintuitive as it may seem, perhaps we need to face what we are afraid of the most: the cold, the hunger, the sweat, tears, and blood. We need *to feel* these things to know we're still alive and breathing.

○

What direction would our lives have taken had we *not* followed through with our excursion on the Appalachian Trail and succumbed to our initial anxieties and fears? We assuredly would have a little less debt, more money in the bank, and perhaps more secure jobs, but I'm here to say I'm glad we chose an adventurous risk over the mundane and predictable security.

I thought it appropriate to revisit some of the questions I posed in the prologue before our hike and lend an answer to them in hindsight:

Q: What is this lifestyle like?

A: It's one of the most challenging (physically and mentally) yet liberating things we've done in life, and we do not regret it one bit. To prove to ourselves that we could live minimally in a fulfilling way has been deeply rewarding. The overarching lesson taken from this experience was to learn that the beginning of any journey will always be riddled with worry and fear, encouraging us not to go through with it, but that we, too, possess capabilities crafted into us by endless generations of evolution and cultural innovation that enable us to not only survive but thrive when challenges confront us.

Q: Did we enjoy it?
A: Undeniably yes.
Q: Did we hate it?
A: Undeniably yes. There were some incredibly stressful times, but fortunately, they weren't nearly as frequent as the good times. Take this balance to heart.

Q: Who did we meet?
A: I never expected to meet so many people with so much unconditional love, kindness, and openness in their hearts. The trail attracts and creates such a spectacular vision of humanity, a powerful sense of belonging and connectedness, that it feels quite surreal for a time, but eventually becomes the norm.

Q: What did their stories entail?
A: I was most taken aback by the inspiring stories so many openly shared with us. Many of the people we met were shaped by tragedy and suffering, but were also coupled with courage, hope, and optimism.

Q: How much did we change?
A: This one is still difficult to answer because I'm not quite sure how to gauge something like this, but I have gained greater confidence in myself and my abilities to always improve and push myself despite physical or mental hardships. I opened up to people more, which is always a struggle for the introverted. As for Hilary and me, we've connected far more intimately than we ever could have realized. Before this, we were separated for nearly six months as Hilary was studying abroad. So we went from being completely separated to seeing each other 24/7, which seemed to be the ultimate test of our relationship, and we're still together after 13 years, now happily married with our son, Walden.

Q: How often did we fight?

EPILOGUE

A: 1…2…87 times, I believe. I'm not sure how frequent it was, but compromise is very much a crucial thing to learn for couples or groups on such an excursion, and I think we managed to overcome our obstacles well, especially in the last couple of months.

Q: If we don't finish, does that mean we failed?

A: Not at all. We began the trail with a purist mentality, thinking we needed to cover every square inch of the trail to reveal all its secrets and for us to gain some proverbial full enlightenment of the experience. This isn't so. The prevailing motto rings true: "It's all about the journey, not the destination." Those who wander teach us that adventures should not be prepackaged experiences with a rigid set of goals to tick off, but left entirely open to allow, whatever happens, to happen. I don't feel guilty about our decision to end where we did. One of the major lessons from the trail and life itself is that so many unexpected things are going to occur, and some of those things are going to prevent you from obtaining deeply passionate goals. Like a Stoic philosopher or Buddhist monk, we must tune in to the things we have control over, and for those that we don't, don't worry about them. I've always struggled with things that went contrary to what I had planned, and to some extent, I still suffer the anxiety of it. However, I've come to accept more and more that these kinds of things are always going to occur in life, and the best I can do is accept and adapt when things are beyond my control. We set out for an adventure, and that's exactly what we had. The destination became a trivial matter in the end anyway, and I think that was one of the more salient things we both learned from the trail.

Q: Is this something worth doing?

A: Without a doubt, yes. I wrote this long-winded book on why it was, after all. There is an endless supply of experience and values to be drawn from hiking the trail, and that is not an exaggeration. I've done my best to relay this message throughout this book, but there are still many lessons that are difficult to capture in words alone. However, if you learn to venture forth on your own adventures, you will see what I mean.

Q: Were there regrets?

A: None. Well, perhaps starting with 60 pounds on my back was dumb.

Q: Were there rewards?

A: They were ceaseless and beyond words.

Q: Is this dangerous?

A: Irrelevant.

I still stand firmly behind the words written down the day we made our summit of Katahdin: *Whatever goal or dream one imagines pursuing, make it a reality because pure imagination alone can never fathom the truth and beauty of something left undone.*

○

You feel small when you walk a long way. The earth enhances to a size unrecognizably more vast and diverse than once assumed. Its inhabitants become more remarkable and no longer fit into neat, preconceived biases. It then becomes pretty silly to try to even brand individuals a certain way. Our previous apprehensions about this world severely come under scrutiny, and we begin to wonder if all this time, many of those fears and anxieties were lying to us, concocted by someone or something trying to keep us in place. We feel a little tricked and betrayed by a society and culture that seems bent on spooking us.

EPILOGUE

Where did those fears come from? Why were we so susceptible? Many things happen when we break away from the normalcy of everyday life to choreograph our adventures. We're less likely to conform to the consensus of what things are supposed to be feared and avoided. There is a sense that adventure and the need to explore our world is not just some trivial matter after all, say a vacation we need once in a while to decompress before returning to work, but something existential, intricately woven into our biology, evolution, and identity of being humans.

Society has had many great leaps forward in technology, communication, scientific discovery, medicine and health, social organization, and endless improvements to our well-being. So too do many problems persist as a consequence of modernity and human nature. We've designed an industrial and consumerist socioeconomic system dependent on finite, diminishing resources amidst a growing population and a destabilizing climate. Social inequality continues to limit human potential in seemingly inexorable ways. Fear seems to be getting the better of us, as we incessantly stay glued to our televisions and the internet. The lessons of those who wander encourage us to step back, breathe more deeply, and take more adventurous action in our lives—to witness more direct experiences. As we trek across the landscape and encounter Earth's many cultural perspectives, we become a little braver, a little more sensible, a little more informed, and a little more thoughtful and charitable to one another.

For a lot of us, the apocalypse seems imminent. When we examine the common themes comprising the modern media-industrial complex along with our contemporary popular culture, it often depicts a very unsettling future with humanity itself as the self-destructive villain, and we fall victim to a culture of fear, suffering from obsessive safety disorder. It must be said that many of these portrayals are merely based on fears that are often misconstrued and biased, filtered through the news that naturally selects for the worst aspects of humanity and what popular culture has discovered to attract us the most. Internally, this negativity is what our brains are primed to pay attention to the most. In the end, the world is largely how we perceive it. If all we perceive is violence, hatred, and misery, then the world is indeed violent, hateful, and miserable. However, we are not powerless. We are not helpless. We are not polluted. We are not parasites of the earth. We are not doomed. These jaded views come largely from sources beyond our immediate experiences, not from our own. And the future is yet to be written. We have agency, the ability to boldly act and re-engineer ourselves and the world. If we do not see the world for what it is, if we fail to interact and engage, if we are not compelled to gain new experiences, if we do not attempt to make connections with others, if we do not obtain the perspectives adventures can teach, if we suppress this innate urge within us—then we will only continue to succumb to such misperceptions, cynicism, and powerlessness. What's more, is that we'll passively allow our world to unfold with policies and customs predicated on such fears and misunderstandings. We'll become apathetic or nonchalant to the banning of groups in desperate need of our help and sympathy, and to the building of walls that will cloister us away from one another, all at our own expense, as we unwittingly suffer from our obsessive safety disorder.

Many people *must* live through an experience and feel it personally before understanding sets in. I obtained this poignant but subtle insight from a philosophy professor who stated that it is rare that one can simply *tell* someone something; that what they needed was to be *shown*, to see things, and to feel things for themselves directly. As captivating as our modern technology and culture are, there are still physical and emotional experiences that they cannot possibly substitute for. Technology is a supplement, not a surrogate for experiencing the world. The only way of reaching those experiences is *by making the journey and seeing it for ourselves with all our senses present.*

Our path to discoveries and new adventures has not ceased, nor has the path become too trodden. It is still vitally important for us as individuals and as a collective species to fill our time with new thrills in adventure. We can overcome irrational or unreasoned fear through wandering. Extensive travel will not exactly eliminate our fears, but in the end, it will result in having a more realistic and healthy relationship with what fear is and what it is not. From attempting to hike a new trail in your home county to daring to travel abroad for the first time to seeing some of those 1,000 places before we die, we inevitably feel a surge of empowerment and a connection with something deeply ingrained in our blood, some inexplicable source of adventure. If we are informed, well-prepared, and act wisely, there will be little left to fear and no adventure we cannot undertake.

END

NOTES

1 Mark Kelley, "Murder on the Appalachian Trail," August 1, 2014. http://adventurepossible.com/adventure/murder-on-the-appalachian-trail/

2 Bruce Chatwin, *Anatomy of Restlessness*, (New York: Viking, 1996), p. 75.

3 Alain de Botton. *The Art of Travel*, (New York: Vintage International, 2004), p. 9.

4 Bruce Chatwin, *Anatomy of Restlessness*, (New York: Viking, 1996), p. 102.

5 Ross E. Dunn, *The Adventures of Ibn Battuta: A Muslim Traveler of the 14th Century* (Berkley: University of California Press, 1986), pp. 30-1.

Chapter 1: Those Who Do Not Wander: Arriving Without Traveling

6 Emphasis added.

7 U.S. Department of Transportation, Federal Highway Administration (2024, October 3). *3.2 Trillion Miles Driven On U.S. Roads In 2016.* www.fhwa.dot.gov/policyinformation/statistics/2022

8 https://www.bts.gov/topics/national-transportation-statistics

9 The Chapman University Survey on American Fears (2016, October 11). *Fear of Terrorism Impacts Travel Plans, Everyday Lives of Americans.* https://blogs.chapman.edu/wilkinson/2016/10/11/fear-of-terrorism-impacts-travel-plans-everyday-lives-of-americans/

10 U.S. Department of State, Bureau of Consular Affairs (2017, February

17). *U.S. Citizen Deaths Overseas.* https://travel.state.gov/content/travel/en/international-travel/while-abroad/death-abroad1/death-statistics.html

11 *Ibid.*

12 National Travel and Tourism Office (2017, February 17). *U.S. Outbound Travel.* https://travel.trade.gov/outreachpages/download_data_table/2015_Outbound_Analysis.pdf

13 Sidney W. Mintz, *Sweetness and Power: The Place of Sugar in Modern History* (New York: Penguin Books, 1986), pp. 202-203.

14 Rebecca Solnit, *Wanderlust: A History of Walking* (New York: Penguin Group, 2000), p. 10.

15 U.S. Department of State, Bureau of Consular Affairs (2023, February 21). *Valid Passports in Circulation (1988-2022).* https://travel.state.gov/content/passports/en/passports/statistics.html

16 Department of Homeland Security, U.S. Customs and Border Protection (2023, February 21). *Western Hemisphere Travel Initiative.* https://www.cbp.gov/travel/us-citizens/western-hemisphere-travel-initiative

17 National Travel and Tourism Office (2017, February 17). *U.S. Outbound Travel.* https://travel.trade.gov/outreachpages/download_data_table/2015_Outbound_Analysis.pdf

18 Luis A. Vivanco and Robert J. Gordon, *Tarzan was an Ecotourist…and Other Tales in the Anthropology of Adventure* (New York: Bergham Press, 2006), pp. 217-234.

19 Lawrence H. Keeley, *War Before Civilization: The Myth of the Peaceful Savage* (New York: Oxford University Press, 1996), pp. 164-5.

20 National Travel and Tourism Office (2017, February 17). *U.S. Travel Abroad.* http://travel.trade.gov/outreachpages/download_data_table/2012_US_Travel_Abroad.pdf

21 U.S. Department of State, Bureau of Consular Affairs (2023, February 21). *Valid Passports in Circulation (1988-2022).* https://travel.state.gov/content/passports/en/passports/statistics.html

22 National Travel and Tourism Office (2017, February 17). *U.S. Travel Abroad.* http://travel.trade.gov/outreachpages/download_data_ta-

ble/2012_US_Travel_Abroad.pdf

23 "Where Will Americans Travel in 2015?," *New York Times*, January 11, 2015. https://www.nytimes.com/2015/01/11/travel/where-will-americans-travel-in-2015-.html?_r=1

24 Department of the Interior, National Park Service (2017, February 17). *Annual Visitation to National Parks*. https://www.nps.gov/aboutus/faqs.htm

25 National Travel and Tourism Office (2017, February 17). *U.S. Travel Abroad*. http://travel.trade.gov/outreachpages/download_data_table/2012_US_Travel_Abroad.pdf

26 American's State Parks (2017, February 17). *State Park Facts*. http://www.americasstateparks.org/About

27 Abbey, Edward. *Desert Solitaire: A Season in the Wilderness*. (Ballantine Books: New York, 1971) pp. 63-4.

28 "How to Score a Middle Fork of the Salmon River Permit and Plan the Ultimate Trip," *Paddling Magazine*, October 23, 2024.

29 "Why more Americans don't travel abroad," *CNN*, February 4, 2011. http://www.cnn.com/2011/TRAVEL/02/04/americans.travel.domestically/

30 "America's Great Passport Divide," *The Atlantic*, March 15, 2011. https://www.theatlantic.com/national/archive/2011/03/americas-great-passport-divide/72399/

31 *Ibid.*

32 "The Average Cost of Airfare: How Much Is a Plane Ticket?" *The Motley Fool,* April 14, 2025. https://www.fool.com/money/research/average-cost-of-airfare/#:~:text=86%20on%20average).-,International%20airfare%20price%20statistics,to%20FCM%20and%20Corporate%20Traveler.

33 "The Average Cost of a Vacation in 2025: Trends and Statistics," *The Motley Fool,* April 2, 2025. https://www.fool.com/money/research/average-cost-of-a-vacation/#:~:text=On%20average%2C%20the%20daily%20cost,trip%20costs%20%24923%20per%20day.

34 "Don't Toss That Sour Milk! And Other Tips To Cut Kitchen Food Waste," *NPR*, September 23, 2015. https://www.npr.org/sections/the-salt/2015/09/23/441460163/don-t-toss-that-sour-milk-10-tips-cut-food-waste-in-your-kitchen

35 Juliet B. Schor, *The Overspent American: Why We Want What We Don't Need* (New York: Basic Books, 1998) p. 68.

36 *Ibid.*, p. 80.

37 "Why Americans Don't Travel Overseas," *Nomadic Matt*, October 10, 2017. http://www.nomadicmatt.com/travel-blogs/why-americans-dont-travel-overseas/

Chapter 2: Those Who Wander: The Restless Few

38 Zach Davis, "21 Appalachian Trail Statistics That Will Surprise, Entertain and Inform You," *REI*, July 28, 2015. https://www.rei.com/blog/hike/21-appalachian-trail-statistics-that-will-surprise-entertain-and-inform-you

39 "2,000-milers," *Appalachian Trail Conservancy*, February 22, 2023. http://www.appalachiantrail.org/home/community/2000-milers

40 David Brill, *As Far As the Eye Can See: Reflections of an Appalachian Trail Hiker,* (University of Tennessee Press: Knoxville, 2020), pp. 53-4.

41 David Reich, *Who We Are and How We Got Here: Ancient DNA and The New Science of the Human Past* (New York: Vintage, 2018), p. 82.

42 See Ralph Linton, *The Tree of Culture* (New York: Alfred A. Knopf, 1955), p. 46; White, Leslie A., *The Evolution of Culture: The Development of Civilization to the Fall of Rome* (New York: McGraw-Hill, 1959), p. 271, 320-1, 334.

43 Ralph Linton, *The Tree of Culture* (New York: Alfred A. Knopf, 1955), p. 46. Emphasis added.

44 Bronislaw Malinowski, "Kula: The Circulating Exchange of Valuables in the Archipelagoes of Eastern New Guinea," *Man*, 20: 97–105, July 1920.

45 George Simmel, "The Adventure" In *Simmel on Culture: Selected Writings,* edited by David Frisby and Mike Featherstone, London: Sage, 1997, p. 226.

46 *Ibid.,* p. xvi.

47 Jon Krakauer, *Into Thin Air* (New York: Anchor Books, 1997), p. 23.

48 Robert Moor, *On Trails: An Exploration* (New York: Simon & Schuster, 2016), p. 245.

49 David Brill, *As Far As the Eye Can See: Reflections of an Appalachian Trail Hiker,* (University of Tennessee Press: Knoxville, 2020), pp. 54-5.

50 Alain de Botton, *The Art of Travel,* (New York: Vintage International, 2004), p. 150.

51 "Safety," *Appalachian Trail Conservancy,* February 22, 2023. https://appalachiantrail.org/explore/plan-and-prepare/hiking-basics/safety/

52 "Mark Sanford extramarital affair," *Wikipedia,* February 22, 2023. https://en.wikipedia.org/wiki/Mark_Sanford_extramarital_affair

53 Earl V. Shaffer, *Walking With Spring* (West Virginia: Appalachian Trail Conference, 2004), p. 8.

54 "Warrior Hike," *Warrior Expeditions,* February 22, 2023. http://warriorhike.org/

55 Mihaly Csikszentmihalyi. *Flow: The Psychology of Optimal Experience* (New York: Harper & Row, 1990), p. 4.

56 Joshua Slocum, *Sailing Alone Around the World* (New York: Dover Books, 1956), p. vii.

Chapter 3: Perspectives Through Adventure: Grappling With Change and Continuity

57 Luis A. Vivanco and Robert J. Gordon, *Tarzan was an Ecotourist...and Other Tales in the Anthropology of Adventure* (New York: Bergham Press, 2006), p. 3. Emphasis added.

58 *Ibid.*

59 *Science*, Vol. 352, No. 6288 Special Issue: Urban Planet, pp. 904-47.

60 See TED talk on procrastination by Tim Urban, creator of the science and technology blog *Wait But Why*: https://www.youtube.com/watch?v=arj7oStGLkU

61 Alvin Toffler, *Future Shock* (New York: Bantam Books, 1990), p. 75.

62 Steven Pinker, *The Better Angels of our Nature: Why Violence Has Declined* (New York: Penguin, 2011), p. 657.

63 Olivia Solon, "The God Complex: How Big Data Will Fuel a New Religion," *Wired*, March 2017.

64 Rebecca Solnit, *Wanderlust: A History of Walking* (New York: Penguin Group, 2000), p. 251.

65 *Ibid.*, p. 253.

66 Hans Rosling, Ola Rosling, and Anna Rosling, *Factfulness: Ten Reasons We're Wrong About the World—And Why Things Are Better Than You Think* (New York: Flatiron Books, 2018), p. 62; Steven Pinker, *Enlightenment Now: The Case for Reason, Science, Humanism, and Progress* (New York: Viking, 2018), pp. 132-3.

67 Ulysses S. Grant, *Personal Memoirs, Chapter II,* February 22, 2023. https://americanliterature.com/author/ulysses-s-grant/book/personal-memoirs-of-us-grant/chapter-ii

68 Rebecca Solnit, *Wanderlust: A History of Walking* (New York: Penguin Group, 2000), p. 257.

69 Paul Salopek, "Mapping Police Stops on a World Walk," *National Geographic*, November 12, 2015. https://www.nationalgeographic.org/projects/out-of-eden-walk/articles/2015-11-mapping-police-stops-on-a-world-walk/

70 This is contested in the data presented by Steven Pinker's *Enlightenment Now*, p. 249 that demonstrates an overall decline in the number of work hours over the last century and a half suggesting we work 22 hours fewer now. Also see pages 255-6 on increased leisure time.

71 Rebecca Solnit, *Wanderlust: A History of Walking* (New York: Penguin Group, 2000), pp. 257-259.

72 This is a useful GIS tool and fascinating way to compare historic maps with the present to see how the landscape has changed over time: https://ngmdb.usgs.gov/topoview/

73 Paul Zweig, *The Adventurer: The Fate of Adventure in the Western World* (New York: Akadine Press, 1999), pp. 5-6.

74 Ibid., p. viii.

75 Gordon S. Wood, *The Radicalism of the American Revolution* (New York: Vintage Books, 1993), p. 347.

76 Aries, Philippe, and Georges Duby. *A History of Private Life: From Pagan Rome to Byzantium.* (Cambridge, Mass.: Belknap Press 1987), p. 188.

77 Allen Abramson and Robert Fletcher, "Recreating the vertical: Rock-climbing as epic and deep eco-play, *Anthropology today,* 23.6 (2007): 3-7.

78 Johan Huizinga, *Homo Ludens: A Study of the Play Element in Culture* (London: Beacon Press, 1966), p. 13.

79 Bertrand Russell, 'What I Believe' in *Why I Am Not a Christian* (New York: Simon & Schuster, 1957), p. 85.

Chapter 4: A Nation Suffering from OSD (Obsessive Safety Disorder): Context for Our Brave New World

80 Robert M. Sapolsky (1994), "Individual differences and the stress response," *Seminars in Neuroscience,* Vol. 6, No. 4, pp. 261-269.

81 Hans Rosling, Ola Rosling, and Anna Rosling, *Factfulness: Ten Reasons We're Wrong About the World—And Why Things Are Better Than You Think* (New York: Flatiron Books, 2018), pp. 50-1.

82 "500 Million But Not A Single One More," *Effective Altruism*, December 9, 2014. https://forum.effectivealtruism.org/posts/jk7A3NMdbxp65k-cJJ/500-million-but-not-a-single-one-more; Sophie Ochmann and Max Roser (2018) – "Smallpox." Published online at OurWorldInData.org. Retrieved from: https://ourworldindata.org/smallpox

83 See Errol Morris's 2016 op-doc *The Demon in the Freezer* on the question of smallpox's continued existence in controlled facilities.

84 "Who Saved the Most Lives in History?" *Science Heroes*. http://science-heroes.com/

85 Joshua S. Goldstein, *Winning the War on War: The Decline of Armed Conflict Worldwide* (Dutton/Penguin Books, 2011), pp. 310; U.S. Department of Defense (2018). "DoD Releases Fiscal Year 2018 Budget Proposal," Retrieved from: http://comptroller.defense.gov/Portals/45/Documents/defbudget/fy2018/fy2018_Press_Release.pdf

86 Luis A. Vivanco and Robert J. Gordon, *Tarzan was an Ecotourist...and Other Tales in the Anthropology of Adventure* (New York: Bergham Press, 2006), p. 4.

87 Frank Furedi, *The Culture of Fear Revisited* (London: Continuum, 2006), p. 26.

88 Lenore Skenazy, "Suburban Mom Handcuffed, Jailed for Making 8-Year-Old Son Walk Half a Mile Home," *Reason*, November 16, 2022. https://reason.com/2022/11/16/suburban-mom-jailed-handcuffed-cps-son-walk-home/

89 Frank Furedi, *The Culture of Fear Revisited* (London: Continuum, 2006), p. 26.

90 Luis A. Vivanco and Robert J. Gordon, *Tarzan was an Ecotourist...and Other Tales in the Anthropology of Adventure* (New York: Bergham Press, 2006), p. 4.

91 "Christopher Hitchens [2005] Why Orwell Matters." *YouTube*, uploaded by The Hitchens Archive 24 April 2014, https://www.youtube.com/watch?v=rY5Ste5xRAA

92 Frank Furedi, *The Culture of Fear Revisited* (London: Continuum, 2006), p. 5.

93 *Ibid.*, p. 25.

94 Paige Pfleger, "Thumbs Up, Then and Now: Hitchhiking Stories from the Road," *NPR*, August 9, 2015. http://www.npr.org/2015/08/09/430079847/thumbs-up-then-and-now-hitchhiking-stories-from-the-road

95 For advice on safely hitchhiking in the United States see: https://www.nomadicmatt.com/travel-blogs/hitchhike-across-united-states/

NOTES

96 "The United States Spends More on Defense than the Next 9 Countries Combined," Retrieved from: https://www.pgpf.org/article/the-united-states-spends-more-on-defense-than-the-next-9-countries-combined/

97 International Institute for Strategic Studies, *The Military Balance* (2018). https://www.iiss.org/en/publications/military%20balance; Stockholm International Peace Research Institute, *SIPRI Military Expenditure Database* (2018). http://www.sipri.org/research/armaments/milex/milex_database

98 Barry Glassner, *Culture of Fear: Why Americans Are Afraid of the Wrong Things* (New York: Basic Books, 2009), p. xii.

99 *Ibid.*, p. xiv.

100 Frank Furedi, *The Culture of Fear Revisited* (London: Continuum, 2006), p. x.

101 "Terrorism," Retrieved from https://ourworldindata.org/terrorism

102 Steven Pinker, *Enlightenment Now: The Case for Reason, Science, Humanism, and Progress* (New York: Viking, 2018), p. 193.

103 *Ibid.*, p. 197.

104 "Motor vehicle fatality rate in U.S. by year," *Wikipedia*, February 22, 2023. https://en.wikipedia.org/wiki/List_of_motor_vehicle_deaths_in_U.S._by_year

105 Linda Qui, "Fact-checking a comparison of gun deaths and terrorism deaths," *PolitiFact*, October 5, 2015. http://www.politifact.com/truth-o-meter/statements/2015/oct/05/viral-image/fact-checking-comparison-gun-deaths-and-terrorism-/

106 Hans Rosling, Ola Rosling, and Anna Rosling, *Factfulness: Ten Reasons We're Wrong About the World—And Why Things Are Better Than You Think* (New York: Flatiron Books, 2018), p. 121.

107 Centers for Disease Control and Prevention, *Suicide Data and Statistics*, February 22, 2023. https://www.cdc.gov/suicide/suicide-data-statistics.html

108 *Science* 6 May 2016 Vol. 352 Issue 6286 p. 634.

109 Nina Martin and Renee Montagne, "The Last Person You'd Expect To Die In Childbirth," *NPR*, May 12, 2017. https://www.npr.org/2017/05/12/527806002/focus-on-infants-during-childbirth-leaves-u-s-moms-in-danger?utm_source=facebook.com&utm_medium=social&utm_campaign=npr&utm_term=nprnews&utm_content=20170512

110 Death Penalty Information Center, *Executions by State and Year*, February 22, 2023. http://www.deathpenaltyinfo.org/executions-year

111 Centers for Disease Control and Prevention, *Chronic Disease Data*, February 22, 2023. http://www.cdc.gov/chronicdisease/overview/

112 MedHelp, *Common Causes of Death*, February 22, 2023. https://www.medhelp.org/general-health/articles/The-25-Most-Common-Causes-of-Death/193?page

113 Daniel Gardner, *The Science of Fear: How the Culture of Fear Manipulates Your Brain* (New York: Penguin) 2009), p. 13.

114 Gavin de Becker, *The Gift of Fear* (New York: Dell Publishing, 1997), p. 150.

115 Gwyneth Cravens, *Power to Save the World: The Truth about Nuclear Energy* (New York: Vintage Books, 2007), p. 271.

Chapter 5: Our Ancient Brains Meet the Brave New World: Evolutionary Baggage and Cognitive Bias

116 Steven Pinker, *The Better Angels of Our Nature: Why Violence Has Declined* (New York: Penguin, 2011), p. 128.

117 See Steven Pinker's *The Better Angels of Our Nature: Why Violence Has Declined.*

118 Lawrence H. Keeley, *War Before Civilization: The Myth of the Peaceful Savage* (New York: Oxford University Press, 1996). For a synthesis of Keeley's findings and the parallels and differences of human violence compared with other great ape species see Lectures 1-3 on the free Open Yale Course 'Global Problems of Population Growth' taught by Professor Robert Wyman: http://oyc.yale.edu/molecular-cellular-and-developmental-biology

119 Joshua S. Goldstein, "Think Again: War," *Foreign Policy*, August 15, 2011. http://foreignpolicy.com/2011/08/15/think-again-war/; Joshua S. Goldstein and Steven Pinker, "War Really is Going Out of Style," *New York Times*, December 17, 2011. https://www.nytimes.com/2011/12/18/opinion/sunday/war-really-is-going-out-of-style.html?_r

120 *Ibid.*, p. 179.

121 Lawrence H. Keeley, *War Before Civilization: The Myth of the Peaceful Savage* (New York: Oxford University Press, 1996), p. 169.

122 Gavin de Becker, *The Gift of Fear* (New York: Dell Publishing, 1997), p. 327.

123 Steven Pinker, "The Dangers of Worrying About Doomsday," *The Globe and Mail*, February 24, 2018. https://www.theglobeandmail.com/opinion/the-dangers-of-worrying-about-doomsday/article38062215/

124 Hans Rosling, Ola Rosling, and Anna Rosling, *Factfulness: Ten Reasons We're Wrong About the World—And Why Things Are Better Than You Think* (New York: Flatiron Books, 2018); Steven Pinker, *The Better Angels of Our Nature: Why Violence Has Declined* (New York: Penguin, 2011); *Enlightenment Now: The Case for Reason, Science, Humanism, and Progress* (New York: Viking, 2018); Joshua S. Goldstein, *Winning the War on War: The Decline of Armed Conflict Worldwide* (Dutton/Penguin Books, 2011); Mihaly Csikszentmihalyi. *Flow: The Psychology of Optimal Experience* (New York: Harper & Row, 1990), p. 1; Greg Lukianoff and Jonathan Haidt, *The Coddling of the American Mind: How Good Intentions and Bad Ideas Are Setting Up a Generation for Failure* (New York: Penguin Group, 2018).

125 Frank Furedi, *The Culture of Fear Revisited* (London: Continuum, 2006); Daniel Gardner, *The Science of Fear: How the Culture of Fear Manipulates Your Brain* (New York: Penguin) 2009); Barry Glassner, *Culture of Fear: Why Americans Are Afraid of the Wrong Things* (New York: Basic Books, 2009).

126 Wikipedia, *List of Cognitive Biases*, June 23, 2023. https://en.wikipedia.org/wiki/List_of_cognitive_biases

127 Barry Glassner, *Culture of Fear: Why Americans Are Afraid of the Wrong Things* (New York: Basic Books, 2009), p. xxiii.

128 Gavin de Becker, *The Gift of Fear* (New York: Dell Publishing, 1997), p. 31.

129 *Ibid.*, p. 10.

130 Daniel Gardner, *The Science of Fear: How the Culture of Fear Manipulates Your Brain* (New York: Penguin) 2009), p. 17.

131 Daniel Kahneman, *Thinking Fast and Slow* (New York: Macmillan, 2011), p. 301.

132 *Ibid.*

133 Gavin de Becker, *The Gift of Fear* (New York: Dell Publishing, 1997), p. 44.

134 Greg Downey and Daniel H. Lende, *The Encultured Brain: An Introduction to Neuroanthropology* (Massachusetts: MIT Press, 2012), pp. 103-137.

135 Frank Furedi, *The Culture of Fear Revisited* (London: Continuum, 2006), pp. ix-x.

136 Hans Rosling, Ola Rosling, and Anna Rosling, *Factfulness: Ten Reasons We're Wrong About the World—And Why Things Are Better Than You Think* (New York: Flatiron Books, 2018), p. 14.

137 Daniel Gardner, *The Science of Fear: How the Culture of Fear Manipulates Your Brain* (New York: Penguin) 2009), pp. 67-8.

138 *Ibid.*, pp. 125-7.

139 Paul Rozin and Edward B. Royzman (2001), "Negativity bias, negativity dominance, and contagion," *Personality and Social Psychology Review.* 5 (4): 296–320.

140 *Ibid.*

141 J. R. Averill, (1980), "On the paucity of positive emotions". In K. R. Blankstein, P. Pliner, & J. Polivy (Eds.), *Advances in the study of communication and affect*, Vol. 6 (p. 745). New York: Plenum.

142 Steven Pinker, *Enlightenment Now: The Case for Reason, Science, Humanism, and Progress* (New York: Viking, 2018), p. 48.

143 Daniel Gardner, *The Science of Fear: How the Culture of Fear Manipulates Your Brain* (New York: Penguin) 2009), p. 3.

144 *Ibid.*; Gerd Gigerenzer, "Out of the frying pan into the fire: behavioral

reactions to terrorist attacks," *Risk Analysis,* April 26, 2006. https://www.ncbi.nlm.nih.gov/pubmed/16573625

145 Frank Furedi, *The Culture of Fear Revisited* (London: Continuum, 2006), p. 33.

146 Amos Tversky and Daniel Kahneman (1973), "Availability: A Heuristic for Judging Frequency and Probability," *Cognitive Psychology 5,* 207-232.

147 Daniel Gardner, *The Science of Fear: How the Culture of Fear Manipulates Your Brain* (New York: Penguin) 2009), p. 49.

148 Haidt, Jonathan, *The Righteous Mind: Why Good People Are Divided By Politics and Religion.* (New York: Vintage Books, 2012), p. 364.

149 Jonathan Glover, *Humanity: A Moral History of the 20th Century* (Connecticut: Yale University Press, 2012), pp. 141-8.

150 *Ibid.,* p. 33.

151 *Ibid.,* pp. 31-9.

152 *Ibid.,* pp. 342-3.

153 "List of cognitive biases," *Wikipedia,* February 22, 2023. https://en.wikipedia.org/wiki/List_of_cognitive_biases

154 Steven Pinker, *The Better Angels of Our Nature: Why Violence Has Declined* (New York: Penguin, 2011), p. xxii.

155 *Ibid.* p. xxvi.

156 For an in depth look on this topic see Steven Pinker's *The Better Angels of Our Nature: Why Violence Has Declined.*

157 See Steven Pinker's *The Better Angels of our Nature* and *Enlightenment Now* along with Hans Rosling's *Factfulness* and Joshua Goldstein's *Winning the War on War* for a subset of the "progressive literature."

158 Supplementary list of "progress literature" titles: *Mass Flourishing; The Great Surge; The Great Convergence; The Big Ratchet; The End of Doom; Getting Better; The Moral Arc; Abundance; The Great Escape; The Improving State of the World; The Case for Rational Optimism; The Infinite Resource; The Progress Paradox; Progress; The Rational Optimist; Utopia for Realists; The Expanding Circle.*

159 Chris Michaud, "One in seven thinks end of world is coming: poll," *Reuters,* May 1, 2012. http://www.reuters.com/article/us-mayancalendar-poll-idUSBRE8400XH20120501

160 Rebecca Riffkin, "Americans Name Terrorism as No. 1 U.S. Problem," *Gallup,* December 14, 2015. http://www.gallup.com/poll/187655/americans-name-terrorism-no-problem.aspx

161 Hans Rosling, Ola Rosling, and Anna Rosling, *Factfulness: Ten Reasons We're Wrong About the World—And Why Things Are Better Than You Think* (New York: Flatiron Books, 2018), p. 121.

162 *Ibid.,* p. 141.

163 *Ibid.,* p. 69.

Chapter 6: Media and the Modern Paradox: Paranoia and Confusion in the Age of Information

164 Alvin Toffler, *Powershift* (New York: Bantam Books, 1990), p. 328.

165 Barry Glassner, *Culture of Fear: Why Americans Are Afraid of the Wrong Things* (New York: Basic Books, 2009), p. xxviii.

166 *Ibid.,* p. xxix.

167 Martin Gurri, *The Revolt of the Public and the Crisis of Authority in the New Millenium* (San Franscisco: Stripe Press, 2018), pp. 20-1.

168 "Big Data, for better or worse: 90% of world's data generated over last two years," *Science Daily,* May 22, 2013. http://www.sciencedaily.com/releases/2013/05/130522085217.htm

169 *Ibid.*

170 Alvin Toffler, *Future Shock* (New York: Bantam Books, 1990), p. 161 and *The Third Wave* (New York: Bantam Books, 1990), p. 158.

171 Alvin Toffler, *Future Shock* (New York: Bantam Books, 1990), p. 161.

172 See Clifford Geertz's essays in *The Interpretation of Culture* for an in depth look into symbolic anthropology.

173 "BS is everywhere by Jon Stewart" *YouTube,* uploaded by Mohammed

NOTES

Husnat, August 21, 2015, https://www.youtube.com/watch?v=lz3jn-wbSFAU

174 David Bornstein and Tina Rosenburg, "When Reportage Turns to Cynicism," *New York Times*, November 14, 2016. http://www.nytimes.com/2016/11/15/opinion/when-reportage-turns-to-cynicism.html?_r=1

175 Letter from John Adams to James Warren, May 12, 1776.

176 Alvin Toffler, *Powershift* (New York: Bantam Books, 1990), p. 326.

177 Frank Furedi, *The Culture of Fear Revisited* (London: Continuum, 2006), p. 60.

178 Hans Rosling, Ola Rosling, and Anna Rosling, *Factfulness: Ten Reasons We're Wrong About the World—And Why Things Are Better Than You Think* (New York: Flatiron Books, 2018), p. 211.

179 Alvin Toffler, *Future Shock* (New York: Bantam Books, 1990), pp. 156-7.

180 Sisyphus, the reader may recall from Greek mythology, due to his trickery and hubris in declaring himself more genius that Zeus was condemned to roll a giant boulder up a steep hill merely to watch it roll down and must repeat the process for eternity. The term *Sisyphean* is used metaphorically to refer to tasks that are futile and seemingly endless. However, as Albert Camus declared in *The Myth of Sisyphus*, though life may be absurd, "One must imagine Sisyphus happy."

Chapter 7: Agents of Fear: Responsibility, Trust, and the Choices We Make

181 See https://oyc.yale.edu/philosophy/phil-181/lecture-1 for a good illustration of the Trolley Problem and variations of this moral conundrum.

182 Paul Salopek, "Lost and Found (Alas) in Jeddah," *National Geographic*, July 9, 2013. https://www.nationalgeographic.org/projects/out-of-eden-walk/blogs/lab-talk/2013-07-lost-and-found-alas-jeddah

183 *Ibid.*, p. xvii.

184 "Great Pacific Garbage Patch," *National Geographic*. https://education.nationalgeographic.org/resource/great-pacific-garbage-patch

185 Frank Furedi, *The Culture of Fear Revisited* (London: Continuum, 2006), p. ix.

186 *Ibid.*, p. 4.

187 Max Roser (2015) – "Trust." Published online at OurWorldInData.org. Retrieved from: http://ourworldindata.org/data/culture-values-and-society/trust/

188 Justin McCarthy, "Trust in Government to Protect Against Terrorism at New Low," *Gallup*, December 11, 2015. http://www.gallup.com/poll/187622/trust-government-protect-against-terrorism-new-low.aspx?g_source=fear&g_medium=search&g_campaign=tiles

189 Barry Glassner, *Culture of Fear: Why Americans Are Afraid of the Wrong Things* (New York: Basic Books, 2009), p. xx.

190 Robin S. Rosenberg, "Abnormal is the New Normal," *Slate*, April 12, 2013.

191 Jean M. Twenge, W. Keith Campbell, and Nathan T. Carter (2014), "Declines in trust in others and confidence in institutions among American adults and late adolescents, 1972–2012," *Psychological Science*, 25 (10), 1914-1923.

192 Josh Morgan, "The Decline of Trust in the United States," *Medium*, May 20, 2014. https://medium.com/@slowerdawn/the-decline-of-trust-in-the-united-states-fb8ab719b82a#.w03nqxu3n

193 *Ibid.*

194 *Ibid.*

195 U.S. Bureau of Labor Statistics, *American Time Use Survey*, February 17, 2017. http://www.bls.gov/tus/charts/chart9.pdf

196 *Ibid.*

197 F. Thomas Juster, Hiromi Ono, and Frank Stafford, "Changing Times of American Youth: 1981–2003," *Institute for Social Research*, November 2004. https://www.researchgate.net/publication/260403511_Changing_times_of_American_youth_1981-2003

NOTES

198 Victoria J. Rideout, Ulla G. Foehr, and Donald F. Roberts "Generation M2: Media in the Lives of 8–18-Year Olds," The Henry J Kaiser Family Foundation Report (2010). http://www.kff.org/entmedia/8010.cfm

199 Chris Weller, "Here's Why It Feels Like You Have No Free Time, In One Chart," *IFLScience*, May 18, 2017. http://www.iflscience.com/editors-blog/heres-why-it-feels-like-you-have-no-free-time-in-one-chart/

200 Rhitu Chatterjee, "Americans Are A Lonely Lot, And Young People Bear The Heaviest Burden," *NPR*, March 1, 2018. https://www.npr.org/sections/health-shots/2018/05/01/606588504/americans-are-a-lonely-lot-and-young-people-bear-the-heaviest-burden

Chapter 8: The Tradeoffs of Adventure, Part I: The Benefits of Wandering

201 Gregory N. Bratman, J. Paul Hamilton, Kevin S. Hahn, Gretchen C. Daily, and James J. Gross (2015) , "Nature experience reduces rumination and subgenual prefrontal cortex activation," *PNAS* 2015 112 (28) 8567-8572. http://www.pnas.org/content/112/28/8567

202 *Ibid.*

203 Terry Hartig and Peter H. Kahn Jr. (2016), "Living in cities, naturally," *Science* Vol. 352 No. 6288, 938-940.

204 Ruth Ann Atchley, David L. Strayer, and Paul Atchley (2012), "Creativity in the Wild: Improving Creative Reasoning through Immersion in Natural Settings," *PLOS ONE* 7(12): e51474. https://doi.org/10.1371/journal.pone.0051474

205 Frances E. Kuo and Andrea Faber Taylor (2004), "A potential natural treatment for attention-deficit/hyperactivity disorder: evidence from a national study," *American Journal of Public Health*, 94(9), 1580–1586. https://www.ncbi.nlm.nih.gov/pmc/articles/PMC1448497/

206 Visit https://www.nomadicmatt.com/travel-blogs/why-solo-travel/ for further advice and links on solo traveling.

207 Bill Bryson, *A Walk in the Woods: Rediscovering America on the Appalachian Trail* (New York: Broadway Books, 1998), p. 55.

208 Alana Semuels, "We Are All Accumulating Mountains of Things," *The Atlantic*, August 21, 2018. https://www.theatlantic.com/technology/archive/2018/08/online-shopping-and-accumulation-of-junk/567985/

209 *Ibid.*

210 *Ibid.*

211 *Ibid.*

212 The term suggested here is most inferred from the work of Victor Turner, more specifically the definition of *existential* or *spontaneous communitas*.

213 Peter Singer, *The Expanding Circle: Ethics, Evolution, and Moral Progress* (New Jersey: Princeton University Press, 2011), p. 120.

214 Frans de Waal, *The Age of Empathy: Nature's Lessons for a Kinder Society* (New York: Random House, 2009), pp. 203-4.

Chapter 9: The Tradeoffs of Adventure, Part II: The Challenges of Wandering

215 William H.R. Rivers, "The genealogical method of anthropological enquiry. *Sociological Review*, 3:1-11 (1910) in *Readings in Kinship and Social Structure* edited by Nelson Graburn (New York: Harper & Row Publishers, 1971).

216 Bronislaw Malinowski, *The Argonauts of the Western Pacific* (Illinois: Waveland Press, Inc., 1984), p. xvi.

217 Joseph Epes Brown, *The Spiritual Legacy of the American Indian* (Bloomington, Indiana: World Wisdom, 2007), p. 46.

218 Joe Watkins, "Bone Lickers, Grave Diggers, and Other Unsavory Characters: Archaeologists, Archaeological Cultures, and the Disconnect from Native Peoples," *The Oxford Handbook of North American Archaeology* (New York, Oxford University Press, 2012), p. 29. For an in depth look into the effects of Native American and European contact and governmental policies, see *The Emergent Native Americans*, edited by Deward E. Walkder, Jr., (Boston: Little, Brown and Company, 1972).

219 Anti-tourism protests break out in Spain, Italy and Portugal. (2025, June

15). Retrieved from https://community.ricksteves.com/travel-forum/general-europe/anti-tourism-protests-break-out-in-spain-italy-and-portugal

220 Deborah McLaren, *Rethinking Tourism and Ecotravel* (Connecticut: Kumarian Press, 2003), pp. 3-5.

221 *Ibid.*, p. 20.

222 *Ibid.*, p. 10.

223 *Ibid.*, pp. 66-7;71.

224 *Ibid.*, p. 27.

225 *Ibid.*, pp. 28-31; 68-71;82-5.

226 See https://travelmaps.state.gov/TSGMap/?extent=-63.232725541,17.983292283,-62.898785524,18.149091721

227 Deborah McLaren, *Rethinking Tourism and Ecotravel* (Connecticut: Kumarian Press, 2003), pp. 33-4.

228 U.S. Department of Agriculture, Forest Service, "Land Areas of the National Forest System" February 23, 2023. https://www.fs.usda.gov/land/staff/lar-index.shtml

229 U.S. Department of Agriculture, Forest Service, "National Visitor Use Monitoring Survey Results: U.S. Forest Service National Summary," February 23, 2023. https://www.fs.fed.us/recreation/programs/nvum/pdf/508pdf2015_National_Summary_Report.pdf

230 U.S. Department of the Interior, National Park Service, "NPS Stats," February 17, 2017. https://www.nps.gov/aboutus/faqs.htm

231 *Ibid.*

232 U.S. Department of the Interior, Bureau of Land Management, "Public Land Statistics," February 17, 2017. https://www.blm.gov/public_land_statistics/pls14/pls2014.pdf

233 Jon Krakauer, *Into Thin Air* (New York: Anchor Books, 1997), pp. 47-8

234 *Ibid.*, p. 48.

235 Valene L. Smith (editor), *Hosts and Guests: The Anthropology of Tourism* (Philadelphia: University of Pennsylvania Press, 1989) pp. x-xi.

236 "WWOOF," *Wikipedia*, February 23, 2023. https://en.wikipedia.org/wiki/WWOOF; see also http://wwoofinternational.org/

237 Deborah McLaren, *Rethinking Tourism and Ecotravel* (Connecticut: Kumarian Press, 2003), pp. 42-3.

238 *Ibid.*, p. 92.

239 *Ibid.*, p. 93.

240 Bratton, Susan Power. *The Spirit of the Appalachian Trail: Community, Environment, and Belief on a Long Distance Hiking Path* (Knoxville: University of Tennessee Press, 2012) pp. 140-141.

SELECTED BIBLIOGRAPHY

Aries, Philippe, and Georges Duby. *A History of Private Life.* Cambridge, Mass.: Belknap Press, 1987.

Abbey, Edward. *Desert Solitaire: A Season in the Wilderness.* New York: Balantine Books, 1971.

Bratton, Susan Power. *The Spirit of the Appalachian Trail: Community, Environment, and Belief on a Long Distance Hiking Path.* Knoxville: University of Tennessee Press, 2012.

Brill, David. *As Far As the Eye Can See: Reflections of an Appalachian Trail Hiker.* Knoxville: University of Tennessee Press, 2020.

Brown, Joseph Epes. *The Spiritual Legacy of the American Indian.* Indiana: World Wisdom, 2007.

Bryson, Bill. *A Walk in the Woods: Rediscovering America on the Appalachian Trail.* New York: Broadway Books, 1998.

Camus, Albert. *The Myth of Sisyphus.* New York: Vintage Books, 1983.

Chatwin, Bruce. *Anatomy of Restlessness.* New York: Viking, 1996.

———. *The Songlines.* New York: Viking, 1987.

———. *In Patagonia.* New York: Penguin Group, 1988.

Cravens, Gwyneth. *Power to Save the World: The Truth about Nuclear Energy.* New York: Vintage Books, 2007.

Csikszentmihalyi, Mihaly. *Flow: The Psychology of Optimal Experience.* New York: Harper & Row, 1990.

De Becker, Gavin. *The Gift of Fear*. New York: Dell Publishing, 1997.

De Botton, Alain. *The Art of Travel*. New York: Vintage International, 2004.

De Maistre, Xavier. *A Journey around My Room*. United Kingdom: ALMA Classics, 2017.

De Waal, Frans. *The Age of Empathy: Nature's Lessons for a Kinder Society* (New York: Random House, 2009)

Defoe, Daniel, and Michael Shinagel. *Robinson Crusoe: A Norton Critical Edition*. New York: Norton, 1994.

Donald, Merlin. *Origins of the Modern Mind: Three Stages in the Evolution of Culture and Cognition*. Massachusetts: Harvard University Press, 1991.

Downey, Greg, and Daniel H. Lende, eds. *The Encultured Brain: An Introduction to Neuroanthropology*. Massachusetts: MIT Press, 2012.

Dunn, Ross E. *The Adventures of Ibn Battuta: A Muslim Traveler of the 14th Century*. Berkley: University of California Press, 1986.

Furedi, Frank. *The Culture of Fear Revisited*. London: Continuum, 2006.

Gardner, Daniel. *The Science of Fear: How the Culture of Fear Manipulates Your Brain*. New York: Penguin, 2009.

Glassner, Barry. *Culture of Fear: Why Americans Are Afraid of the Wrong Things*. New York: Basic Books, 2009.

Glover, Jonathan. *Humanity: A Moral History of the 20th Century*. Connecticut: Yale University Press, 2012.

Goldstein, Joshua S. *Winning the War on War: The Decline of Armed Conflict Worldwide*. New York: Penguin, 2011.

———.*The Real Price of War: How You Pay for the War on Terror*. New York: New York University Press, 2005.

Gould, Carol Grant. *The Remarkable Life of William Beebe: Explorer and Naturalist*. New York: Island Press, 2004.

Gurri, Martin. *The Revolt of the Public and the Crisis of Authority in the New Millennium*. San Fransisco: Stripe Press, 2018.

Haidt, Jonathan, *The Righteous Mind: Why Good People Are Divided By Politics and Religion*. New York: Vintage Books, 2012.

SELECTED BIBLIOGRAPHY

Kahneman, Daniel. *Thinking Fast and Slow*. New York: Macmillan, 2011.

Keeley, Lawrence H. *War Before Civilization: The Myth of the Peaceful Savage*. New York: Oxford University Press, 1996.

Krakauer, Jon. *Into Thin Air*. New York: Anchor Books, 1997.

———. *Into the Wild*. New York: Anchor Books, 1996.

———. *Classic Krakauer: Essays on Wilderness and Risk*. New York: Anchor Books, 2019.

Linton, Ralph. *The Tree of Culture*. New York: Alfred A. Knopf, 1955.

Lukianoff, Greg and Jonathan Haidt. *The Coddling of the American Mind: How Good Intentions and Bad Ideas Are Setting Up a Generation for Failure*. New York: Penguin Press, 2018.

Malinowski, Bronsilaw. *The Argonauts of the Western Pacific*. Illinois: Waveland Press, Inc., 1984.

McLaren, Deborah. *Rethinking Tourism and Ecotravel*. Connecticut: Kumarian Press, 2003.

Mintz, Sidney W. *Sweetness and Power: The Place of Sugar in Modern History*. New York: Penguin Books, 1986.

Moor, Robert. *On Trails: An Exploration*. New York: Simon & Schuster, 2016.

Pinker, Steven, *The Better Angels of Our Nature: Why Violence Has Declined*. New York: Penguin, 2011.

———. *Enlightenment Now: The Case for Reason, Science, Humanism, and Progress*. New York: Viking, 2018.

———. *The Blank Slate: The Modern Denial of Human Nature*. New York: Penguin, 2002.

———. *How the Mind Works*. New York: Norton, 1997.

Reich, David. *Who We Are and How We Got Here: Ancient DNA and The New Science of the Human Past*. New York: Vintage, 2018.

Rosling, Hans, Ola Rosling, and Anna Rosling. *Factfulness: Ten Reasons We're Wrong About the World—And Why Things Are Better Than You Think*. New York: Flatiron Books, 2018.

Sapolsky, Robert M. *Behave: The Biology of Humans at Our Best and Worst*. New York: Penguin, 2017.

Schor, Juliet B. *The Overspent American: Why We Want What We Don't Need*. New York: Basic Books, 1998.

Shaffer, Earl V. *Walking With Spring*. West Virginia: Appalachian Trail Conference, 2004.

Singer, Peter. *The Expanding Circle: Ethics, Evolution, and Moral Progress*. New Jersey: Princeton University Press, 2011.

Simmel, Georg. "The Adventure." In *Simmel on Culture: Selected Writings*, edited by David Frisby and Mike Featherstone, London: Sage, 1997.

———. "The Stranger." In *The Sociology of Georg Simmel*, edited by Kurt Wolff, New York: Free Press, 1950.

Slocum, Joshua. *Sailing Alone Around the World*. New York: Dover Books, 1956.

Smith, Valene L., ed. *Hosts and Guests: The Anthropology of Tourism*. Philadelphia: University of Pennsylvania Press, 1989.

Solnit, Rebecca. *Wanderlust: A History of Walking*. New York: Viking, 2000.

Toffler, Alvin. Future *Shock*. New York: Bantam Books, 1990.

———. *Powershift*. New York: Bantam Books, 1990.

———. *The Third Wave*. New York: Bantam Books, 1990.

Vivanco, Luis A., and Robert J. Gordon, eds. *Tarzan was an Ecotourist…and Other Tales in the Anthropology of Adventure*. New York: Bergham Press, 2006.

Waldinger, Robert, and Marc Schulz. *The Good Life: Lessons from the World's Longest Scientific Study of Happiness*. New York: Simon & Schuster, 2023.

Wood, Gordon S. *The Radicalism of the American Revolution*. New York: Vintage Books, 1993.

Zweig, Paul. *The Adventurer: The Fate of Adventure in the Western World*. New York: Akadine Press, 1999.

INDEX

Abbey, Edward, 37–38
adventure
 anthropology of, 88
 costs of, 41-44
Afghanistan, 145, 156
agency, 111, 231-234, 242, 245-251
 American travel patterns, 35-41, 45
anomie, 72
anthropology
 of wandering, 11
anxiety, 3, 5, 8, 31, 57, 66, 93, 95, 140, 158, 165-167, 170, 173, 181, 188, 191, 201, 209, 218, 228, 230, 246-247, 257, 262-263, 268, 316, 324
Appalachian Trail Conservancy, 74
Argentina, 1
Aristotle, 227
artificial intelligence (AI), 98, 204, 244 See also effects of technology
attention, 28, 31, 47, 76, 86, 90-9, 94, 104, 148, 151-152, 168, 171, 176, 171, 180-182, 186, 204, 211, 232, 238, 249, 253, 264, 268, 326
attention deficit hyperactivity disorder (ADHD), 262
Australia, 59, 62

availability heuristic, 182-186, 192
awe, 19, 65, 135,

Bangkok, 35
Battuta, Ibn, 10
Baxter, Percival Proctor, 20
beatnik, 141, 256
Belfast, 266
Belize, 315
Benedict, Ruth, 12
Bloomington, 256
Bourdain, Anthony, 279, 300, 309
brain, 5, 75, 89, 102, 131, 140, 147, 159, 161-193, 199, 200, 202, 221, 223, 229, 262
Bratton, Susan Power, 304-305
Brill, David, 68-71
Britain, 35, 114, 210
Brown, A.R. Radcliffe, 12
Brown, John, 144
Brown, Joseph Epes, 288-289
Bryson, Bill, 15, 271-272

Canada, 33, 35
Cancún, 35
Chatwin, Bruce, 7, 10

Chile, 1
China, 59, 62, 133, 147, 292
cognitive bias, 161, 167, 175, 182, 237-238
Colorado, 266, 314-315
community, sense of, 47, 59, 68, 70-71, 77, 241, 259, 264, 267, 275-276
communitas, 275-276
confirmation bias, 183-186, 192, 239
Conrad, Joseph, 105
Csikszentmihalyi, Mihaly, 81, 285
culture
    of fear, 8-10, 131-132, 136, 138, 142-144, 147, 164, 168, 174-175, 201-202, 213-214, 225, 232, 235-237, 254, 320, 326
    of safety, 123, 136, 141, 146, 159, 175, 181. See also Obsessive Safety Disorder
Curie, Marie, 307

Dartmouth, 256
Davis, Wade, 108
De Becker, Gavin, 149, 153-154, 168-169, 173
De Botton, Alain, 8, 73
De Waal, Frans, 277-278
defense spending, 132, 142-143
depression, 209, 262
DiCaprio, Leonardo, 35
distance
    importance in travel, 24, 34, 47, 97, 101, 264
Doyle, Sir Arthur Conan, 105

Earhart, Amelia, 11
ecotourism, 266, 314-315
Egypt, 62, 166, 169
Emerson, Ralph Waldo, 85, 140, 309, 314
evolution, 10-12, 88-89, 127, 130-131, 161, 169, 170-176, 179, 183, 185, 199, 322, 325
Epic of Gilgamesh, 12

fear, perceived, 6, 126, 191, 220, 228, 257, 268, 308
Forster, E.M., 242-246
France, 59, 317
Frost, Robert, 257
Furedi, Frank, 138-139, 161, 173, 181, 213-214, 237. See also culture of fear

Gagarin, Yuri, 11
Gardner, Daniel, 147-148, 171-172, 177, 180
Georgia, 15
Germany, 59
Gigerenzer, Gerd, 180
Glassner, Barry, 143, 168, 201, 240
Glover, Jonathan, 185
Going, 42
Goldstein, Joshua S., 151-152, 188
Gordan, Robert J., 88-89, 135
Grant, Ulysses S., 100
gratitude, 273
group polarization, 183-186, 192, 238
Guatemala, 315
Gurri, Martin, 203

INDEX

habituation, 93, 175-177, 186, 192
Hanover, 218, 256, 275
Haidt, Jonathan, 184
Harper's Ferry, 144
Hemingway, Ernest, 89
Hesiod, 115
hitchhiking, 140-141
historical context, 36
hiking,
    benefits of, 255, 261-263
Hitchens, Christopher, 36, 137
hominin, 11, 27, 62-64, 104, 260-261, 311
Homo erectus, 11
Homo ergaster, 11
Humans of New York, 219
Huizinga, Johan, 118-119
Hundred-Mile Wilderness, 17, 50, 55, 120, 163, 266

identity, 47, 71, 115, 264, 312, 325
idleness,
    concept of, 111-116, 119
Iliad, 13
Indiana University, 1, 171, 256, 270
indigenous peoples, 104, 287, 294-295, 300
Indonesia, 104, 292-293
Iran, 147
Iraq, 145, 156
Ireland, 59
Israel, 156, 278
Italy, 43, 315

Japan, 59

Kahneman, Daniel, 172-173, 182
Keeley, Lawrence, 34, 151-152
Kenya, 293
Kerouac, Jack, 141
Knoxville, 315
Krakauer, Jon, 70, 296-297, 311, 316

labor, 112-116, 119, 290-293, 299, 307
leisure vs. work, 112-115, 119. *See also* work ethic
Levi, Primo, 76
Lévi-Strauss, Claude, 12
Lewis and Clark, 10, 22, 116, 135
Libya, 145, 155
life satisfaction, 46
Linton, Ralph, 64-65
London, 35

MacKaye, Benton, 70
Maine, 15-16, 25, 49, 162, 229, 266, 279- 280-283, 317
Maine Appalachian Trail Club (MATC), 50
Malinowski, Bronislaw, 12, 65, 287-288
Massachusetts, 144, 220
Max Planck Institute, 181
McCandless, Christopher, 311-317
McLaren, Deborah, 255, 289-291, 293, 299-301
media-effects theory, 201
media,
    mass, 199, 212-214
    social, 85, 157, 164, 192, 202-204, 236- 241, 253, 320
Mead, Margaret, 12
Mexico, 33, 35, 166, 317

Millinocket, 16
mindfulness, 93, 230, 273-274
Mintz, Sidney, 29-30
Monson, 17, 50, 123, 126-127, 162, 266
Montana, 315
Moor, Robert, 70
Moorish Proverb, 137
mountains, 40, 56, 57, 65, 71, 279-283
   K2, 75
   Mount Everest, 133, 158, 298
   Mount Greylock, 144, 220
   Mount Katahdin, 15-19, 49-55,
      69-70, 120, 163, 317, 324
   Mount Moosilauke, 25
   Mount Springer, 15, 70
   Mount Washington, 282-284
Myanmar, 293
Muir, John, 89

National Park Service, 35, 219
Native Americans, 116,
   See also indigenous peoples
negativity bias, 178-179, 186, 192
Nevada, 141
New Hampshire, 218, 229, 256,
   279, 281
New Jersey, 141, 195, 220,
New York, 141
New York City, 91
New York Times, 154, 208
nature,
therapeutic effects of, 261-268, 274-278
Nigeria, 145
North Carolina, 165

odds of dying (OOD) 147
Odyssey, 13
Orwell, George, 137
Obsessive Safety Disorder (OSD),
   123, 136,141, 146, 159, 175, 181

Paine, Thomas, 210, 224
Pakistan, 145, 147
Palin, Sarah, 43
passports
statistics on, 33-35, 41, 44
Patterson, Kaleo, 293
Pennsylvania, 141-142
Pinker, Steven, 97, 123, 145-146,
   150-151, 154, 164, 187-188
place, 24, 34, 47, 97, 101
Polo, Marco, 10
Pomelo, 42
Philippines, 69, 293
Protestant Ethic, 112-118 *See also*
   Max Weber
Proust, Marcel, 85
Puerto Vallarta, 35

Reich, David, 61-62
resilience
and adventure, 54, 240-241, 248, 269
risk,
   actual, 6, 126, 268
   calculated, 138
   concept of, 133-136
   importance of, 88-89, 134-136,
      138-139
Roosevelt, Theodore, 89, 135
Rosling, Hans, 161, 164, 175, 188-
   190, 192, 214

INDEX

Royzman, Edward, 178-179
Rozin, Paul, 178-179
Russell, Bertrand, 119

Sagan, Carl, 49, 106, 195, 212, 229, 260
Salopek, Paul, 101-102, 190-191, 233-234
Schor, Juliet B., 43-44
Shaffer, Earl, V., 77-78
Shay's Rebellion, 144
Shenandoah National Park, 79, 307, 314
Saudi Arabia, 147
Simmel, Georg, 66, 87-88
Singer, Peter, 277
Slocum, Joshua, 81-82
Solnit, Rebecca, 29-32, 99-103
Sri Lanka, 293
Stewart, Jon, 207-208
Switzerland, 59
Syria, 145, 155

technology,
effects of, 21, 25-32, 39-40, 85-86, 97-101, 119, 136, 153, 172, 223, 242, 246-247, 252, 269, 273, 276, 305, 325-327. *See also* Alvin Toffler
Tennessee, 315
terrorism, 145-150, 155-156, 173, 180, 188, 237, 240
The Beach, 35
Thoreau, Henry David, 1, 44-45, 89, 94, 253, 312
Tibet, 293
TikTok, 147 *See also* social media
time, 24, 34, 47, 97, 101

perception of, 93-94
Toffler, Alvin, 96-99, 195, 199, 204-205, 212-215
trail
 magic, 50, 128, 219
 name, 50-51, 69, 71, 196
 trust, 46, 59, 70, 170, 178, 200-204, 208, 239-245, 247, 251, 254, 263, 269-270, 294
Tversky, Amos, 183
Twain, Mark, 23, 302
Twitter/X, 199, 202, 213, 215, *See also* social media
Tyson, Neil DeGrasse, 106

United Kingdom, 35
Universal Declaration of Human Rights, 279, 304
University of Tennessee, 315
University of Vermont, 88
Utah, 141, 317

Virginia, 79, 310, 314

walking
 as meditation, 229-230
 history of, 27-33
wandering
 anthropology of, 11
Western Hemisphere Travel Initiative (WHTI) 33
West Virginia, 144
Whymper, Edward, 282
Wilson, E.O., 241
Weber, Max, 112. *See also* Protestant Ethic

Wood, Gordon S., 113
World Wide Opportunities on Organic Farms or Willing Workers on Organic Farms (WWOOF), 298
work ethic, 14, 112-115, 119
Wyoming, 2, 141, 199, 317

Zweig, Paul, 110-111, 115

www.ingramcontent.com/pod-product-compliance
Lightning Source LLC
LaVergne TN
LVHW030315070526
838199LV00069B/6470